# BLACK TULIP

# BLACK TULIP

The Life and Myth of Erich Hartmann,
the World's Top Fighter Ace

ERIK SCHMIDT

**CASEMATE**
*Philadelphia & Oxford*

Published in the United States of America and Great Britain in 2020 by
CASEMATE PUBLISHERS
1950 Lawrence Road, Havertown, PA 19083, USA
and
The Old Music Hall, 106–108 Cowley Road, Oxford OX4 1JE, UK

Hardcover Edition: ISBN 978-1-61200-824-0
Digital Edition: ISBN 978-1-61200-825-7


A CIP record for this book is available from the British Library

Printed and bound in the United States of America

Typeset in India for Casemate Publishing Services. www.casematepublishingservices.com

For a complete list of Casemate titles, please contact:

CASEMATE PUBLISHERS (US)
Telephone (610) 853-9131
Fax (610) 853-9146
Email: casemate@casematepublishers.com
www.casematepublishers.com

CASEMATE PUBLISHERS (UK)
Telephone (01865) 241249
Email: casemate-uk@casematepublishers.co.uk
www.casematepublishers.co.uk

*The typeface used on the cover is Futura, which was designed in 1927 by German Paul Renner. In 1933, Renner was removed from his post because of his anti-Nazi views. His influence far outlasted the Third Reich, however, and in 1969 Futura was used on the plaque left on the moon by the Apollo 11 astronauts.*

*For the kiddos, who are everything.*

# Contents

*Acknowledgments*                                                    xi
*Introduction*                                                       xiii


**Part One: Inheritances**
1      "The Force That is Devoted to Death"                          3
2      Harmony                                                       7
3      "The Demolition Function"                                     17
4      *Jugend*                                                      25
5      Into the *Luftwaffe*                                          37

**Part Two: Hartmann's Wars**
6      Kills                                                         57
7      Against Stalin's Falcons                                      73
8      Recognition and Attrition                                     81
9      Into Captivity                                                93
10     The East and the West                                         111
11     Old Gray Ghosts                                               123
12     Last Flights                                                  141

**Part Three: Stories Told**
13     Marketing the *Wehrmacht*                                     151
14     In Their Words                                                169
15     The Production of Meaning                                     181


*Conclusion*                                                         189
*Bibliography*                                                       193
*Endnotes*                                                           197
*Index*                                                              209

Out beyond ideas of wrongdoing and rightdoing, there is a field. I'll meet you there.

—RUMI

Erich Hartmann. (Bundesarchiv, Bild 101I-502-0195-09A/Sperling)

# Acknowledgments

Writing isn't such a solitary thing after all. This has been a long process, and I've had great helpers along the way. I'm grateful for all of them.

Mike Magnuson helped launch this. As a teacher, he helped me improve my language and focus on what really matters: the difficult bits, the conflict, the grit of the thing. As a friend and fellow history nut, he gave me enthusiasm and showed me that I could, and should, do it.

There were many other educators. Stephen Kuusisto taught me to observe myself thinking, a necessary writing lesson. Elinor Langer was the first person to ask me about Erich Hartmann and his black tulip, and I benefited from her allegiance to Strunk and White. (Full stop.) Seth Cotlar, even earlier, showed us all how a diligent and passionate historian does this important work.

Everything orbits around family. My wife's patience with this creative process, to which she doesn't quite relate but supports anyway (a measure of generosity in a partner), has been crucial, as have her business sense and organization. She has given an enormous amount to this project over a span of years. My kids, who arrived after I'd started this book, have driven me forward and given me focus. More than anyone else in the whole world, they're the ones for whom I'll always try to do my best work. And my parents, my original editors, taught me to love learning and to always ask questions, especially of myself. Their lessons have served me everywhere.

And then there are those who have provided so many other contributions, large and small, whether or not they knew they were doing it. Museum curators, friendly archivists, fellow writers, patient German helpers, curious family and friends: they've allowed me to sit in Messerschmitt cockpits, put on the cotton gloves and handle amazing pieces of history, and wrap my mind around what this project could, and needed to, become.

# Introduction

Every moment in history is just as complex as the moment we're living in right now.

—John Biewen[1]

Look at them: they were so young. And yet they were so incredibly, historically, deadly.

When people talk about history's best fighter pilots, they usually talk about the *Luftwaffe*'s *Experten*—those coolly efficient men whose performances in World War II can stretch believability. Plenty of people, with plenty of justification, would call them the finest cohort of pilots produced by any air force, in any war, ever. And given how much air combat has been digitized and depersonalized in the last few decades, they will almost certainly never be matched.

Erich Hartmann is the highest-scoring *Experte* of them all. Over two and a half years at war, the rock-jawed *Luftwaffe* blonde claimed 352 enemy aircraft shot down over the frostbitten Eastern Front. *One pilot, three hundred fifty-two enemies destroyed.* By contrast, the top American ace of the war, Dick Bong, scored "only" 40 kills in the Pacific Theater. There are a few good reasons for the discrepancy that have nothing to do with talent, the biggest among them being Hartmann's target-rich environment and the Germans' policy of keeping their aces at the warfront until they were killed, captured, or the war ended (they didn't rotate out after predetermined tours). Hartmann was one of the fortunate ones for whom the end of the war came before death or debilitation.

His knack for staying out of other men's crosshairs meant that he survived a staggering 1,404 combat missions, 825 of which put him in the company of enemy aircraft. His kill total makes a little more sense when you do the math: Hartmann averaged one kill for every 3.99 missions, or one for every 2.34 missions that involved air combat. Other pilots—albeit for briefer spans of time—posted higher averages. And with each month that went by, Hartmann acquired even more know-how, initiative, and success. It probably isn't a stretch to say that by the end of the conflict he knew his enemy's planes and tactics far better than most of the pilots flying them did.

His survivability also came from unusual mental and physical endurance, as well as the many talents he developed early on, when the Germans took their time training recruits in dogfighting, aerodynamics, and mechanical systems. The difference between *Luftwaffe* pilot training in 1941 and 1945 is drastic; many of Hartmann's younger peers who arrived at the front later in the war were thrown into cockpits with not much more than a run-through and a wish of good luck. Because of this, Hartmann was also a teacher. He and the other old hands (this is relative: Hartmann was a seasoned 23 years old in 1945) had to teach the new pilots how to fly and survive in the thick of it all. Sometimes they succeeded.

Hartmann also had an unusual gut-level understanding of aircraft and airpower, that intangible "right stuff" that all the great pilots seem to have. He always said that he could *just sense* when something was wrong with his plane well before any cockpit gauge reported it to him. This was undoubtedly true. The pilot's sixth sense doesn't seem mystical at all to anyone who knows piloting.

In the fight, Hartmann was calculating and coolheaded, wasting neither bullets nor wingmen. He was always more of a tactician than a brawler, and he tended to skirt around risky situations and only attacked when the odds were favorable (which was often). Any guru of air combat, from the early aces of World War I to today's Top Gun instructors, would admire Hartmann's diligent application of the timeless rules of engagement: *Attack from the sun. Seek the higher altitude to conserve speed and energy. Fly with your head, not your muscles.* He believed in those principles and adhered to them more completely than almost anything else in his life.

Throughout the war, Hartmann tangled with the full spectrum of enemies, and he defeated them all. These included hundreds of hapless, unseasoned Soviets hamstrung by subpar equipment and training, as well as their elite squadron mates, whom Hartmann considered some of the fiercest and most dangerous pilots of the war. In general, Soviet pilots acquired a reputation for being unwise and ill-prepared, and this was sometimes true (though it was also influenced by unreflective bias), but Hartmann also acknowledged their refinements and strengths as soldiers.

His postings took him all over the Eastern Front, from the early days in the Russian south to the *Wehrmacht's* final retraction back within German borders, where it was finally snuffed out as the Western and Eastern Fronts converged. Hartmann's 352nd kill came on the very last day of the European war, and that engagement is a good window into his experience as a hunter. It took place early in the morning over the city of Brno in what is now the Czech

Republic. By this point, Soviet fighter pilots could frolic with impunity above the smoldering cities because the airspace was all but empty of Germans—the *Luftwaffe* had been crushed and the conflict had ground to a halt. Hitler was dead somewhere in Berlin.

One Yak-7 pilot was celebrating his country's victory with a lazy loop above the firestorms below. With typical good timing, Hartmann dropped in behind him in his Messerschmitt Bf 109, undetected, and squeezed off a burst of gunfire that sent the clueless Yak pilot tumbling to the ground. The engagement took all of a few seconds. Hartmann's kills usually were this fast, and his appearance usually was this surprising to his victims. The other Soviets in the area, suddenly aware that they had been ambushed, reeled in confusion. Hartmann resisted any temptation to engage more enemies and continued diving toward a lower altitude, throttle wide open, where he could dash away camouflaged against the trees. While he sped toward base, he glanced back toward his six o'clock and saw that the Americans were arriving over Brno in their glistening, bare-metal P-51 Mustangs. To Hartmann's surprise—maybe amusement—the Allied fighters had begun dogfighting furiously with each other. (Were the Mustangs and Yaks mistaken? Or just anticipatory?) Either way, Hartmann left them to it. He flew on to complete his last mission and await the ground forces poised to overrun his airfield.

The Eastern Front, we know, was one of the most gruesome theaters of war in history. It was mind-numbingly desolate; vast almost beyond comprehension; usually either frozen or covered by infinite muck; and, to a rigidly trained and indoctrinated German, foreign in a hundred difficult ways. The campaign in the East was Germany's signature strategic catastrophe, but it was also, oddly, the key to Hartmann's success. Despite the crushing turn of fortunes at Stalingrad, Moscow, and elsewhere, Hartmann flew above it all free to engage endless streams of advancing Soviet fighters and bombers. The same industrial revival that made the Soviet air force a viable opposing force to Hitler also made Hartmann's airspace saturated with targets, and day after day he soared above the gristly realities of the ground war into duels that he and the other airmen still had the luxury of calling chivalrous.

Hartmann is also one of a handful of *Luftwaffe* pilots known for using a unique paint scheme on their planes—and his is a fitting metaphor for an unusual, elusive, shadowy life. The black tulip, as he called it, was a visual signature that made him stand out among all the other German aircraft sprayed with those murky mottles of gray and green. It wrapped around the nose of his Bf 109, drenching it in stark black. Set off by thin outlines of white, the saw-toothed tulip design was angular, mechanistic, menacing. Although

Hartmann actually only used it for a while, he, like the Red Baron before him, gained a permanent mystique that aligned him even more with the dark, incisive *Luftwaffe*. The Soviets called him the Black Devil, and eventually Stalin put up a bounty on his head.

To Hartmann's surprise, opposing pilots started fleeing when they saw his tulip-nosed plane leading a formation, leaving him without as many targets. This actually hurt his kill pace, so he loaned his personal plane to younger recruits to give them a little immunity while he went up in an anonymously marked 109. They learned to fly their aircraft better, and his victories accelerated.

By several measures, then—kill total, outright skill and natural talent, expert application of the techniques of war—Hartmann's was the most impressive career any fighter pilot has ever had, presuming as we do that each kill marking stenciled onto a fuselage or a rudder is another sign of prestige and refinement.

Despite the wartime drama and success, what happened after the war is actually what makes Hartmann such an interesting and relevant historical character. According to the terms of surrender in the East, he and thousands of other German combatants were handed over to the country they had fought against, regardless of where, or to whom, they surrendered. May 1945 saw Hartmann, stripped of his airborne weapon and seniority, thrust into the jowls of the Soviet prison system, even though he surrendered to the U.S. 90th Infantry Division. Hours after he had capped his legendary career with his last victory, he became a captive of the Soviet Union, and every promise in his life, every bit of personal and professional momentum he had built as a soldier, evaporated in a field near the Czech town of Pisek.

He stood that day in the open dirt with a few hundred German families and refugees. As soon as the Soviets took command of the situation, they resorted to the kind of barbarism and abuse you might hear about but hate to really imagine. The Americans hadn't even left the scene before, as Hartmann recalled later, the Soviet soldiers beat, raped, killed, and humiliated dozens of German women and children. All through the evening and that first endless night, the shocked and furious German men were held back by rifle barrels. Some, in desperate attempts to throw off the abusers, were shot dead on the spot for aggressing. Eventually, a Soviet officer arrived and put an end to the carnage by summarily hanging his own soldiers. There was relief among the captives then, but also a new wariness about the brutal institution they had just entered.

A pattern of abuse and retribution had been established, and these were to be the most obvious norms in Hartmann's subsequent 10 years of captivity.

For a decade he zigzagged the Soviet countryside, moving from camp to camp and occasionally enjoying the (relative) benefits afforded to top officers, which included adequate food and limited mail correspondence with the outside world. But he also spent months in solitary confinement, endured starvation (some of it self-imposed as protest), and sat through bewildering interrogations meant to get him to confess to war crimes or proclaim his allegiance to the Soviet Union so they could use him as a trophy.

When he returned in 1955 to what had become West Germany, he weighed 100 pounds. Looking at photos of him at this time, it's as though portions of his soul, not just his body, had been extracted and never filled back in. Hartmann had become hardened to the world, fortified in his hatred of the Soviets—he always said that only the promise of returning to his family had sustained him. His reunion with Ursula, his wife and best friend since schooling, was gentle and sweet; his reintegration into the shockingly modern West German society was arduous.

And that's why the creation of the new West German air force was so timely. Just at the time when Hartmann was returning home, his country was embarking on the cautious process of rearming. This would never be the same kind of military he was used to—it was intentionally constrained by civilian authorities, bureaucratic, complex, wary of its past. And yet it was modern in many ways, which was another kind of discomfort for the old ace. But it gave him a mission again. His peers told him it was his best available vocation, and his family did not interfere, leaving the decision completely to him. As soon as he was more or less recovered, he agreed to join up and re-learn the air combat skills at which, a few years earlier, he had literally been more accomplished than anyone on earth.

In some ways, this second flying career was more conflicted and hazardous than his first, strange as that is to say. His run-ins with leadership started right away when his incoming rank was manipulated, possibly by civilian overseers with grudges (or so claim his fawning early biographers). Over the following decade-plus, Hartmann aided his enemies by committing a series of procedural and judgmental errors that made him seem like even more of a relic from the bad old days. Despite his ceremonious entrance into the *Bundeswehr* ("civil defense") as commander of West Germany's first all-jet fighter wing, *Jagdgeschwader 71*, named for Manfred von Richthofen, his reputation and influence wilted. By the late 1960s he was on his way out, and he quietly accepted an early retirement after being relegated to pushing papers around a desk, the worst possible form of exile for a born-and-bred fighter pilot. By then he had been leapfrogged in rank by younger officers whom he had trained.

Finally—crushingly—there was just nowhere for Erich Hartmann to go but home.

He never needed to despair, though. Starting when his second career was faltering, he, like many of his *Luftwaffe* peers, had his public legacy recrafted for him by a closely aligned group of writers (mostly American, mostly military, mostly men) who were keenly, often personally, invested in his welfare and reputation. These commentators wrote enthusiastically about the nobility of his airborne fight, the universality of his duty to country, and his general character—all while omitting the obvious and thorny issues of Nazism and Hartmann's diligent service under Hitler. They hated the slow spiral toward obsolescence that had defined his most recent years in the *Bundeswehr*, so they added shape, color, and drama to his life story. These writers were the experts of their time because of their proximity to Hartmann and the other reclusive *Wehrmacht* veterans, most of whom, for obvious reasons, limited their interviews and public conversations to people whom they trusted. In an era of public skepticism, these writers and their subjects were fellow travelers of a sort, each, in his own way, arguing for the valor they believed had existed in the German ranks during Hitler's war of racial extermination. Sometimes they did so convincingly; other times, not so much. Either way, too few commentators beyond this core group provided contrasting investigations into these Germans' careers, convictions, or personal lives. A peculiar, and very intentional, view of the war and the war-makers filtered into the marketplace.

In a handful of leading works, richly retold dogfight stories spilled onto book pages and created a comfortably clean view of these *Luftwaffe* aces, much like what happened with the other branches of the *Wehrmacht*. Along the way, the commentators did Hartmann the favor of assigning him personal traits with which no red-blooded Westerner would argue. Here was a tough-as-nails freedom-seeker who had been swallowed into the Soviet camps and then soared out of them, a man whose fighting values would have put him at home in the U.S. Army Air Corps or the Royal Air Force at any time. Hartmann's storytellers endowed him with all the proper rugged-individualist, anti-Communist tendencies. He scoffed at mediocrity and bureaucracy, we hear; he was fiercely independent and charmingly stubborn. He even spoke with a drawl that people said reminded them of mid-century American cowboy movies.

This interpretation became the default one as the first salvo of books spawned more, and those in turn generated countless magazine articles, all restating the same central thesis: that these Germans were unimpeachable knights of the air, and that National Socialism was an inconsequential distraction along their path to glory rather than the pathway itself. This moral conclusion was history's best available truth about German combatants like Hartmann for 60 years.

Today, the original writers' omission of the most obvious and troublesome questions in Hartmann's life serves to make those matters all the more conspicuous. What about Hartmann's time as a Hitler Youth leader, or the indoctrination he was subject to as a young man? Or the Nazi ideals that leeched into the *Luftwaffe* and the other branches of the *Wehrmacht*? Or the corroding nationalism and militarism that dictated his life and have remained relevant topics in this century? Exploring these issues doesn't necessarily condemn Hartmann—the presence of indoctrinated hatred doesn't define its impact on every person subjected to it—but they do invite moral ambiguity into a narrative that was always so much more useful in black-and-white. In the Cold War's early innings, the middle ground wasn't where you went to find your heroes.

There were plenty of cultural and political tugs acting on those writers, of course, which influenced their frames of reference and drove their creative output. For one thing, they were of fairly uniform background. They were often military officers or commentators who had turned to writing popular literature after establishing a primary career elsewhere; they were not professional historians in a traditional sense, nor were they attached to academic institutions or subject to substantial critical review. Some of them were vulnerable to doing what most historians today are trained not to: using history to advance a set of preexisting convictions rather than letting the history suggest what those convictions should be.

It's worth remembering that many of their literary celebrations were at least partially rooted in real character traits. Hartmann really was a gruff, decisive, purposeful man, especially as he presented himself years after the Third Reich had crumbled. Bureaucrats got under his skin like splinters. He called things as he saw them, at times famously and to the detriment of his professional reputation. To the insiders who have created and protected Hartmann's legacy over the years it has felt authentic, even urgent, to focus on these palatable parts of his character and frame them as the dominant ones. Their hero-building seems to grow from something resembling protectiveness—a fear, maybe, that Hartmann and the other *Wehrmacht* fighters have always been one uncharitable interpretation away from ruin. You can see that their feelings for their *Experten* were deep, personal, and maybe even reasonable under their cultural and historical circumstances. But that doesn't mean they were correct.

## Weil im Schönbuch, Germany and the "What" of This Book

Just north of Hartmann's hometown of Weil im Schönbuch in southwestern Germany, there's a horizon of hillside, green and undulating and covered with wheat. In the summertime, scattered copses are all that disrupt the landscape, rolling as it does into the distance until the colors get lost in the haze. You can listen to the hush of a million wheat buds slapping each other in the breeze, or to little squadrons of birds chattering back and forth. This is a peaceful, tranquil place.

The feeling dissipates when you remember what used to go on here. Hills like these were where Nazis watched German youngsters become glider pilots. It was a perfectly nefarious program: the budding aviators, seven, 10, 13 years old, had already been earmarked as those who would pilot the fighters and bombers in service of Hitler's lustful conquests. The boys strove for their first aerial victories—over the whipping wind, the topography, their instructors' stopwatches—in the way any youngster follows the lure of adventure. But they were ignorant of the master plans that propelled their education.

It's a sad realization, really, that Germany's youngsters were the most important raw war material Hitler ever needed. He extracted them from childhoods of far different and gentler potential so they could feed his hateful machine.

Weil im Schönbuch, population 10,000, is an easy half-hour from Stuttgart by train, and I went there late one spring morning thinking that if I could get closer to where Hartmann grew up and lived, I could get nearer to him as a person. I stepped off at the tiny main station and walked down along *Bismarckstrasse* toward a compact central square. This airy space is the social heart of the place, and when I arrived it was scented by the local bakery, which puffed out the best possible advertisement for the day's *Brötchen*. A flock of schoolchildren wearing hats ambled along the worn cobble stones in the low, early-season sun, their brightly colored backpacks cinched close.

Across an elbow in the road, a young woman was serving Italian lunches at a sidewalk cafe. She looked to be 18, was absolutely brunette, and was working alone on the slow shift, humming along to a Bryan Adams song on the radio, then to a Don Henley one. Every so often she'd duck inside the building to a small corner booth, where she sat next to a tomato-stained man of 50 (the owner, I assumed) who kept two glasses of pilsner filled.

I sat at a table outside, facing the square, and the waitress came by right away. In atrophied German, I gave her a greeting and an order for coffee. While she walked away I wondered what she might think of her town's most famous departed soldier. By this time, Hartmann had been dead almost 20 years; the waitress might have been born after his funeral, I figured, and probably after town leaders had named a street after him. *Hartmannstrasse* lies to the north near the cemetery road, and it's lined by colorful, neat houses. Maybe she'd wonder, as other characteristically forthright Germans already had, why a youngish American researcher like me would have any interest in, or anything to say about, an old German like him.

She came back just as I'd taken out my pen and recycled-paper notebook, and she threw me a knowing smile. I agreed with a grin: "Yes, I'm here for information." I jumped right in, asking her about Hartmann without any clumsy chit chat. My lack of fluency with the language felt like an excuse to cut to the chase.

She responded in very good English that yes, naturally, she knew who Erich Hartmann was. He was "the flyer," she said, stretching her arms into airplane wings and wagging them. She asked if I'd seen his house and his gravesite, both of which I had. I gathered that she had a surface-level understanding of his story but not a deep attachment to it: talking about Hartmann seemed perfunctory for her, like she was being asked to be a tour guide and didn't really care to.

I asked if she learned about him in school.

"Oh no, not in school," she said, quickly. "But we all still know about him. And all the rest."

She pointed across the street toward a war memorial that lists the names of the local men killed in both world wars. She didn't know that I'd taken pictures of it minutes earlier, noting that the nearby statue, a dirty-bronze sculpture of a helmeted soldier kneeling and holding another who'd been wounded, had brought up surprising emotions. It had made me think about families, and how drastically the world wars depleted a couple of generations. For such a small town, the list of the dead is surprisingly long.

I also noticed that all those soldiers were grouped together—there was no separate category for those who had died performing Hitler's missions as opposed to those of Kaiser Wilhelm II before. Later I questioned why I had been surprised by that.

"A town hero, then?" I asked.

"Oh, yes," she said.

"What do people around here say about him? Do they still talk about him?"

She shifted her weight. "Yes, we sometimes do ... He lived in this town his whole life."

By now, her tone translated to some variety of impatient. I suspected that she was used to outsiders but not pesky interviewers. Just then, a nearby door opened and a voice came from inside the building. An older man. My waitress stood straighter and moved her pen to hover above her order pad, a decisive signal.

"Now, what do you want to eat?" she asked.

I didn't push her, fearing that she'd been caught off-task. I gave her my order, watched her head inside, and picked up my notebook to make some scribbles. More than anything, I had new questions. When I was done jotting down notes, I stared for a while into the earthy coffee she'd left behind.

I took a couple insights from that conversation. First was the realization that I wasn't solely (or even primarily) researching Erich Hartmann. I was researching Erich Hartmann's story, which is a different kind of thing. I knew that his story had been authored, originally, in the 1960s, in a fervent and purposeful way, and I was interested to see how it had echoed all the way to the present. Any biographer attempts to help readers see into a life, but this project was going to have to help them see into the ways people have made meaning of that life over the decades. I wasn't sure how to start. While Hartmann would be the main character, his fans, critics, and storytellers would have to play supporting roles. Even my waitress might.

The second takeaway, to be honest, was that I hadn't managed the interview very well. This was the start of the project; had I interviewed the woman with years of practice under my belt, I might have gotten more out of her. More spontaneity, more personal insights, less of a script. I might have even gotten to the owner with the tomato stains.

The more I've thought about this over time, the more comfortable I've become with it. My purpose, in this moment at the cafe, wasn't to "solve" Erich Hartmann so much as it was to figure out Erik Schmidt—to wrap my mind around a project as a curious (and at least somewhat guided) outsider willing to do some self-inspection before coming up with some grand declaration about my subject. There was something fundamental going on for me—I was beginning to understand history not as the systematic lining-up of facts (as many of us remember it from schooling), but as an adventure, where each biography or article or spoken memory says as much about the author as it does the subject.

Among the questions that gnawed at me once my waitress had left were several about the purpose of this project. Why, I wondered, did I feel such a compulsion, an urgency, to pursue Hartmann? I'm no hero-worshipper and I'm no muckraker; it was neither of those things. But it must have been something.

Sitting there with my coffee, I glanced up toward the sun, still ascending—the same sun Hartmann used to fly in front of in dogfights to conceal himself. I could almost see him up there, turning, sprinting, evading.

Almost.

## Loveland, Colorado and the "Why" of This Book

Here was a perfect summer night, where the fragrant air lingered and the last sunlight clung to the tops of the Rocky Mountains like gold dust. I was on my way to a street festival in downtown Loveland, Colorado, that had been billed as a celebration of the 1940s. I imagined live music with a horn section, ice cream, and lots of old stories told about this most consequential of decades. There's a shrinking number of people left who lived through it, and I expected to listen carefully and smile often.

When I walked around the last corner and could finally see what was going on in the cordoned-off street, I was delighted. The music, the community, and the folding chairs were all there, as expected, but *the entire street was lined with tanks*. Military armored vehicles, restored and preserved in their 1940s-era camouflage and markings, crouched near the curbs in the fading light. People strolled beneath the giant gun barrels, apparently without a passing thought about what a historical monument this event had temporarily become.

I learned later that the city had contracted with a local collector of military materiel, and his vehicles, of several nationalities, were all parked along the street just as precisely as if they had been brought in by the operators who had first taken them to war. Once I got close to them I could sniff that intoxicating, vaguely combustible smell that lingers around old military equipment—leftover gasoline and 70 years' worth of lubricants and solvents. These old tools of war still had life in them, and as I inspected each of them I dragged my fingers across their cold steel armor, letting my nails catch on the chipped layers of matte camouflage paint. I checked the straightness of the rivet lines, observed the tight wobbles in the weld seams, and mentally measured the thickness of the armor plating. I grinned at the olive-drab pragmatism of these old designs.

Surprisingly, there were several vehicles from the *Wehrmacht* on display. They wore paint of varying colors and freshness, and one standout had recently been resprayed in a desert tan, likely representative of the African theater (it might have been a Nashorn tank destroyer, but I can't be sure of that). There was a man standing inside it, a volunteer wearing a full reproduction German military uniform. His upper half poked out of the vehicle's opened interior compartment, and he was chatting with locals, answering questions about what this strange, boxy, heavy vehicle was. Backlit by a street lamp, he was leaning out and over the edge of the exterior armor, his left hand on an inert land mine mounted on the outside of the plating. The round mine was a foot wide and colored charcoal gray, which made it stand out against the camouflage. The volunteer's other hand rested near a stenciled German cross marking that announced the vehicle's nationality. He was explaining how the land mine worked with the casualness of a grocer showing off a peach.

And then, in a flash of streetlight reflection, I saw the patch of the *Waffen-SS* sewn onto his shirt collar. This was no ordinary German uniform: it was the uniform of Hitler's most vitriolic, fanatical combat troops. I stopped in my tracks. The metallic thread of that jagged, dual-lightning-bolt-shaped symbol leapt out under the gloomy lighting, and while the man shifted and gestured, the symbol appeared frozen to me, focusing and projecting the surrounding light, not the least bit dulled by time.

A gurgle of revulsion built in my chest. Had the volunteer looked my way, he probably would have been confused to see me scowling there. I was, briefly, under the physiological influence of feelings and ideas that were buried somewhere deep in me and seldom brought out: *That uniform should insult everyone on this city block. Why would he flaunt that trash? This is how evil gets normalized.*

Let's not overestimate the sophistication of my response. This was visceral, pre-rational, and judgmental. Truth is, I knew little about the event and even less about the man in the tank; there was no reason to think he was any different than the countless mild-mannered military re-enactors out there doing what they enjoy. Almost immediately, I became interested not just in the cultural/historical scene playing out in front of me, but in my own reaction to it. I was a spectator to myself, considering what factors had come together to create this strange experience. Revulsion subsided and fascination rose.

I came to understand that the influences operating on me then were probably the same that act on all of us in some way. Family, culture, schooling, vocation, whatever conceptions of the world are hardwired in our brains—these things make us who we are, and they exert themselves in many ways throughout our lives. In this case, I was experiencing a legacy of my family and upbringing that I had never felt so powerfully.

It had started when I was a kid, when I gained a basic understanding of Hitler and the war through family. In my German grandparents' household, where I spent time around the holidays and in the summers, I heard about the scourge of Nazism in brief, definite moments: *Hitler was a fool and a crook.*

*Remember that not all Germans were Nazis.* My family on both sides, as far as I know, is predominantly German, and my father's side is where the lineage is clearest. His close relatives followed a circuitous route from Germany to Ellis Island in the years before World War I: first to Russia, which at the time was offering lucrative land grants and tax benefits to Germans who were willing to relocate and provide labor, and then, when that didn't pan out, back across Europe and over the Atlantic. As a youngster I enjoyed a hodgepodge of German and Russian influences in language, food, and family memory. There was a moral weight to those old memories, too, and an intuitive defense of the homeland—the ordinary Germans and the nationality they shared.

Until I was standing in front of that insignia, I never understood how deep these influences went.

The night in Loveland shaped this book in two dominant ways. First, it gave me my urgency. The *Waffen-SS* symbol was a glaring reminder that Nazism, like all sorts of hate, has never really been extinguished. I held no more animosity toward the volunteer in the tank than I did toward the inert steel he was standing on, but his showing me that symbol was, in a way, a wakeup call. Symbols connote very real things—sometimes horrible things that get sanitized and elevated to mythologies while the rest of us aren't paying attention.

Second, the experience reminded me of the distinction between preserving history and understanding it. You hear museum curators and military buffs talk about the need to *preserve* history's remnants—artifacts, equipment, documentation, tanks on a street—and that's crucial, but it's only ever seemed like half the job to me. It's one thing to preserve a *Waffen-SS* symbol; it's another thing to greet it with the context and detail to grasp its meaning, origins and applications, and relevance today. The best historians have always helped us judge for ourselves not just the *what* of history, but the *why* and the *what now*.

So I'll be direct. It's one thing to preserve Erich Hartmann's life story as it's been handed to us. It's quite another to understand that story's origins, meanings, authors, successes, failures, and consequences. It's still another hard thing to truly understand the man behind the storytelling. I don't know yet if that's actually doable.

Here's my plan. You'll see me diverge occasionally, as much as is needed, from a linear biographical account of Hartmann's life. You can obtain one of those elsewhere. There is context to be understood, questions to be asked, and my goal with this book is not (spoiler alert) to inform you of "what kind of man" Hartmann was at his deepest core and then move on to yet another dogfight scene. No, my goal is show that if you want to understand any man or woman from history, you have to look in places other than their core. You have to reckon with their peculiar cultural, intellectual, and philosophical inheritances, all of which combine, like pieces of clay layered onto a sculpture during its formation, to make them who they are. We're all subject to this, so I imagine understanding Hartmann's life might help us understand our own. I hope it might also help us use his unique slice of history to make better decisions for ourselves today and tomorrow. Enough certainly is at stake.

I'll do my best. We start with war.

# Part One

## Inheritances

## CHAPTER I

# "The Force That is Devoted to Death"

Death stands at attention, obedient, expectant, ready to serve, ready to shear away the peoples *en masse*.

—Winston Churchill

France, 1918. Springtime. Low altitude.

These are the waning days of World War I, and defeat closes in on Germany like ink seeping into a map. The Americans have shed their neutrality and are mobilizing. Ten thousand fresh souls a day replenish the Allied armies, bearing down on the fatigued German forces. The catastrophic end is unavoidable.

Manfred von Richthofen, above it all, flies on undeterred.

At this moment, he streaks past the River Somme in a Fokker Dr.1 triplane bearing the black crosses of the German Flying Corps. The Fokker can manage 110 miles per hour, and Richthofen's plane is painted crimson red, the flagrant opposite of camouflage. He's just taken fire from a pilot to his rear, but he's shaken him off. Now he focuses on the British fighter at his 12 o'clock, weaving, banking, pitching. It moves in and out of his crosshairs, but Richthofen follows patiently, keeping his position, waiting for the right moment. He knows he is only seconds away from his 81st aerial kill.[1]

But now, a .303 bullet arcs up from a ground-based artillery unit. In an instant, this speck of lead pierces the Fokker's fabric skin, enters Richthofen's body at his right armpit, and exits at his left nipple, two inches higher, after ricocheting off his spine. The bullet has punctured several vital tissues in his torso and released a flood of blood into his chest. This sends alarms to his brain, signaling catastrophic damage and producing searing pain. The Fokker's nose falls below the horizon as Richthofen slumps toward unconsciousness. The Red Baron is going to die today. The only question is how long it will take.

Most historians now agree that it took just long enough for him to crash-land his aircraft, more or less intact, in a field near the country village of Vaux-sur-Somme northeast of Amiens. Richthofen wouldn't have seen the locals who flocked to his damaged Fokker so they could rip away bits and pieces as souvenirs. This was an iconic aircraft—loved by many, hated by others, recognized by almost everyone who knew what an airplane was. Richthofen was already notorious throughout Europe and beloved by his German propagandists. People on both sides of the front wanted a piece of him.

The looters were fast and thorough. Some of Richthofen's personal items, including his scarf, a monogrammed handkerchief, and his leather flying boots, disappeared and were never accounted for. People cut away patches of the red fuselage and wings, hurrying away with doped-fabric mementos. (Karma, maybe: Richthofen had made a habit of removing patches of his victims' planes.) Eventually, British authorities arrived at the wreckage, too. They were desperate for any engineering clues about Richthofen's impressive three-winged fighter, so they saved a sample of its motor oil and shipped it back across the Channel for study by chemists.[2]

Soon after, the British organized an elaborate burial, a notable act in a war that had left so many of the dead strewn anonymously in the trenches. A lengthy procession through the town of Bertangles was led by a dozen riflemen and included an infantry platoon and a line of spectators.[3] Richthofen's enemies were putting him on display, but this was no exhibition of the hated—they believed there was something special about him, and they were honoring him as they would honor one of their own. Although some critics would later accuse the British of staging the event as a self-congratulatory show of their own chivalry, this was, in all likelihood, an earnest demonstration of respect for a hero.[4]

They buried Richthofen in the local cemetery half a mile from town, in the shadow of a hemlock tree. Someone made a cross from his wooden propeller and pounded it into the ground near a metal plaque commemorating him.[5] The plaque was eventually stolen, too, but from that day on, Richthofen's legend wasn't going anywhere. He wasn't yet known as the Red Baron—back then the Germans called him the Red Battle Flyer—but his exploits were etched into people's historical consciousness as soon as the drama of his death spread through the news. The esteemed British publication *The Aeroplane* described him as "a brave man, a clean fighter and an aristocrat." It noted that his enemies "will be pleased to hear that he has been put out of action, but there will be no one amongst them who will not regret the death of such a courageous nobleman."[6]

Richthofen's legend is made richer because nobody knows exactly who killed him. Today there is general consensus that the fatal bullet came from an unidentified soldier on the ground, but at the time of the engagement, the pilot who'd been pursuing Richthofen, a Canadian named Roy Brown, was given official credit for the kill. This was despite the obvious geometric challenge of creating a sideways and upward bullet trajectory (as discerned from Richthofen's autopsy) while firing from above and behind his aircraft. And while other pilots would have considered the errant credit a career boost, Brown was tormented by it. After he watched Richthofen crash, he brought his plane in for a landing near the Fokker and walked to the wreckage.

"The sight of Richthofen as I walked closer gave me a start," he wrote in a letter home. "He appeared so small to me, so delicate ... Blond, silk-soft hair, like that of a child, fell from the broad, high forehead. His face, particularly peaceful, had an expression of gentleness and goodness, of refinement.

"Suddenly I felt miserable, desperately unhappy, as if I had committed an injustice ... In my heart, I cursed the force that is devoted to death."[7]

Another theory of Richthofen's death says that he wasn't actually shot until after he had crash-landed his damaged plane. The bullet entered his torso when he reached up to heave himself out of the cockpit, the theory goes.[8] This is plausible, in part because the .303 bullet was something of a universal ammunition. It was used in many types of guns at the time, so identifying the projectile that killed Richthofen does little to identify who or what shot it.

Probably, the verdict will always depend on who's telling the story.

There's one thing nobody argues about, however. Manfred von Richthofen was the origin of a species, a prototype for the elite fighter pilot that exists in our imaginations to this day. He was the clearest model for Erich Hartmann and the *Experten*. He really was, as *The Aeroplane* noted, an aristocrat and a nobleman according to his heritage, and his widely publicized exploits above the trenches cemented the image. We still assume these men (and, recently, women) belong to a special group. They're highly trained, innately skilled, grounded in precious and distinctive soldiering traditions. They all, apparently, aspire to what Richthofen managed to show us, just briefly: chivalry in precarious coexistence with killing.

Richthofen's story, like all of them, gets more complicated the more you know about it. It was convenient, for instance, that the editor of *The Aeroplane*, C. G. Grey, the influential man who helped spread Richthofen's legend across the Channel and far abroad, was an ardent German apologist and, later, a Nazi sympathizer. He once wrote that Germany was "'the first line of defence against Eastern barbarism'. If the British 'only had some of the racial pride and the spirit of nationalism and the aggressive spirit which moves Germany today,' they would be much better off."[9] Little had Richthofen known that his prowess in the air would contribute, through no action of his own, to the congealing spirit of hate in Europe.

There were other aerial pioneers, of course: Eddie Rickenbacker from the United States, Albert Ball from Great Britain, William Bishop of Canada, Max Immelmann and Oswald Bölcke of Germany, and many more. These aviators all stood in contrast to the dehumanizing, catastrophic effects of the war elsewhere. Remember that World War I, on a wider view, was most notable for indiscriminate and mechanized death, not romanticized duels from the old days. Aviation historian Mike Spick writes that in World War I, battlefields "became moonscapes of mud and shell craters ... Not only was the slaughter on an unimaginable scale; it was almost completely anonymous."[10] John Keegan, in his history of the war, observes that "the First World War inaugurated the manufacture of mass death that the Second brought to its pitiless consummation."[11] This echoes a point made by historian and Holocaust scholar Omer Bartov, who has said that the "sustained industrial killing of nameless soldiers" in World War I foreshadowed the application of "industrial" methods to kill masses of targeted and undesirable civilians in World War II.[12]

On the World War I battlefields, with groups of soldiers shelled into oblivion at once, the long-held notion of an honorable fight began to break apart. Artillerymen had no idea whom they were killing. To many, the old notion of looking your enemy in the eye and conducting a respectable battle wasn't just quaint; it was becoming tactically unreasonable.

So where was the antidote, the people wondered, to all this dehumanization—thousands of bodies at a time, lifeless, accumulated in heaps, covered with dirt and drained of their color and their identity and their purpose? Could there ever be such a thing?

Yes: he was in the sky, far above it all.

## CHAPTER 2

# Harmony

Nation states have all used the heroic ideal to propagate and perpetuate codes of moral conduct … and systems of economic, social and political control.

—M. GREGORY KENDRICK[1]

By the spring of 1922, Germans were used to grieving. In Stuttgart, locals walked the gravel paths of the *Schlossplatz*, the city's central square, and remembered the day just four years earlier when Germany had been handed the most humiliating and total defeat in its history. They could gaze up at the regal statue of Concordia, the Roman goddess of harmony atop her giant concrete pillar, and wonder how the land she oversaw could ever retrieve such a feeling again.

Harmony. The longing ran deep.

It was the most unharmonious of times. The aftereffects of World War I were almost as wrecking as the attrition that had taken place in the trenches, and hyperinflation had already made bacon and milk more effective currencies than anything that could be printed on paper. People really did use worthless *Deutschmarks* as wallpaper, and on payday they hurried to stores carrying their cash in laundry tubs so they could buy whatever they could before the currency's valuation was reset again. Nobody quite knew what it was going to mean to be a German in the 20th century.

Erich Alfred Hartmann was born just after Easter. His family wasn't particularly well-off or landed, but in the dreariness of their time they had one crucial privilege: mobility. For them, enduring Germany's inter-war troubles was a choice, and they opted not to. The boy who would grow into the greatest German ace of all time spent his toddler years wandering a completely different part of the world and soaking up something resembling a carefree boyhood. His first words might well have been in Chinese.

He owed it to a seasoned and educated father, a former army medic who had survived World War I with his health and a marketable skill set. Within a year of the Armistice, Dr. Alfred Hartmann was engaged to an arrestingly youthful blonde named Elisabeth Machtholf, and he built a family medical practice in Weissach, near Stuttgart in the German south. Alfred gained clout, and the role as a healer seemed to come naturally enough. He was unambiguously professional and carried himself conservatively. His dark suits showed precise tailoring and his small eyeglasses suggested sophistication, but they also softened him. He was the patriarch, but not necessarily the ruler. Alfred rarely smiled in photos, unlike his gregarious son, but there was always something warm and assuring beneath his formality. Family stories recall his appetite for quiet philosophizing at home.

Dr. Hartmann had a cousin at the German consulate in Shanghai, and talk of international intrigue and happier financial prospects there made Alfred consider a drastic relocation.[2] It was curiously reasonable, given the German political and economic situation: The family would need to bear the long trek, but they could expect security—everyone needs a doctor—and adventure in China. Such a vastly different country and culture might give them a chance at normalcy.

Their journey began in September 1924, covered a quarter of the globe, and spanned languages, climates, and governments. Initially, Alfred went ahead alone to set up a viable practice before the rest of the family came. He bought land on a small, grassy island on the Xiang River, a tributary of the Yangtze near the city of Changsha (where his medical practice was located), a few hundred miles inland of Shanghai. Back in Germany, Elisabeth cared for her two boys, saw to the business of their departure, and managed the home. Erich was in a 3-year-old's knee socks when they boarded an Asia-bound ocean liner to join Alfred.

If Alfred conveyed solidity, Elisabeth emanated raw agency. She was poised, assertive, utterly competent, and quietly attractive. It was she, not Alfred, who gave Erich the physical architecture that kept him seeming younger than he was his entire life, and it was she who shepherded her boys aboard the *Adolf von Baeyer* (named after the Nobel-laureate chemist who did his pioneering work through the late 1800s) with the coolness that would also be attributed to her eldest boy.

It was also she who, at a later date, would give him his lust for flying. Though it was of no use in China or at the nadir of the German economic depression, Elisabeth Hartmann was an accomplished pilot. Her passion would be one of the most critical inheritances young Erich ever received.

Aboard the ocean liner, Elisabeth could be found squinting in the sun, sons at arm's reach, eyes focused on what lay beyond. In old photos and her limited testimonies of the period, she appears elusive—she is the most desirable supporting character in Erich's early story but remains distant to us today, especially in these years (her audacity would be made clearer a couple decades later). Her gaze suggested wonder at what lay beyond the horizon, but didn't give much else away.

China met the Hartmanns' hopes for financial success and adventure. Alfred became a popular townsman (he noted that the Chinese tended to pay their bills on time),[3] and the children grew attached to their nanny, Zauma, whom they would later remember cheerily. Zauma helped reveal the human side of her otherwise quiet employer, too. She once got Alfred into traditional Chinese garb during a lesson or a celebration—it isn't clear whether it was a bout of playfulness on his part or something he was forced into, but the typically composed doctor looked thoroughly, and endearingly, befuddled.[4]

Before long, conflict and uncertainty followed the Hartmann family. In 1927, the Chinese Civil War began, forcing a split between the Nationalists and the insurgent Communists, and the danger to outsiders rose quickly. As the war intensified, many Chinese began resisting or demonizing foreigners, and street violence became commonplace. One of the few memories of China that Erich ever talked about was when he saw a group of partisans carrying signs that read "Foreign Devils Out."[5] Elisabeth, more gruesomely, remembered the day Alfred found the severed heads of several English friends perched atop some fence posts.[6]

At the same time, Alfred's professional prospects were souring, despite his status and Germany's noncommittal stance on China. By 1928, the Hartmann parents admitted the need to return home. Elisabeth packed up her sons and headed for the rail lines that fed into the Trans-Siberian Railroad (the reasons for rail instead of ship travel aren't clear), while Alfred stayed behind to ride it out and keep accumulating wages. For the second time, he would be alone 5,000 miles from home; for the second time, Elisabeth and the boys would find their way as a trio. This trip didn't go so well.

One of the major stops en route was in Moscow, where Elisabeth ventured out to explore the station for food, leaving the boys in their seats. After just a few minutes of a stop that was supposed to last an hour, the train lurched to life with Erich and Alfred sitting alone, with no idea where their mother was. Alfred cried in his seat as the train moved in slow motion, while wide-eyed Erich tried to reassure his younger brother that everything would be fine and *Mutti* would return soon, as she had promised. Erich would have been just tall enough to see out of the train's windows, scanning the crowd for the familiar sight of his mother, thinking just a few minutes into the future and imagining permanent estrangement from his family.

Fortunately, Elisabeth heard the premature train whistle, dropped a sack of goods, and dashed after her sons. The huge inertia of the rail cars worked in her favor, and she made it to the last one before it accelerated away from the station. She jumped aboard, heaving herself up by the railing, and when she crashed through the doors toward her boys, they sat stunned in their seats. Years later, she would compare the harrowing boarding scene to something out of the American "Old West."[7]

Young Erich couldn't have known at the time that the Moscow scare wasn't going to be his last, or even most frightful, experience on a Russian railway.

Back in Stuttgart, Elisabeth waited for word from Alfred, which took several months to arrive. In his letter, however, Alfred wasn't laying out his return plans. Instead, he was making the case that Elisabeth and the boys should travel back to China and give the whole thing another shot. Although Germans at the end of the 1920s were in the so-called golden years of the Weimar Republic—the hopeful but illusory period of stability before the government's collapse—doubt and discontent still circulated. Liberal democracy wasn't particularly natural to Germans at the time: the country had only been unified 50 years earlier, and many would have felt more comfortable under the watch of Germany's original authoritarian unifier, Bismarck. From Alfred's point of view, conditions had seemed to settle down a little in China, and he wondered if the prospects there were still at least as good as those in Germany. Maybe he still hung onto some version of the wanderlust that had drawn him there in the first place.

Elisabeth smothered the idea. "I will not return to China," she responded, "and I am looking now for an office for you near Stuttgart, where you can settle down and practice medicine safely."[8] Dr. Hartmann complied, and the family settled close to where they had begun. The town of Weil im Schönbuch (just "Weil" to them) was the community that would serve them for the rest of their lives. Shortly after they arrived, they built a spacious house not far from the town hall. It was a blockish three-story building, whitewashed, with one compelling architectural flourish: a concave roofline that suggested Asian influence.

Nobody has ever seemed to ask how the China experience affected Erich Hartmann's personal development or his worldview. This was a highly unusual path for a child of Hitler's Germany to have taken, and while he said almost nothing about these things later on, at least publicly, there are still reasons to take the question seriously. Modern researchers have plenty to say about how experiences abroad can equip youngsters with intercultural and cognitive skills that they might not otherwise practice. Could Hartmann have used the China experience as a lens through which to interpret later events in Germany? Would he have warily recalled "Foreign Devils Out" when he saw the same xenophobic sentiment spread into his schools? Would the experience have changed how Alfred and Elisabeth raised their sons? Or was China little more than a colorful flourish to a family firmly rooted in tradition and in search of stability?

We won't know, but the China experience nevertheless underscores one of the Nazis' most important successes: the winning of German boyhood. Erich Hartmann's first six years show us the range of possibilities available even to someone born into the mess of inter-war Germany, but the years that followed reveal how thoroughly the Nazis snuffed those possibilities out.

Hartmann was too young to know it, but Hitler had something else going for him in 1928: the momentum of German history. After all, that Hartmann house, curious roofline and all, was built squarely on a road called *Bismarckstrasse*.

## Hildebrand and Heroism

In the old Germanic legend, recorded during the 4th century BC, a distinguished soldier named Hildebrand encounters a difficult dilemma. We don't have the full written manuscript of *Hildebrandsleid*, but the plot of the drama is clear enough to scholars. Hildebrand initially comes up against a new young enemy named Hadubrand, who bristles with power and is similarly renowned. According to custom, the two must duel, with their armies standing by as spectators. Only one will survive.

What only Hildebrand and the reader are allowed to know is that the two fighters are father and son. "Now my own child will cut me down with his weapon," Hildebrand observes. "Or I shall be his doom."[9] This is the cruel outcome of Hildebrand's successes in battle up to this point. "I was always placed in the first battle-line," he says, "and before no fortress was I felled." His 30 years of dominance have only served to position him in this dire confrontation.

And there's the central dramatic question: can Hildebrand, the father, kill his son simply because that is what is expected of him? Yes, it turns out. The text of *Hildebrandsleid* is incomplete and ends before we learn the outcome of the battle, but, according to one interpretation, the story only makes logical sense if Hildebrand carries his task to its conclusion and succeeds in killing his son.[10] Regardless of the outcome, it is clear that Hildebrand at least *attempts* to kill his son because of his established social framework and the armies looking on at the confrontation, whose expectations he is obliged to meet.

This deeply uncomfortable climax highlights a crucial theme in the ebbing ideal of the Germanic hero: the protection of order. Historian Brian Murdoch has observed that for the Germanic heroes of the old days, "to be a *good* warrior is simply to do his appointed task properly, and he cannot (or at least he ought not to) set out to be a hero in more recent [individualist] senses of the word."[11] On the surface, you might think Hildebrand was showing us something resembling the modern, individualist heroic path, as described by Joseph Campbell *et al*: there was the journey, the disruptive obstacle, the battle, the solitary victory. But what really matters are his motivations—the *why* of this heroic tale. Hildebrand killed his son not for individual glory or because he hated him, but because doing anything else would not have made much sense within his social and political framework. His victory, strange as it sounds, was a victory for harmony.

There are examples from other well-known tales. Some scholars interpret the monsters in *Beowulf* (an Old English story rooted in Germanic paganism) as threats to the hero's political framework and the social order. Murdoch says: "[D]uring the period of the poem—in which two rulers, Hrodgar and Beowulf[,] rule for fifty years apiece—the political balance was maintained, and the respective peoples lived, therefore, in happily uninteresting times."[12]

Happily uninteresting times. Now apply this framework to those youngsters who came of age under the influence of Nazism. It wasn't just the propaganda, empire-building, and ethnocentrism that influenced their worldview. There were always other influences, as you would imagine with any generation—ones that reached deeper and farther back into their shared history and sense of belonging. To them, the *Wehrmacht*, the marches, and the flag-waving—and yes, even the dictator—were, in some way, natural. "Over all else in Germanic writings about the hero," Murdoch says, "is the acknowledgment of a need for stability."[13] To those insulated by their desirable racial identities, as the Hartmanns were, Hitler and the *Wehrmacht* promised precisely that. In many ways they delivered it early on.

Historian M. Gregory Kendrick uses social science to reiterate Murdoch's earlier assessments of traditional heroism and how it changed over time. "Heroism in [earlier societies] was largely about taking actions aimed at protecting, preserving, or transcending [the] centuries-long status quo," he writes.[14] As a result, those who were labeled heroes were often the ones fending off outside invaders, rebellions, or disruption. This was due in part to the hierarchical nature of many older cultures and nation-states, where the value of the average individual wasn't the focus it is today. The polity and the order were what mattered, and only a select few were situated to defend it. But all of this began to change with industrialization, the Enlightenment, and the democratization of developed economies. Modern hero narratives eventually began to support the growing belief, Kendrick adds, that "we celebrate ... anyone who is both unordinary in some fashion and yet very much a part of that great herd within which we all live and work."[15] Just about anyone, in other words, simply by encountering the circumstances of their lives head-on, could become a hero.

Erich Hartmann obviously occupies a confused place in all of this. His early choices and behaviors, at the time of his upbringing and during World War II, were essentially compliant—he excelled at following exactly the path laid out for him. They also seem to support those distant cultural and social inheritances: harmony, stability, and retrieving a mythical national cohesion from the past. These were, of course, foundational parts of Hitler's promises to his country. The humiliation of Versailles was always on his and his citizens' minds (even though Germany would have imposed similarly harsh terms on its enemies if it had won), and Hitler's fanatical march to war felt not like a needless reprisal of the earlier catastrophe, but a necessary international correction.[16] Hitler was able to sell his messages of hate, obedience, and collective struggle not because those messages were always amazingly well crafted, but because they were sellable at the time.

When you listen to Hitler's early speeches, you hear about reclaiming what was old, beloved, and solid, and  of delivering to the German people the moral, military, and cultural stability that was rightly theirs. You hear about vanquishing the outsiders and the traitors who had led Germany astray after World War I. You hear about home, the German heart, and the country's special place under heaven. Hitlerian fascism didn't promise a new nation so much as it promised, at long last, the old one. Or at least something that resembled people's memories closely enough that it felt authentic.

But the influences of Richthofen and the new individualists promised something more in the rarified air above the battlefield. They promised individual achievement, chivalry, and independence. This duality—the old collective values plus the new individualist ones—is part of what makes the German aviators of World War II so fascinating relative to other soldiers. Their worldview contained both, which is one reason they were able to conduct themselves with such purpose, clarity, and effectiveness.

## Yes, Iron and Blood

Germans today are of mixed feelings about their original dictator. On one hand, Otto von Bismarck was the craftsman of the nationalism, militarism, and racial and cultural insularity that Hitler later exploited. But he also created the modern welfare state, cultivated noteworthy democratic norms, and possessed distinctive, maybe even revolutionary, qualities as a statesman. In 1933, all these things seemed compatible and desirable. If Germans craved a revival at that time, it was the Bismarckian ideal they longed for; if and when Erich Hartmann set out to retrieve that celebrated, harmonious past, this was probably his reference point.

Bismarck's leadership had as much to do with where he had come from as where he thought he was going. The Prussians were warriors, and armed conflict was, forever it seemed, the most durable organizing tool among the scattered German polities. (As Napoleon is credited with saying: "Prussia was hatched from a cannon-ball.") But Bismarck was no simple chest-beater. Many say he helped create Realpolitik, a political philosophy that defers, sometimes ruthlessly, to desirable practical effects instead of ideology or first principles.[17] He made war for the outcomes, engineering conflicts with Denmark, Austria, and France that Prussia could easily win. In the process, he redrew the map of the homeland and nurtured a productive, unifying nationalist fervor to sustain the recent unification. It mattered little that he was officially subordinate to the Kaiser, Wilhelm I. In every practical sense, he made the chancellorship the highest prize.

Historians have observed that Bismarck lacked many of the typical traits we assume of national leaders. He had no long military record, no real social privilege, and few useful religious connections—but he still grabbed people with his presence and his conviction in a way that none of his contemporaries ever could. This was, in large part, because Bismarck was a very particular type of hero, a hybrid figure who blended old notions of social order with an emerging, modern emphasis on individual gravitas.

Today, historians call this heroic vitalism. The expression refers to a singular, powerful leader who uses a cult of personality and (typically) coercive military and/or police force to achieve control and compliance in the citizenry. This hero scoffs at softness, egalitarianism, and intellectualism. He is almost exclusively masculine. He rallies his countrymen by concocting a dazzling public persona that affords him a morally elevated position relative to the populace he controls. There's a reason the word "vitality" has a slightly biological feel, too: it's about muscle, verve, red blood surging through the veins, endurance.

Kendrick observes that, on a practical level, heroic vitalism relies on "an odd amalgam of illiberal politics, romanticism, violence, and utopian reveries."[18]

Heroic vitalism of Bismarck's variety also understands violence to be a natural part of the political process. Bismarck started wars, won them, and through the bloodshed unified the chronically fragmented Germanic states. It's true that he had more nuanced skills as a statesman than many people understand, but his political legacy will always boil down to iron and blood. This was intentional. Bismarck—and especially the idolizing totalitarians who followed him—imagined "a new heroic age that was reactionary—atavistic actually—in its political and social arrangements, and wildly utopian in its aims and aspirations for the human future."[19] One reason Hitler's lustful dreams of *Ubermenschen* and a new Germanic utopia didn't seem completely crazy to people was that he didn't really invent them.

Bismarck left plenty of subtle influences as well. For example, long after he had completed his own (brief and maybe even unwanted) military service, he wore his military uniform in office. Governing in uniform was not the expected practice for a chancellor, but it ennobled Bismarck, lending refinement to an otherwise gruff and unspectacular-looking man. Some historians talk about the "fetishization of uniform" that Bismarck helped to spawn, and it could be that he unwittingly foreshadowed those grandiose speeches in 1930s Nuremberg, with the goose-stepping, flag-waving, and cheering, by so effectively wielding his own martial image. Later dictators stayed fond of drab fabrics and brass.[20]

The Bismarckian worldview was not the cause of German anti-Semitism, but it provided fresh soil in which it could grow. Most staunchly nationalist platforms include hostility toward "the other," and Bismarck supported the idea that there were proper Germans, and then there were all the others. This was an emotionally powerful truth even prior to World War I because it fitted with the combative narrative the proudly unified Germany had been writing for itself all along. It permeated popular rhetoric in the way rugged individualism permeated Americana as the United States pushed at its western frontier during that same time period. The possibilities—and the urgency—seemed boundless.

The German culture was shaped by plenty of other influences that tugged the country toward dictatorship. As the novelist Eric Vuillard put it:

> They were too cramped for space in Germany—and since no one is ever completely satisfied, and people are always turning toward hazy distant horizons, and a touch of megalomania overlaid with paranoid tendencies makes the slope even slipperier; and since, on top of that, they had already had the delirium of Herder and the addresses of Fichte, Hegel's "spirit of the people" and Schelling's dream of a communion of hearts, we can say that the notion of *Lebensraum* was really nothing new.[21]

The philosopher and literary critic Johann Gottfried Herder, as a reminder, helped give Germans their conception of nationality and the nation-state, kindling a quiet skepticism toward other historical cultures. And it was Johann Gottlieb Fichte who gave the people their nationalistic rallying cry in the era of Napoleon. Here Vuillard is invoking a swirl of insular, pride-afflicted influences that have bobbed and floated to the surface all along the turbulent course of German history—just as similar influences are visible in many other countries.

Still, for Germans, virulent anti-Semitism was a choice and a departure from precedent. Richard Evans, in his inches-thick treatment of the rise of Nazism, notes that "the Jewish story in the late 19th century was a success story … and Jews were associated above all with the most modern and progressive developments in society, culture and the economy."[22] A familiar related fact is that Bismarck trusted his finances for decades to a Jewish advisor named Gerson Bleichröder. But as the new century arrived, an economic bubble burst, the blaming started, and commentators who might otherwise have been relegated to the fringe stepped into the mainstream. These writers and critics, opportunistic and shape-shifting, wondered aloud whether Jewish people's hardships weren't quite proportional to the rest of the populace. In some cases, where Jewish businesspeople had achieved vaulted positions, they had seemed insulated, as if they were elite insiders in some quiet scheme of economic manipulation. This economic rationale was eventually coupled with the pseudo-scientific notion that there must be something cold, some baseline nefariousness, making its way through these non-Aryans' bloodstreams. Eventually, the Nazis' biological racism, at times ripped off from Darwin and customized to support the cause, formalized a bigotry with which many Germans were already vaguely familiar. The depth of this moral evil and empirical error has grown clearer with each passing year, but in any historical period, hatred seeps into a fragile society like water into concrete. The more cracks, the more seepage.

And then Erich Hartmann was ready for school.

## CHAPTER 3

# "The Demolition Function"

I have seen what war does to children, makes them killers or victims, robs them of their parents, their homes, and their innocence—steals their childhood and leaves them marked in body, mind, and spirit.

—WILLIAM BROYLES, JR[1]

*Coriolanus*, says writer Anthony Lane, is among Shakespeare's grimmest work. An edition of the tragedy published for German schoolchildren in 1934 compared the Roman warrior to Hitler himself, since Coriolanus' goal was to "lead the people back to health ... 'just as Adolf Hitler in our days wishes to lead our beloved German fatherland.'"[2] Ignore the fact that Coriolanus turns against his beloved Rome. Ignore the blood and grime of his methods.

Hitler's Nazism was not just a regurgitation of old Bismarckian militarism. It was a gristlier perversion. When the party took hold, it pushed mixed ideals whose rapid adoption by so many Germans has remained an obvious historical puzzle. These were, in part, backward-looking ideals, since they supported the dismissal of the Weimar Republic's liberal rationalism in favor of a more emotive traditionalism. But they were also forward-looking, since the *Gleichschaltung* (roughly: streamlining or coordination of the citizenry, meaning the extermination of some for the sake of others) demanded modernization in infrastructure, technology, rhetoric, even mass media. The scheme was something that had never existed before. Ignore the stench of oppression and mass murder.

All of this was coalescing just when Hartmann was coming of age. In April 1928, three years after Hitler had formalized his ideas in *Mein Kampf*, Hartmann entered the local *Volksschule*. This was no Nazi institution yet, but it normalized some of the behaviors that interested the Nazis the most. Hartmann was academically uninspired, but he shone in physical drill and sports. His younger brother, Alfred Jr., remembered later: "He was stronger than me in every way. He was sports-minded, athletic and accomplished ... In fact, there was nothing in the sporting line at which he did not excel or could not excel if he tried it."[3] Old photos show that Erich had a sport for every season, barreling off ski jumps in one shot and collecting swimming awards in others. His adventurousness charmed his teachers, who remembered him for his good behavior and obedience.[4]

The German dictatorship arrived in 1933, when Hartmann was 11 years old. When political fragmentation and disillusionment led President Paul von Hindenburg to appoint Hitler as Chancellor in January that year, Hitler immediately called new national elections, hoping to consolidate a majority of the vote. On election day in March—which saw an 89 per cent voter turnout—the Nazis received 43.9 per cent of the vote, courtesy of inflamed propaganda, widespread violence, and intimidation from Hitler's henchmen and the still-young *Schutzstaffel* (*SS*). This was short of their goals but enough for the Nazis to break 50 per cent with their nationalist allies.[5] From there it took some further suppression of the Nazis' enemies to ensure passage a few weeks later of the Enabling Act, which required a two-thirds majority of legislators and gave Hitler dictatorial powers in the name of order and security. Among the political parties still operating in Germany, only the Social Democrats voted against the Act. Their spokesman, Otto Wels, gave a dissenting speech in which he defended "the principles of humanity and justice," but when he did it he carried a cyanide capsule in his pocket, fearing that he would either be shot or tortured for the display. He wasn't, but he was forced into exile and stripped of his citizenship.[6]

Over the years, people have begun to see Hitler's ascendency for what it was: the lawful arrival of a party leader promising ambitious national rebuilding, safety from nefarious outsiders, and a return to Germany's glory days. Germans' acceptance of Hitler was catastrophic, but it wasn't an otherworldly phenomenon. It was a substantially democratic one, which is part of why it remains such a sore in our consciousness.

And the Nazis acted quickly once they'd found their foothold. The Enabling Act was passed within several weeks of the March elections, and the reorientation of German institutions began immediately. One of the first targets was the education system.

## Teaching the Dictatorship

In 1936, Hartmann entered a strict, National Socialist-run boarding school at Rottweil known as the National Political Reformatory. Its main building sat heavily among straight lines of trees and boasted all the fortified brick halls that one might expect of it. Enrolled boys were allotted one bed and one chair, and the motto, Hartmann remembered, was "discipline and cleanliness."[7] Militaristic structure and ritual displaced exploration and inquiry. Hartmann's lack of an obvious intellectual spark made him a desirable pupil, since Hitler despised nothing in his youth more than braininess. At institutions like Rottweil, "self-confidence and national pride were to be inculcated in German youth, instead of 'scholastic slime'," writes historian Lisa Pine. "Hitler thus placed great emphasis upon the importance of physical training."[8]

Victor Klemperer, a frequently cited diarist of the Nazi years, expressed Hartmann's tutelage thus:

> For Hitler, the development of character quite explicitly has to take second place; in his view it evolves more or less automatically when the physical dominates education and quashes the workings of the mind. Last of all in his pedagogical programme … comes the training of the intellect and its provision with knowledge; it is only countenanced with reluctance, and is viewed with suspicion.[9]

This approach was, in part, a reaction to the Enlightenment ideals many Germans associated with the leaders of the failed Weimar government. There was a spirit of rebellion in the citizenry against the progressive academic types, especially among young men and women who came of age under the influence of the warring youth groups that were in place prior to the Hitler Youth. Hitler noticed this opportunity. Universities suffered when their coursework was curtailed, their academic terms were compressed, and their professors—some the most seasoned minds in Germany's communities and inheritors of world-class intellectual traditions—were fired or marginalized through intimidation or other methods. Klemperer, for example, had taught Romance studies at the Technical University of Dresden until his dismissal in 1935. He resumed teaching in East Germany after the war.

The Nazis suppressed jazz, tore out artwork that didn't fit their philosophy and called it degenerate, and burned books by the millions while kids like Hartmann looked on. Non-Jewish citizens watched with some trepidation, but also with constant propaganda about the so-called principles behind the changes. There were some notable exceptions to the cultural wipeout, including the performing arts, which were allowed to continue only partially neutralized. Propaganda minister Joseph Göbbels was sensitive to the balance between realigning the citizenry and alienating it.

German education by the mid-1930s was, consequently, a sham. Schools stayed administratively detached from the Nazi Party, but this division meant less and less as time went on. Curricula were rebuilt to fit the National Socialist plan, and teachers who were thought of as dangerous to the cause were replaced. Some of the others, many of whom might have been uninterested in National Socialism, experienced sudden upward mobility now that so many undesirable teachers were gone and attributed it to the efficacy of the Party. And while leaders postured as if they were making concessions to teachers and schools (they supposed that they were making gestures of goodwill, it seems, by not wholly overrunning the institution), the reality was that schooling for boys and girls was exactly what National Socialism demanded it be. It was just subcontracted.

The lessons Hartmann and the others were subjected to are stunning in hindsight. Nazi science purported to show how Hitler's racist policies were validated by heredity. New history texts—which, says historian Gilmer Blackburn, served a "demolition function" in that they cleared the way for a racial-revisionist understanding of Germany—focused overwhelmingly on the chest-beating triumphs of the nation's past, its larger-than-life leadership figures, and the nefarious suppression of the Germanic spirit by foreign influences.[10] Geography formalized the image of the "eternally wandering Jew" in contrast to the rooted, expansionist German. Even mathematics socialized young people to think of Jews and other outliers as financial problems. Aside from having to calculate the trajectories of mortar shells, students solved problems like how much money over a hypothetical lifetime of 45 years a "cripple," an "alcoholic," and a "deaf and dumb person" would cost the state to keep alive.[11] It's easy to imagine a bigoted teacher rocking his head back and forth in front of the class: "That's a lot of our money, children. We can't let that continue, can we?"

The takeaway here is not that young German minds were blank slates easily influenced by Hitler's bluster and cinematic appeal. These youngsters, like any others, were influenced by the truth content that was packaged for them, and it came from many directions. The organization and resources of the German state ensured that the children overwhelmingly encountered Hitler's version of reality, that it was normalized through education, and that it was delivered by trusted sources. If modern-day curricular experts could look at those discarded lesson plans or leftover notes on blackboards, they would probably conclude that the Nazis were teaching intuitive and vocational thought processes more than integrative or critical ones; it fitted their scheme, discouraged dissent, and prepared students for the tasks of German expansionism, such as laboring and soldiering. It wasn't just about giving young people a way of looking at the world; it was giving them an expectation for what their job in that world would be. As a way to produce an equipped workforce and ready soldiers, it worked just fine, but as a method of empowering thinkers, dreamers, and intellectual risk-takers, it was worthless. Today we recognize this as institutionalized oppression.

Reinhard Heydrich, one of the most venomous Nazis, was in charge of bringing about the so-called Final Solution for Jews in what was then Czechoslovakia. In 1942, he mused that "the teaching profession is a breeding ground for opposition ... It must be destroyed."[12] This was essentially a practical declaration. He and others who sought to stifle informed dissent proceeded confidently, creating the policies and practices that smothered a generation of thinkers and creators. Little did they know, or care, that they were orchestrating a dour betrayal of some of their home country's proudest and most enlightened traditions and achievements.

The missing piece in this part of Hartmann's upbringing is the type and degree of influence his parents had over his schooling and understandings of the world. Although his recollections of this time period are fragmented and not very detailed, a couple of conclusions spring naturally from them. One was that his childhood, despite the ruthless organization of the Nazi state, still included all the familiar, innocuous mileposts: experimenting with black powder in chemistry class, building boy-sized gliders and jumping off the roof with them, sports, and girls. As researchers Sönke Neitzel and Harald Welzer remind us, Germans' acceptance of Hitler wasn't actually predicated on zombie-like conformity and mass brainwashing, but rather on the seepage of evil into a constant and comforting sense of normalcy: "The Third Reich consisted first and foremost of a multitude of mundane everyday factors that structure people's lives in every imaginable society. Children went to school, and adults went to work or to the unemployment office."

They continue: "The Nazi regime ended freedom of the press, censored criticism, and created a highly conformist public sphere." But, they say, raising a finger against simplifying a complicated reality, the *private* sphere was another matter.[13] In households like the Hartmanns', dissent and divergent opinions were never destroyed. It was through normal, private discussion that Germans maintained coherence in their world views and their day-to-day activities so they could proceed with life.

The Hartmann dinner-table conversations, then, were probably like millions of others then and since. This was a capable and intelligent family that had conceived and executed the bold plan to relocate just a couple years earlier; these were diligent members of their community who seem to have been driven by practicality as much as ideology. Just as there is no evidence to say that no Hartmann family member ever held a Nazi belief, there also is no reason to suppose they were all open adherents.

Rudi Florian, a German who was 10 years old in 1944, recalls these private conversations in his own family during the Hitler years. "Though [my parents] did not like the Nazis, they did not dare to openly oppose them either," he writes. "They chose instead the path of passive resistance like so many others did for their own safety." When Florian had to join the Hitler Youth, his mother helped him evade the meetings by saying he had to stay home to care for his sister. The officials who came to the Florian house to ask about Rudi's whereabouts eventually got tired of the excuse and stopped trying. Florian credits his family's Catholicism for their clearheaded, if quiet, opposition to the Nazis. He has spoken widely about the horrors of the Holocaust and the need for vigilance against hate groups that still occupy the periphery of our governments and discourse.[14]

Here, again, is one of the sad realizations that come from studying the Nazi regime. It's one profoundly evil thing for people to openly and viciously eradicate others and their identity as a culture. It's quite another for an ideology to enter, drip by drip, into the lives of other Germans who weren't similarly vulnerable, conditioning them to comply or at least not to speak out. Florian quotes Nobel Peace Prize winner Elie Wiesel here: "Whenever and wherever human beings endure suffering and humiliation, take sides. Neutrality helps the oppressor, never the victim. Silence encourages the tormentor, never the tormented."[15] The problem, today as in 1933 or 1944, is that it's easier to believe this idea than it is to enact it.

## Graduation

In the spring of 1937, Erich Hartmann transferred to the *Hochschule* at Korntal, a small community to the north of Stuttgart, where he finished his *Abitur*, roughly the equivalent to an American high school diploma. According to him, Korntal was a relief from the iron-clad military structure at Rottweil, where leaders relished in victimizing students. One of his old instructors at Korntal, Kurt Busch, remembered Hartmann readily 30 years after the fact, noting that he was "straightforward, open and honest," even if he was prone to a "certain impulsiveness."[16]

Hartmann's original biography, *The Blond Knight of Germany*, suggests that Korntal was a deliberate move away from the Nazi flag-waving and militarism of Rottweil, but even it was overrun. There is a school at Korntal today, and in its historical background information its administrators note that in 1937, the same year that Hartmann arrived, "the streamlining of schools" took place. What had once been the Higher School for Boys of the Evangelical United Brethren Korntal had its "former school and home directors ... replaced."[17] Busch and at least some of the other teachers were allowed to remain through the changes, but the happy innocence of the institution isn't so certain. In a photo of Busch kept by Hartmann's family, he smiles into the camera with a swastika prominently banded around his left arm. A caption to the photo mentions that Busch was the leader of the boarding school, suggesting that if the Nazis had replaced the rest of the leadership with hand-picked servants, Busch must have convinced them of his suitability somehow. The specifics are uncertain.

The most notable milepost for Hartmann during this period was romantic. While at Korntal, he developed a feverish crush on a brunette named Ursula Pätsch, and every record available suggests that he pursued her single-mindedly. Her parents initially disapproved of the match, since she was 15 and he was two years older, and Hartmann also had to contend with rival boys. But "Uschi," as he liked to call her, became convinced that he was the right boy after much courting and after he (literally) beat another prospective boyfriend into submission. Their courtship featured all the classic teenage zeal and blunders. Here's Hartmann:

> At this time, Uschi had another admirer. I made a great mistake of taking her out on a date, to a film at the cinema, and I lost track of time. I brought her back very late, and her parents gave her a three-month restriction ... she was not to have any contact with me because I was a bad influence.

But he found a way:

> Uschi used to take dance lessons, and she went to this studio ... I would wait around the corner, and then when [her parents] left I would go in. This was how we still met. The teacher finally became tired of seeing me there and asked me to leave. So, I paid and signed up for the dancing classes! We called ourselves Romeo and Juliet, but Uschi said that she was not going to kill herself over me, so I could forget about that.[18]

Incidentally, the mention of Shakespeare gives us another window into how the Nazis reframed cultural influences that were impractical to eliminate or ban. In this case, they did it by claiming Shakespeare as one of their own. He was more German than English, they said (with utter seriousness). The party argued the point in an official document called "Shakespeare: A Germanic Writer."

The lovebirds' affinity for each other endured as months turned into years, and before long Ursula would have her nickname painted in wavy script on the side of a Messerschmitt fighter. This romance, and the dedication that kindled it, is one of the lighter and more private storylines that run through Hartmann's life. It shows ambition where his academic pursuits did not, charming bullheadedness that would become more evident as he aged, and the influence of a love interest in a dreary wartime environment. It also confirms that Germany's young people were complex, vulnerable, feeling individuals. Hartmann and the others, after all, were someone's children. At the outset they were no more homogeneous or shallow-minded than young people from other time periods or places, and despite Hitler's best work, most would never have their identities fully overwritten by the Nazi code. They loved as fiercely as they fought. They fought because they believed what they were doing was noble—it's what they were taught.

# CHAPTER 4

# *Jugend*

I want a violent, domineering, undismayed, cruel youth. Youth must be all that. It must bear pain. There must be nothing weak and gentle about it ... in this way I can create the new.

—HITLER, *MEIN KAMPF*

In inter-war Germany, the *Hitlerjugend*—Hitler Youth—was neither novel nor particularly extreme. Germans were accustomed to well-organized, combative youth groups that vied for attention and territory with fists, bent pipes, and occasionally ideas. These organizations were outlets for teenage angst, but they also provided purpose and camaraderie in a dreary time largely devoid of those things. Created on July 4, 1926, the Hitler Youth was a refinement of something that had already been invented.

This large-scale involvement among young people grew from the social and economic realities at the time, not just the allure of an ideology or a spirit of rebellion. Historian Michael Kater writes:

> [T]he youth cohort born between approximately 1903 and 1915 was afflicted with various economic, social, physical, and psychological problems. This group of young men and women were between the ages of eighteen and thirty in 1933, when they constituted nearly one-third of the German population. Brought up as children during World War I, they and their mothers were abandoned as the fathers fought in the trenches ... [T]he children's pain was prolonged when the fathers returned from the war as losers who had been thrashed.[1]

Before Hitler was even Chancellor, he was standing in for the father figures of thousands of German households. This paternalistic role was deliberate, and it was crucial to his acceptance.

Erich Hartmann was a quiet but accomplished Hitler Youth member. His public recollections of the experience are thin, and his level of devotion to the organization, as well as the degree to which he adopted its explicitly political, racist, and nationalist tenets, is all but lost in history. In one letter he wrote to Ursula, Hartmann described the upper Hitler Youth leadership as "trash." This seems to be the most explicit reaction he had to the hierarchy, but it's worth noting that he wrote that letter well after the war had been lost, in a Soviet prison camp, where it was sure to be read and censored.[2]

When Hitler came to power, he appointed an ardent young Nazi named Baldur von Schirach as head of the Hitler Youth. Schirach was a slick, inner-circle Party member enamored with Hitler and the National Socialist worldview. He would be convicted of war crimes after Germany's defeat. But his efforts populated the military, filled the factories with able and compliant workers, and nurtured an indoctrinated leadership class that was supposed to be responsible for continuing Hitler's plans after Germany had crushed its enemies.

"Adolf Hitler, we believe in you," Schirach proclaimed in 1934, assuming the voice of his administrators and his youth simultaneously. "[W]ithout you we would be individuals[;] through you we are a nation. You give us the experience of our youth."[3]

It helped Shirach and the other Hitler Youth architects that many of Germany's existing youth groups had compatible militarist aims. For a while there was a leftist faction that included Communists, particularly as the 1917 Russian Revolution came and went, but this faded after it was (literally) beaten into submission by the paramilitary offshoots of the Hitler Youth. Some of the right-wing groups were church-based and others were secular; most already used militarism as their doctrinal glue. They frequently shared a programmatic focus on physical activities like hiking and sports as a way to reinforce rote skill-building and conformity, and they perpetuated the general disdain for the modernity represented by the Weimar government.

Hartmann's biography is inconsistent in how it describes his entrance into the Hitler Youth. In a photo caption of Hartmann in his Hitler Youth uniform, it says that children were automatically conscripted into the organization in 1939, suggesting that Hartmann was merely a member of that unwitting cohort. However, later, it specifies that he became a glider leader in the Hitler Youth in 1937, before mandatory conscription. (By 1937, Schirach had already orchestrated a voluntary membership among boys and girls of 64 per cent of the population.)[4] It is likely that his entrance was even earlier, given that 1937 was the year he received the important promotion. Hartmann says almost nothing about any of this, sadly, and in his later interviews he describes a conflict with the neighborhood bicycle gang with more detail than he ever gave to the Hitler Youth.[5] But, as will become clear later, it is possible to learn more about Hartmann's Hitler Youth experience without his commentary on it.

For Hartmann or anyone else, there was never any doubt about the ultimate purpose of the organization. A 1932 leaflet, distributed to encourage Hitler Youth membership in Kiel, declared:

> On the day of the National Socialist seizure of power begins the German Revolution … Our banners do not carry the slogans of "Moscow," nor "Internationalism" nor "Pacifism." The only name they carry is that of "Germany" and nothing but "Germany."[6]

To that end, Hartmann and the others learned rifle marksmanship, honing their shot and their knowledge of their weapons; they wrestled each other to the ground in camp games meant to toughen them up and fortify their spirits; and, of course, they marched and marched and marched. It is easy to picture the 12-year-olds, according to the schedule set by their local governments, arriving at the drill field to find brand-new camping gear and outfits, air rifles, and all the pageantry of a great excursion. Their leaders are waiting for them. These leaders, all accomplished and approved by the hierarchy, mentor each pupil along the trails when they can't take the long hikes, offering them water and the encouragement they want so desperately from someone they've been steered to admire. With each free breath the groups sing songs of unity and national purpose. The children experience nothing short of infatuation. It sinks in.

One former member, Hermann Graml, who became a respected German historian, recalled being "wooed and flattered beyond limits" by these events.[7] Kater summarizes: "Unlike family, church, and school, the [Hitler Youth] was not weighed down by tradition and taboos and seemed to offer an exciting opportunity for young people to be respected and responsible."[8] It didn't hurt that it allowed the boys comparatively free fraternization with girls.

It is unclear how deeply involved Ursula was, but she would have had a ready-made path under National Socialism, too. Young women were swept into the League of German Girls (*Bund Deutscher Mädel*, or *BDM*), the Hitler Youth's female division, whose training elements were shaped by dominant gender norms and sexist attitudes. Many of these were on display in a program called the *Pflichtjahr* ("compulsory year"), which took city-dwelling young girls and had them do work out in the countryside. The idea was to train them for domestic responsibilities and give them a respect for the homeland, especially since Nazis tended to view cities as paved bastions of depravity that women should avoid.[9] So they got them out into the countryside to see what they should be aspiring to.

Even construction of the *Autobahn* was packaged as a glorious effort to connect Germans with their land. Starting in 1933, this vast public works project was designed not just to connect cities and industry, but to weave throughout the countryside, highlighting the natural wonders and splendor of the German land. For Fritz Todt, whom Hitler put in charge of the *Autobahn*'s development, "they even fulfilled a racial purpose, linking the motor-borne German soul to the authentic woods, mountains and fields of its native land, and expressing the Nordic race's delight in the adventure, speed and excitement provided by modern technology."[10]

Young women were supposed to be health-conscious and fit like their male counterparts, but only so they could perform as suitable bearers of the next generation of worthy German children. This was another justification for the focus on getting outdoors and away from urban impurities. And while their usefulness was based primarily on their fertility, free or premature sexual behavior was a serious social deviation. Unsurprisingly, this rule didn't apply as harshly to male League leaders watching over the girls. Some of them adapted the German acronym for the group, *BDM*, to mean "*Bubi drück Mich*," or "Babe, squeeze me."

And yet the girls, like the boys, found the organization enchanting. They were celebrated members of society, banded together in service of a cause. For many, it became the defining positive experience of their upbringing, a fact that caused a lot of heartache later in life when they understood the evil of the regime they had celebrated. "I can't get the sunshine out of my memories," said one remorseful former *BDM* member.[11]

## Even the Pope

In 2009, the story broke that Pope Benedict XVI, whose given name is Joseph Ratzinger, had been a member of the Hitler Youth. The official response from the Vatican downplayed his experience. "The Hitler Youth is not a significant experience in his life because he was not an active participant. It was just something that was done," said spokesman Rev. Federico Lombardi, after he had botched the story earlier by asserting falsely that Ratzinger had "never, never, never" been involved.[12] Several outlets spent their time examining not just the extent of the Pope's participation, but the awkwardness of the story itself, since it broke just as the Pope was visiting Israel to talk about the Holocaust and meet two important rabbis.

Although Ratzinger and Hartmann's quietness about the Hitler Youth is typical, it isn't universal. Some former members came to terms their experience publicly, reckoning with their guilt, confusion, and, as the *BDM* member above shows, the awkward fondness they still had for parts of the experience. Among them is Alfons Heck, whose boyhood story shared several of the same mileposts as Hartmann's. Heck, who eventually lectured alongside a Holocaust survivor named Helen Waterford, said that his openness was made possible only by years of hard introspection and healing. Heck's memories are honest and detailed, and, even if they don't apply literally to Hartmann's experience—Heck also headed toward the *Luftwaffe* via the Hitler Youth, but he was younger than Hartmann and from a different town—they certainly flesh out the national and programmatic experience in which Hartmann was immersed.

The Hitler Youth worked because it was an emotional and sensory barrage meant to create fascination, meaning, and allegiance. Heck recalls one day shortly after his town's new infantry garrison was opened (that day was immediately declared a civic holiday):

> I belonged to the *Fanfarenzug* then, the drum and fanfare platoon, which always preceded any large units of the Hitler Youth in order to set the marching cadence. Hundreds of Hitler Youth boys were arranged in formation and stood at attention in honor of the flawlessly goose-stepping soldiers. Afterwards, we were inspected by a colonel who wore the blue cross of the *Order Pour le Merite*, Germany's highest World War I decoration for bravery[,] around his neck.[13]

This grandeur was the perfect complement to Hitler's early economic and social successes, which was convincing the grownups that Hitler could actually deliver the rebirth he promised. As Heck put it, his family had become "impressed not with Hitler's political ideology, but with his undeniable success in restoring full employment and economic order as well as social stability in a devastated, beaten-down nation which suffered from a massive inferiority complex."[14] An American journalist at the time put it this way: "I am beginning to comprehend some of the reasons for Hitler's astounding success. He is restoring pageantry and color and mysticism to the drab lives of twentieth-century Germans."[15]

Heck visited Nuremberg for the notorious Nazi Party Congress—the giant political rally marked by massive crowds of youngsters and delirious party supporters flanked by waves of soldiers—and the fervor of the movement swept him up. He made the trip to Nuremberg from his hometown of Wittlich as a member of his district's Hitler Youth delegation. To him, it was worth every minute of the 250-mile train ride. He felt a powerful connection to his *Führer*—a personal connection, even though he had never seen him in the flesh.

This was all according to Hitler's plan, and the intimacy between the youth and the *Führer* was orchestrated even down to the linguistic level. Hitler Youth members were among very few Germans who were taught to refer to Hitler with the casual *Du* form of the German "You" rather than the more customary and formal *Sie*. This distinction doesn't exist in English, but it is significant to German speakers.

This sense of connection also encouraged youths to see the potential heroism in their own lives. The young weren't mere subjects—they were allowed heroic status to the extent that they conformed to Hitler's Aryan ideal and prepared for the sacrifices of war. Erich Hartmann was one of the best possible examples: blond-haired, blue-eyed, and a great physical specimen, he was propelled through Hitler Youth programming by supervisors who recognized his potential.

Like most *Jungen*, Heck was conditioned from a young age—before his formal introduction to the Hitler Youth, even—to accept the doctrines of National Socialism. He recalls his own *Volksschule* and a teacher whose anti-Semitism was venomous and unwavering. "Just observe the shape of their noses," the teacher would say. "If they are formed like an upside down 6, that's usually a good sign of their Jewishness, although some have obstructed such tell-tale signs by their infamous mixing with us."[16] Heck had a close Jewish friend for a while, who, despite his "non-Jewish" features, eventually was forced away from Wittlich. Heck forgot about him as he continued through the program. The boy's name was Heinz.

To the surprise of many people today, the Hitler Youth scheme (and the Nazis' intentions more broadly) was transparent to outsiders. These included many foreign reporters who visited the rallies, and anyone with even a passing interest in the 1936 Olympics in Berlin, where Hitler had aimed to trumpet Aryan superiority on a world stage. When Jessie Owens and others trounced the Germans, Hitler used the experience to heighten the urgency of his racial plans. These were dangerous outliers of other races who simply made genocidal reform all the more urgent, he said. Reactions from abroad were uncoordinated, even if some observers had begun watching Hitler more carefully.

Winston Churchill, for example, was tuned in to Germany's swelling nationalist momentum. "We cannot tell," he wrote in 1934, "whether Hitler will be the man who will once again let loose upon the world a war in which civilization will irretrievably succumb, or whether he will go down in history as the man who restored honor and peace of mind to the great German nation and brought them back, serene, helpful and strong, to the European family circle." He observed that "Hitler's triumphant career has been borne forward not only by a passionate love of Germany, but by currents of hatred so intense as to sear the souls of those who swim upon them."[17]

Ralph Barnes, who became the first American foreign correspondent killed in World War II when his ride in a British bomber ended in a tragic mountain crash, confirmed as early as 1935 the real intentions of the Nazi regime. "With the violently anti-Jewish wing of the Nazi party now apparently in the saddle," he wrote in a September dispatch from Nuremberg to New York, "further anti-Semitic measures, supplementing those decreed by the Reichstag here last night withdrawing citizenship from Jews and forbidding Jewish-'Aryan' (gentile) marriages, are expected to be enacted soon. Reestablishment of the [Jewish] ghetto is now under way ... with the elimination of all the Jews in Germany as [the] ultimate aim."[18]

## Gliding Toward the *Wehrmacht*

Imagine those first flights.

In a glider, at an altitude of even a hundred feet, you see that the fields around you are an abstract collage of greens and browns, a stitched-together blanket spread over the countryside. You detect the subtle, untraceable smells of the cockpit: the leather from the seat pad, the distant lubricants on the control rods, or even whatever natural exhaust comes off a hillside when the wind collides with it. Although the invisible rush of air presses against the control surfaces as a centering force, they still respond dutifully, and initiating a turn takes no more exertion than picking up a pencil from a table. Your body rises and falls whenever the wings are endowed with surplus lift or gasp briefly for a little more. Up here, you're aware that there is no intermediary between you and the foundational laws of physics. Even a pilot who's flown to Mach 2 is likely to tell you that there is no purer or more immersive form of flight than gliding. It's no surprise to other pilots that when Erich Hartmann retired as a much older man, he chose the smallest and most docile planes that took him back to his gliding days to give him access to the sky.

And if you're 11 years old, piloting your own glider is an incredible thrill—which is one way the Nazis got the kids hooked young. By the mid-1930s, state-sponsored gliding programs had sprouted up all over Germany, assigning prestige to the young participants, giving them an outlet for their physical energy and lust for adventure, and creating camaraderie. Above all, these programs were fascinating beyond anything else in the boys' young lives. Elisabeth Hartmann helped organize the Weil chapter in 1936, and she was a natural leader given her status as a pilot.

The basic gliding programs existed under the umbrella of the *Flieger-Hitlerjugend*, the flying branch of the Hitler Youth. But there were several other flying-related organizations created by the Nazis. One was the National Socialist Flyers Corps (NSFK), which was a separate organization but was connected to the Hitler Youth. More enigmatic than the *Flieger-Hitlerjugend*, the NSFK was an outgrowth of an older organization that seems to have been even more explicitly ideological and closely modeled on the *Sturmabteilung* (*SA*)—Hitler's Storm Troopers. This is one reason why, when you spend time researching the *Luftwaffe*, you might see it labeled as the most Nazified of the main *Wehrmacht* branches. While this claim is often asserted and then not really substantiated, there does seem to be a lengthy association between the flying programs of National Socialism, in part because the history of the *Luftwaffe* doesn't predate Nazism in the way the other military branches do. One passage on the NSFK, which seems to be recycled in various places online, offers promising clarity, though it is difficult to validate:

> When Nazi Germany formed the *Luftwaffe*, many NSFK members transferred. As all such prior NSFK members were also Nazi Party members[,] this gave the new *Luftwaffe* a strong Nazi ideological base in contrast to the other branches of the German military, who were comprised of "Old Guard" officers from the German aristocracy.[19]

This is at least plausible. In December 1942, *Flight International* magazine went to some length to describe the special Nazification of the *Luftwaffe*:

> In no other branch of service have the Nazis established themselves so firmly as in the *Luftwaffe*. This was not only because, with the advance of the Nazi Party to power, the *Luftwaffe* was openly and officially established and placed under Göring's orders, but also because in the years prior to 1933 it was the Nazi Party which had created a semi-military organisation for flying, and thus managed to build up a cadre of Nazi-minded and drilled youth for the *Luftwaffe*.[20]

There isn't any obvious reason to doubt the integrity of *Flight International*'s journalism here, but remember that this was during wartime, when writers at *Flight International* might have wanted to leverage the Nazification of the German flyers against them. In 1944, the same publication described Hartmann's activities on the Eastern Front in a dry journalistic style, but added that he was "an ardent member of the Hitler youth[sic]."[21] The word "ardent," presumably a reference to what they assumed to be his ideological fervor, is a subtle flourish that heightens the drama but isn't obviously based on testimony or research.

Regardless of the level of specialness attached to the *Luftwaffe* by Nazi leaders, Kater makes an important basic point about advancing as a Hitler Youth member no matter which branch you were headed for:

> The issue of complicity changes as one focuses on Hitler's youths in their transition from juveniles to young adults ... advancement from the lower [Hitler Youth] ranks was voluntary and necessitated a fair amount of ideological conviction in the Nazi cause, something that

a youth from age sixteen to eighteen could evince as persuasively and sometimes even as eloquently as a diehard Nazi in his early thirties.

He continues into the thorny subject of discussing guilt among these Hitler Youth members:

> It is fair to say that seventeen-year-old [Hitler Youth] leaders with a few hundred charges under their command, in contrast to the ten-year-old underlings, made themselves culpable, to the extent that they knowingly imparted Nazi values to these underlings, inciting them to racial hatred and warfare against Poles, Russians, and Jews.[22]

At his highest Hitler Youth rank, Hartmann was a *Scharführer*. (*Jungscharführer*, as recorded by his wife, Ursula, years later. The preface of *Jung-*, which means "young," does not obviously signify of a different rank. You might wonder if this was a separate designation in the *Jungvolk*, the portion of the Hitler Youth for young beginner cadets, but the *Jungvolk* did not assign its own ranks to members, and Ursula Hartmann also specifies that this was part of the *Flieger-Hitlerjugend*.)[23] *Scharführer* was the fifth rung above the entry-level status of *Hitlerjunge*, so *Scharführeren* almost certainly had to pass certain ideological turnstiles to get to it.

In the most direct sense, then, Hartmann's known Hitler Youth status places him squarely in the company of those Hitler Youth leaders whom historians would label directly culpable for adopting the ideology and filling younger minds with it.

Interestingly, Ursula Hartmann also notes in her book that it was Hartmann's award of the C-level flying license in the *Flieger-Hitlerjugend* (at which point he became an instructor), and his subsequent appointment as a *Scharführer*, that "landed him in the" militant Rottweil National Political Reformatory.[24] Nowhere else is there mention of a causal relationship between Hartmann's Hitler Youth participation and the Nazi administration. If it is the case that he showed enough ideological promise to be recommended for, or assigned to, a place like Rottweil, we might be looking at a more intimate involvement with the Nazis than previously thought.

Of course, it could also be that as Hartmann's flying and leadership skills became more obvious, his ideological conviction needed some help—some "reform"—at a place like Rottweil. This suggests that his devotion to the cause might have actually been *inadequate* for Nazi leaders.

Here it might help to think about other youth organizations, even modern ones, and how there seems to be a balance between what you might call the principles and the practice. At times, the influence of one fades as the other is emphasized, but both always seem to be present and interdependent. It's how these organizations maintain their allure and coherence. The Boy Scouts of America is a good example because it is well-known and well-defined (though not because it should ever be confused with Nazism). In it, the principles are encapsulated in the Scout Oath and Scout Law, and they include duty to God and country, helping others, staying physically and mentally fit, and embodying the ideals of trustworthiness, loyalty, friendliness, *etc.* These are prominent parts of the mental and emotional experience of being a Scout—every Scout memorizes them and is held accountable to adhering to them. In effect, they give the organization its identity and purpose.

The practice, on the other hand, is the programming that happens out there in the world: hiking, camping, skill-building, and so on. These are the most obvious draws for the thousands of Scouts enrolled at any point, but they certainly couldn't sustain the organization unless rooted in the principles.

So, where was that balance for Hartmann? Was he in the Hitler Youth primarily for the principles or the practice? Equally interesting: how static was that orientation over time? You could suppose, with a fair amount of factual backup, that he must have been allegiant to the ideals of the Hitler Youth *at some point*—his upward trajectory within the organization seems to have depended on it. But it's not enough to say that Hartmann was part of the system and therefore must have fully adopted it. That attempt at clarity is just as shallow as saying that he never was influenced by any of it, no matter what the policies said.

This brings up one important related point. A sneaky assumption people tend to make in discussions of Germans and Nazism is that an individual's opinion of the ideology, the leader, or the regime was more or less stagnant: so-and-so was *that kind* of believer, whether they were 13 or 23 or 45. This is especially obvious when people default to talking about "the Germans" as a group, as they often do in conversations about collective guilt. But "the Germans" weren't a herd. Not only is it insufficient to lump all citizens into an ideologically uniform mass; it's also a mistake to ignore individual fluctuations over time. This natural inconsistency, of course, makes all the questions we tend to ask about these people even harder to answer.

From a writer's point of view, this topic is one of the biggest frustrations in Hartmann's story. His biography and related works would have us believe that the Hitler Youth was merely the administrative body that allowed for his ascent into the *Luftwaffe*: "The following year, Hitler came to power, and German aviation began its resurrection."[25] This throwaway transition sentence is essentially how his 332-page biography handles the issue. There is no entry for

"Hitler Youth" in the index of the book, though there is one for "Wristwatches, as World War II souvenirs."[26] This is inadequate and conspicuous, of course. But conspicuousness doesn't confirm anything in particular about Hartmann's lived experience in the organization. We're left wondering.

## *Küken*

Mastering gliding was phenomenally difficult—even physically punishing. In a typical beginner's glider, cadets sat in a metal tube framework, welded as a rudimentary cage open to the airstream. This cage was connected to high-mounted wings and a tail assembly, both of which were covered with semi-transparent doped fabric that showed the wing's internal structure whenever backlit by the sun. Thin cables ran unprotected from the controls between the pilot's legs to the rudder, elevators, and ailerons, and there was often only a fixed skid for landing gear. These aircraft were durable enough for use with young cadets, but were also unforgiving enough to remind them that flying could be perilous at each stage, from launch to landing. Instructors drove home the key concepts of aerodynamics by promoting model building first; alongside the human-operated gliding events, Hitler Youth chapters also held competitions for the best small-scale, hand-launched airplanes.

They called the trainees *Küken*—"chicks"—and often put them in the cockpit alone for their very first flight. Sometimes they were hauled into the air by another airplane, but often they were slung from a rubberized rope. Fellow trainees on the ground could rig the rope to a hook on the front of the glider, grab hold, and catapult the pilot into the air high enough to get over the edge of a hill for a full flight pattern. Once aloft, each cadet had to assess his position relative to the landing zone and use the winds and the lift-giving topography around him to stay airborne. Hilly territory, like the kind found in Weil, made for good, eventful gliding. The contest was typically to stay up for as long as possible—sometimes a half-hour or more—by coaxing the machines into thermal updrafts and managing precious airspeed well enough to avoid stalling or overshooting the target. By judging their sink rate and distance from target, pilots could bring their gliders softly onto a spot in a field the size of a truck bed.

Despite the crudeness of the equipment, the Hitler Youth organizers made gliding an exercise in precision, and the boys thrived on the challenge. They even complied when the most aggravating part of the exercise came: hauling their gliders back uphill after a flight. On good days there was a horse around to help.

If Hartmann's later piloting is any sign, he would have reveled in these challenges. You can imagine him always including some unexpected feat in his flight plan—break the record for longest time aloft when that wasn't actually part of the assignment; make one extra loop along the path to the same old target; side-slip at the right moment to turn an errant landing into a miraculous, soft one. You can also imagine that grin of his, always his visual signature, flashing even more brightly while he was loft, when it was just him and the air and the birds. You can imagine the world's most destructive fighter pilot at peace up there. It's harder to imagine what was in his head.

CHAPTER 5

# Into the *Luftwaffe*

Fight on and fly on to the last drop of blood and the last drop of fuel, to the last beat of the heart.

—Manfred von Richthofen

The *Luftwaffe*, unlike the other branches of the *Wehrmacht*, was created afresh in 1935. But while the Nazis (with Hitler's confidant and former fighter pilot Hermann Göring in the lead) crafted the institution as the shining executor of Hitler's vision, the technologies and strategies of the organization were rooted in developments from World War I. From a technological point of view, the *Luftwaffe*'s aircraft and systems were all descendants of the Fokkers and Albatroses of the earlier conflict. They were infused with an ingenuity and pragmatism that could only have come from experience.

In 1914, there was no such thing as a fighter pilot. Powered flight was barely a decade old, and the frail aircraft riding the gusts were still made of fabric, glue, wood, and wire. In the open cockpits, pilots greased their faces to help them handle the biting winds, and their earliest in-flight weapons included bricks they'd hauled up on their laps hoping to throw them in a useful direction.

A new purpose for the aircraft became obvious as soon as military leaders confronted the carnage of the World War I ground war. And it was the Germans, arguably, who most effectively embraced it, refined it, and made it such a devastating and crucial element of 20th-century warfare.

Manfred von Richthofen's first missions had been as a scout on horseback, and he'd watched as gaggles of soldiers were mowed down in an instant by enemy divisions outfitted with new guns spewing explosive shells. This war was a startling collision of old practices and new killing methods, as demonstrated, for example, by the continued use of horses (Germany mobilized 715,000

This 1938 advertisement reads, "Messerschmitt. Hunters. Destroyers. To win and protect Germany." Note that *Bayerische Flugzeugwerke*, or Bavarian Aircraft Works, is the source of the "Bf" designation of the Bf 109. Willy Messerschmitt took control of the company in 1938, after the Bf 109 had been designed; from that point on, his aircraft received an "Me" designation, as in Me 262. (Firmenlogo, Wikimedia Commons)

horses at the outset of the war)[1] alongside new armored tanks of spectacular agility and destructive power. In one familiar clash of the old and the new, ground troops struggled to coordinate and fire their own weapons because those weapons' power and range required instantaneous communication methods that were still in their infancy.[2]

Richthofen eventually volunteered for flight training not because of any romantic longing for the sky or aircraft—he disliked machines, tools, and "sticky black oil"—but because he found his initial job on the ground to be repulsively outdated.[3]

The first men we'd call fighter pilots were aerial scouts. At the most basic level, they had just traded horses for airplanes, since their main job was to observe enemy troop movements and report back. But it wasn't long before opposing scouts began encountering each other regularly in the air. What probably started as an exchange of hand gestures evolved into pistols carried aloft for a couple of haphazard shots. As these encounters became more regular, people gained a better understanding of their potential value: an enemy scout can't report intelligence very well if you shoot him down first.

Bombers were arriving, too, though not in the swarms we recall from images of World War II. German aircrews called these early bombers "apple crates," and a bomber's need for self-defense was similar to a fighter's need for offense. This paved the way for one of the most consequential advancements in 20th-century warfare: getting a machine gun onto an airplane. It wasn't just a fascinating story of physics and engineering; it was the technological key that allowed the pilots to unlock what was old and noble in war in the face of World War I's modern bloodbath.

By 1914, machine guns had matured technically and could be mass-produced, but only barely. One or two of them could deliver enough lead to send an enemy aircraft tumbling to the ground, but there were several practical problems with installing them. On the one hand, lack of quality control and the violent maneuvers involved in dogfighting often caused these early guns to jam, so pilots needed to be able to reach them while in flight to unjam them. On the other hand, mounting a stationary, forward-firing machine gun within the pilot's reach usually put it on top of the forward fuselage, meaning that the gun would blow off the plane's propeller when it fired. And even if someone could create jam-proof guns, mounting them outboard of the propeller's arc on the wings would mean that they'd need to be calibrated so the separate streams of lead would converge at a central point ahead of the plane, a level of precision that eluded early manufacturers and field mechanics. It probably didn't help that the wings on these early planes were thin and built of flexible wood that changed shape under differing aerodynamic loads—potentially spewing bullets every which way.

The Germans were the first to build a workable system for firing a machine gun through the propeller arc without hitting the blades. Anthony Fokker, who was actually Dutch but studied and worked in Germany, perfected an existing idea by developing the gun synchronizer, which is often inaccurately called the interrupter. By installing it on his *Eindecker* fighter, Fokker proved the concept and ensured its widespread adoption by the Germans, resulting in a brief period of air dominance sometimes referred to as the "Fokker scourge."

Essentially, a synchronizer enabled the engine to mechanically trigger the gun at known points in its rotation. Attached to the engine's camshaft was a rotating cam disc, which intermittently engaged a pushrod that ran toward the gun. When the pilot pulled the trigger in the cockpit, a coupler connected the pushrod to the gun, allowing the pushrod to physically initiate shots according to the rotation of the engine.

The principle was so sound that it lasted for 30 years, all the way through World War II. It only became obsolete when jet engines arrived and fighters stopped having propellers in the first place. At the end of World War II, the German Bf 109K sported two 20mm cannons in the upper fuselage that fired through the propeller arc. These cannons were of an entirely different species than the pea shooters installed on Richthofen's Fokker, but they relied on technology that was fundamentally similar to the synchronizers from 1918.

Fokker, however, didn't want to test his own invention in combat because he hated idea of shooting men with it. The man who tested the synchronizer when Fokker bowed out was Oswald Bölcke, a legendary figure who you might call the first fighter jock. On one memorable mission, Bölcke pursued a French pilot so closely, and with such endurance, that he returned to base and scribbled an enormous report that became known as the founding document of dogfighting. After more experience in air combat and some refinement of his verbiage, these written rules were informally renamed "*Dicta Bölcke*":

1. Try to secure advantages before attacking. If possible, keep the sun behind you.
2. Always carry through an attack when you have started it.
3. Fire only at close range and only when your opponent is properly in your sights.
4. Always keep your eyes on your opponent, and never let yourself be deceived by ruses.
5. In any form of attack it is essential to assail your opponent from behind.
6. If your opponent dives on you, do not try to avoid his onslaught, but fly to meet it.
7. When over the enemy's lines, never forget your own line of retreat.

8. For the *Staffel* [squadron]: Attack on principle in groups of four or six. When the fight breaks up into a series of single combats, take care that several do not go for one opponent.[4]

Anyone familiar with aviation will recognize at least some of these rules; pilots still study versions of them today. They learn to attack with the sun behind them, for example, because the glare prevents an enemy from seeing them well. Turning in to meet an attacker rather than fleeing from him shortens his available engagement time and sharpens the angles between the two flight paths. Today's fighter training programs discuss these rules in terms of vectors and energy maintenance, but Bölcke had gotten most of the concepts right from his own mental notes. He was rewarded with the admiration and trust of those around him.

That admiration also grew from Bölcke's well-known generosity and consideration for others, even (maybe especially) his victims. More than once, Bölcke visited men he'd shot down in war hospitals, exchanging stories and offering his wishes for a fast recovery. Once, he visited a victim at a POW collection station, inviting him to tour his aerodrome as a gesture of goodwill. In 1916, before Richthofen's rise to fame, Bölcke was the most famous pilot in the world, in part because of his public chivalrous gestures.[5]

The transfer of that fame came quickly. Bölcke died in a dogfight with 40 kills to his name. Richthofen, his pupil and admirer, watched him go down from his own cockpit. It wasn't that Bölcke had been shot down, either—he had merely collided with another plane while in formation, which spun his fighter out of control. His funeral procession in France was even more grandiose than Richthofen's would be. Led by the Crown Prince of Bavaria, it attracted 1,000 attendees and drew countless more to the train tracks as his body was shipped by rail from France to Germany for burial.[6]

## 22 Years Later

When spring arrived in 1940, German pilots were a confident lot. They carried a proud tradition rooted in the successes and personas of World War I, and the *Luftwaffe*'s first test in the Spanish Civil War had gone exceptionally well. Poland had just fallen in the war's first violent thrust—this was the reawakening of the *Wehrmacht* as a whole, not just the *Luftwaffe*—and the invasion of France was just around the corner. Hitler and his staffs had every expectation that their young pilots would escort the German ground divisions anywhere they wanted to go, and younger trainees like Hartmann were enticed by the dazzling war stories now that Germany had its first crop of aces since the Treaty of Versailles. Early World War II pilots like Werner Mölders were again injecting glamor into the vocation of being a fighter pilot. Although the Battle of Britain was imminent and would hand Hitler his first real setback (and cost him some of his best pilots), it would be months before the urgency of the attrition set in.

Hartmann graduated from Korntal in April 1940 and turned his eyes immediately to the *Luftwaffe*. There was nothing particularly surprising about his decision to enlist—it was what he had been reared for, and participation in the war was all but inevitable. Although many Germans at the time— Hartmann's father included, apparently—still believed that the war would be over quickly and that Hartmann might not actually see much action, he plunged into a lengthy and arduous training program meant to prepare him for an extended war effort.

Hartmann entered basic training in East Prussia in October 1940. This was a rude awakening for the porcelain-cheeked youngster, who had already discovered at Rottweil that strict drill and instruction didn't come easily. You see him in photos from this time and his lankiness and youth are especially apparent. He looked years younger than the others, as he would the entire war. He was endowed with eyes of great depth and clarity, and his unruly, pure-blond hair never quite stayed put. He was always the kid.

This boyish persona took hold immediately. He quickly received the nickname *Bubi,* or "little boy," which would stick with him his entire career. Some of his peers just substituted that for his first name; they knew him for decades as Bubi Hartmann.

The boyishness was due in large part to his most distinctive feature: that Hartmann grin. His smile was wide, unreserved, and could melt away any sense of hardship or stress, turning an exhausted plane-side photo-op into something playful. In old photos, Hartmann is often the only one grinning; at times it lifts the mood of the entire scene, but other times it just makes him stand out, as if he's the only one who hasn't caught on to the situation. There is an asymmetry to Hartmann's mouth that can seem to signify fatigue or discomfort, a little like when you ask someone to hold a smile for so long that they become aware of their own pose and it becomes stiff. You can tell that Hartmann used his grin often, and that it might have had multiple meanings.

With plenty of time and resources, *Luftwaffe* training was still lengthy and thorough. German fliers at the start of the war were the most proficient in the world because they were exposed to mounds of coursework in engineering, meteorology, aircraft construction, and military aviation history, along with the requisite time spent buzzing through clouds. Hartmann's first military flight took place on March 5, 1941 after basic training. He flew from Berlin-Gatow, an airfield located a patch of forest removed from the German capital city, and his initial flight training lasted almost a year.[7] He checked out in 17 different aircraft before his first flight in the speedy Bf 109 fighter, but everyone knew he wasn't going to end up flying "apple crates."

The Germans used an aerial training sequence much like what you'd see elsewhere. First there were the basic, forgiving biplanes like the Arado 68, which showed instructors if pilots had the intuition and coordination to manage a light aircraft. Then the real sorting took place. After graduation to faster, heavier monoplanes like the Arado 96, which was Germany's standard advanced trainer, pilots were assigned to bombers, transports, or fighters based on aptitude and need. Naturally, the fighter squadrons were highly desired—and difficult-to-acquire—assignments.

Hartmann got his orders to fighter school in late 1941. Here, he grew into a tactician and a marksman—and a careful student of the Bf 109, which by then was firmly trusted as Germany's primary day fighter. The slightly newer Fw 190 was in production by that point, but Hartmann never flew it operationally. It was the 109 all the way.

His first airborne "victim" was a target banner strung behind another airplane. The bull's-eye was painted vibrantly on the fabric so beginners could make it out from a distance, though it usually took a lot of practice to spit the shells out accurately enough to score hits. Consider even the basic physical variables the trainees had to manage: an aircraft inclined to move about in three dimensions; an engine that produces vibrations and the tug of torque; guns and ammunition that choke and misbehave; visibility issues; the pressures of being evaluated by watchful and demanding instructors. This was a test of precision in an environment that fiercely resists such a thing.

On his first run, Hartmann ripped 24 holes in the target with just 50 rounds fired. This was remarkable proficiency. Obviously, all the gliding experience had enabled Hartmann to focus on firing his weapons rather than the basics of keeping his aircraft under control, and from there he progressed easily through the different aircraft and training routines.

After he got his commission as second lieutenant in the spring of 1942, the Hartmann impulsiveness got the better of him. He decided to give an impromptu aerobatics show above his home airfield as celebration for the success, so he buzzed the runway upside down at an altitude of about 30 feet.

When he made his triumphant landing, his stunned and furious superiors hauled him aside, informed him of his infraction and poor judgment, took him off the flight schedule for a week, and cut his pay.

There was one good fortune to come from the experience, however, if you can call it that. The same aircraft Hartmann was supposed to fly that afternoon for another gunnery mission malfunctioned when the next pilot—his roommate—was flying it to the gunnery range. The engine died and the pilot crashed near a railway. He was killed in the wreck.[8] Hartmann's showboating might have saved his life.

His introduction to the 109 had been in the early D model—the chunky-nosed, less-powerful version—but he moved along to the E (prevalent during the Battle of Britain) and then the sleeker F and G models. The G was heavier, faster, and better-armed than other versions, and it would be the type that Hartmann flew for most of the war. He came to know that airplane as soldiers from earlier times had known their horses; success required complete faith in his mount (as fighter pilots have been known to call their planes) and an encyclopedic understanding of its quirks, vulnerabilities, and strengths. The aircraft was an excellent fit for Hartmann's flying personality because it always rewarded incisive, hit-and-run flying. It couldn't always turn with a lift-endowed fighter like the Spitfire, but it was small, powerful, accelerated well, and was hard to see. As far as pilots and their aircraft are concerned, this was one of the best pairings ever made. Fans of Richthofen and his Fokker, or Chuck Yeager and his Mustang, will understand the importance of the man-and-machine pairing.

The Bf 109 was Willy Messerschmitt's masterpiece, one of those bolted-to-gether bits of machinery that seemed to convey a kind of agency—call it a personality—that separated it from its contemporaries. If the Allied fighters were the muscle-bound freedom fighters (consider their names: Mustang, Thunderbolt, Spitfire), the 109, in its trademark mottles of greens and grays, was the knife fighter that did its work in the shadows. It gained a ruthless mystique that perfectly represented the military machine from which it had been born, and plenty of other *Luftwaffe* workhorses have no such character or allure. Maybe it was the metallic "chop-chop" of the Daimler Benz engine, or the cage-like canopy that hinges down over the pilot, almost as if the plane is trapping him in. Or the muscular engine cowling whose aluminum wobbles and bumps are the most aesthetically distinctive part of the airframe. Or maybe those simple, small, angular wings. Whatever the combination of factors, this plane is unambiguously a product of World War II Germany.

From an engineering standpoint, it is appealing not for any obvious grace but for its stripped-down, essential construction—every part in harmony with the others, every function simplified as much as possible. The 109 tempts us toward that most overused German cultural cliché: a design based in aggressive practicality, unadorned with anything superfluous. Utilitarian to the point of being characterless.

Except, with the 109, the utility—the terrible, destructive, pounding utility—is precisely where the character comes from.

The first Bf 109 flew in 1935, and its general shape, purpose, and strengths were fully formed from the start. Over time, it evolved through a long series of upgrades that renewed its usefulness even as newer planes came off other companies' drawing boards. Its makers installed new engines, including one made by Daimler-Benz that endowed the lean fighter with almost 2,000 horsepower. (The American P-47 Thunderbolt, huge compared to the 109, had a few more horsepower but weighed almost twice as much.) They cooked up new armament combinations that made it more lethal. By the end of the war, almost 34,000 Bf 109s had been built—more than any fighter in history and double the number of American P-51s. Along with the British Spitfire, the 109 stayed in production for the entire length of the war as its country's primary day fighter, which is incredible considering that the period from 1939 to 1945 probably encapsulated the most shocking progress in military hardware since humans had begun to fight with one another. If Göbbels wanted a prop for his propaganda campaigns, the 109 was it. All he needed was a few seconds of film showing the 109 raising hell in its operational debut over Spain in 1936, where, in humming swarms, it achieved immediate air superiority in service of its first dictator, Francisco Franco.

The 109's small wings always meant that it had a relatively high wing loading—meaning that there was comparatively little lift available per pound of aircraft weight. In general, this is good for reducing drag and increasing top speed, but it's bad for maneuverability and slow-speed handling. Many pilots, however, swore that the 109 was always able to fare surprisingly well in a turning battle, even against larger-winged adversaries. This was due in part to the 109's forgiving stall characteristics, which allowed pilots to fly the plane aggressively, and at the edge of its performance envelope, for longer. Leading edge slats built into the outboard wings automatically extended under low-airflow situations, which augmented lift just when pilots needed it. The 109's flight surfaces were designed as an extremely well though-out and harmonious structure, and pilots learned quickly how to take advantage of this.

Like any design, however, the 109 had its flaws. Most obvious from the pilot's point of view was the cage-like canopy that used heavy-gauge metal framing to hold together several square panels. It was a far cry from the 360-degree-view, clear bubble canopies fitted to later models of the American P-47 and P-51 fighters. Upgraded models of the 109 introduced a new aft canopy section that gave a slightly improved view to the side and behind, but the effect remained: looking around the sky from the cockpit of a 109 was like staring through scaffolding. Close that canopy over your head and you are immediately confronted with a claustrophobic, rigid environment.

In the cockpit, the 109 felt cold. Whereas American and British cockpits were splashed with color because of the green chromate primer they used, the 109 was painted in a dark matte gray. On the later versions, this was a shade called RLM 66—think of the meanest storm cloud you've seen, darken it a shade, and you're there. As a result, the interior space seemed permanently enveloped in shadow, even though knobs and handles here and there provided sparks of yellow or red. The cockpit structure was a basic aluminum box so small that the pilot's legs were drawn up to waist level, and the sidewalls were only as thick as the sheet aluminum used to construct the fuselage skin. (Small air vents cut out of the sidewalls seem almost perfunctory—you can see daylight around the edges even when they're closed.) A steel-black gunsight was bolted in the pilot's line of vision and projected onto a flat plate of glass a set of crosshairs that predicted where the bullets would travel when fired. Gunsights—a technology that progressed as rapidly and consequentially as machine-gun armaments had in World War I—helped with deflection shooting, which is the practice of aiming at a point in space ahead of an enemy's actual position in order to score a hit. In a turn, a pilot can't aim directly at his target because the target will have moved by the time the bullets get to it. Even with a gunsight, deflection shooting was an inexact science. It's interesting to think that the vast majority of rounds fired in air combat never hit anything until they lost their oomph and pattered into the dirt or ocean somewhere.

The most intimidating problem with the 109 (which persisted through every one of its versions) was its difficult handling during takeoff and landing. This was due to the narrowness and placement of its spindly landing gear. Compared to other fighters, the left and right main gear wheels were positioned very close to the centerline; this, coupled with the fact that the landing gear was placed relatively far forward of the aircraft's center of gravity, made ground loops and other accidents unusually common, especially on the uneven grass and dirt fields throughout the Eastern Front. In a ground loop, a left-right yawing motion can cause one wheel to dig into the ground, which compounds the sideways rotation even more and can result in a dragged wingtip or even collapse of the landing gear.

This was made worse by a factor shared by any powerful single-engine aircraft. Propellers are heavy, and when they rotate so quickly in one direction, all that mass creates torque that pulls the entire aircraft sideways (in the opposite direction—ask Newton). This induced yaw is especially strong on takeoff, when the engine is run up to full power and yet there isn't much corrective aerodynamic stability because the plane isn't going very fast. The yaw tendency, in all airplanes, has to be controlled with pressure on the rudder pedals or else the aircraft might go out of control. In a 1,500hp fighter aircraft, this can take quite some work: one book on the P-40 Warhawk, an American brute that saw a lot of its action in the Pacific theater, said that you could always tell a Warhawk pilot by looking at his thigh muscles.

Why was this design used, then? The 109's landing gear was convenient from construction and maintenance points of view. Unlike many fighters, the gear legs were attached to the fuselage rather than onto the wing structures themselves, meaning that the wings could be removed or replaced without having to hoist the plane off its gear. This had obvious benefits in the field, where heavy equipment was either absent or cumbersome to use. Crews could even roll a wingless 109 onto a rail car if needed.

Although engineers splayed the gear legs outward a few degrees, widening the track of the wheels beyond the leg attachment points, this was only

A Bf 109G-6 takes off, showing the landing gear retraction sequence. Note the missing swastika on the tail of this contemporary warbird restoration (the symbol is banned in Germany). (Kogo, Wikimedia Commons)

ever a partial solution. Hundreds if not thousands of pilots were killed before they even left the ground, and the nature of the 109's landing gear was—strange as it sounds—a tangible contributing factor to the pilot attrition that eventually rendered the *Luftwaffe* impotent. The Germans just kept building 109s, though, unforgiving as they were, and dealt with the losses by taking in more young pilots. It was a process that worked for the first couple years.

## Stories from the Front

Hartmann, ready to venture out to the front, heard tales of valiance and der-ring-do churned out by the German propaganda machine. So did everyone else, including the Americans and their Allied forces—so intent were the Germans on bludgeoning people with their messages that they didn't particularly care who the audience was.

*Der Adler*, the official magazine of the *Luftwaffe*, was a splashy, photo-heavy publication meant to show the saga of the war and follow the soldiers in action. Given the era and the limitations in photography and printing, it was a remarkably attractive product. It was circulated in the U.S. as reportage, in fact, and its writers gleefully described the unusual comradeship of the Aryan warriors they were following. In some of the images, pilots stood beaming next to their mounts, ready for the next mission; in others, creative flight photography captured the fighters and the bombers en route to whatever endeavor lay ahead. "The Air Corps forms the point of the German sword," reported one *Generalfeldmarschall* Milch. "In that branch of the service will be found united the highest qualities of the German aviator spirit and German soldiership."

Replace "German" with "American" or "British" and the verbiage could have been borrowed from elsewhere without any worry. These were ideals that stretched across all those militaries. But the German publication couldn't resist one more flourish:

> Further than that, the German Air Corps is not only in the main a creation of National Socialism, but, as it presents itself to us, would be inconceivable did not the conditions of National Socialism exist. For that reason its development, its mission, and its victories are inseparably connected with our leader Adolf Hitler and with the man who created it as his command, Reich Marshal Hermann Göring.[9]

As we've seen, there is a surprising amount of truth to this.

*Der Adler* is another example of how open the Nazis actually were about their intentions and principles, but it also helps us understand that those principles were not the only guiding ideals in the German military. To Germany's Nazi leaders, the specialness of the *Luftwaffe* was rooted in the National Socialism that was integrated into its mission as an organization, but to the average soldier—and much of the watchful world—its specialness stood, at least occasionally, independent of all that. German military refinement wasn't new, nor had the broader traditions of the *Wehrmacht* been created from scratch by Hitler. To the contrary, its age and durability as an institution is why it performed so well in the war's early days—and why soldiers by the millions joined it in good conscience.

One thing people tend to forget about World War I is how well the German military actually fared, despite its eventual loss—how stable the German military culture was after the defeat. After the Armistice, the organization was dismantled, but its culture and traditions lived on. If anything, they were fortified. This was incredibly useful to Hitler later on.

Basically, Germany didn't lose World War I because its military leaders, soldiers, or tactics were fundamentally subpar. In some important ways, it was the opposite. The *Wehrmacht* relied, for example, on an unusually large and highly skilled officer corps that was able to produce notable victories from the start until well after the Americans entered the war in 1917. The size of the *Wehrmacht*'s leadership pool as compared to other militaries ensured that institutional knowledge was effectively distributed and augmented over time. Historian John Mosier argues that in World War I, this helped the *Wehrmacht* to perform surprisingly well by most accepted tactical measures of combat units—as did its technical superiority at the outset:

> This superiority extended all the way down to the way the ordinary soldier was equipped, starting with the fact that his steel helmet … was infinitely better than that of his opponents. Even a shell's near miss could generate a shock wave that would throw the soldier through the air, turning him into an unwilling missile in which his all too vulnerable head and neck were at risk … [T]he German coal-scuttle helmet protected the back of the neck; moreover, the flared edges transmitted the shock to the shoulders and thus the rest of the body, reducing traumatic head injuries.[10]

Mosier collected these thoughts in a book called *The Myth of the Great War*, in which he argued that the German defeat was tragically misunderstood, that French and British capabilities and performance are often exaggerated, and that historians tend to discount the technical and strategic supremacy of the *Wehrmacht*. Mosier weights the arrival of Pershing's American Expeditionary Forces as the deciding factor that tipped the shaky scales once and for all, ensuring the German loss. Although he has been accused of "overstatement" and "temerity," and a maybe a distracting lust for the Germans, Mosier offers seriousness and depth where *Wehrmacht* apologists do not.[11] Distill his work to its most elemental messages and you'll be reminded of how enduring the *Wehrmacht*'s heritage of strength and sophistication was. Iron and blood indeed.

Because Germans placed so much faith in their military professionals, the shattering loss of World War I seemed inexplicable, and they blamed not the military but the civilian decision-makers who eventually capitulated. Their befuddlement was compounded by the fact that the war didn't take place on German soil, a fact that kept it distant and hard to grasp. Unlike World War II, World War I left no German towns in ruins—so where could the loss have come from?

Emile Fayolle, a prominent French general, observed of the German homeland: "Everything breathes order, prosperity, and wealth. Germany is not at all destroyed. If left alone, she'll start the war all over again in ten years."[12]

Enter, now, the widespread and oft-repeated "stabbed in the back" myth of the German defeat. This was propagated first by nationalist commentators at home who blamed Germany's full acceptance of blame and crushing reparations not on the military, but on cowardly civilian government leaders. The end of the war coincided with the overthrow of the German monarchy and the installation of the weak-kneed Weimar Republic—a course of events that would have bothered German traditionalists even in the absence of a war. The military, they said, had done its job nobly. But the civilian leaders and influencers had stabbed the *Wehrmacht* and the non-ruling class in the back through flaccid diplomacy and underhandedness. You won't be surprised to hear that Jews were special targets of this blame. Cartoonists, ever the gauges of public appetite and attitude, reinforced the myth with caricatures of Jews literally stabbing German soldiers in the back as they lay prone on the battlefield.

What replaced the old order only exacerbated the discontent. John Keegan describes how Germany's "pre-war dissatisfactions paled beside those that overcame it in the aftermath of Versailles":

> Forced to disgorge the conquests of 1870–71 [under Bismarck] … [Germany was] humiliated by a compulsory disarmament that reduced its army to a tiny gendarmerie, dissolved its battlefleet altogether and abolished its air force … The high-mindedness of the liberal democrat government of Weimar helped to palliate them not at all; its very political and diplomatic moderation, in the years when its economic mismanagement ruined the German middle class … fed the forces of extremism to which its principles stood in opposition.[13]

And here's the confounding character of Erich Hartmann's chosen employer, disassembled as the organization might have been following World War I. The feeling of unfairness that came along with its loss in World War I created revulsion among the former soldiers, and it was directed at the institutions and events that defined the new Germany, most notably the Weimar government, the Allied powers, and of course the Treaty of Versailles. This pushed the *Wehrmacht* veterans in two directions simultaneously: back toward the strict guiding principles embedded in their old group culture, and toward the emerging Nazi regime that promised a resurgence and renewed purpose for the military. The *Wehrmacht* had been reimagined by leaders as a Nazi proof point—the final argument for German supremacy along racial and cultural lines, not just military.

## The Nazification Question

One of the most obvious questions about the *Wehrmacht* as a whole is how Nazified it became after Hitler's arrival, specifically in the officer corps. This is still an ambiguous and contentious topic, and it gets harder once you separate the branches and look at them individually. As an umbrella organization, was the *Wehrmacht* a Nazi factory whose members have gotten off too easily over the years, or did it stand more or less independent of the ideology, protected by its own history and culture of professionalism? Or was it somewhere in between? Here's Mosier:

> Few of them were committed National Socialists; indeed, the more they were faced with government demands, the more they resisted them. But at the same time, they had bought into Hitler's premise and accepted his goals to the extent that they understood them. Freeing Germany from its shackles—breaking out of the cave into which they believed the country had been imprisoned—restoring it to its rightful place in the sun, eliminating the social disorder that plagued the Weimar Republic, and reclaiming the lost territories were the aims they shared with Hitler, and indeed most Germans.[14]

Neitzel and Welzer write:

> Above all, [*Wehrmacht* soldiers] were oriented around a military and wartime frame of reference in which ideology played only a subordinate role. But they also waged war within the frame of reference of their society, a National Socialist one, which in certain situations led them to act in radically inhumane fashion. Nonetheless, to perpetrate atrocities—and this is what is most disconcerting—soldiers did to need to be either racist or anti-Semitic.[15]

These passages are eloquent expressions of profound ambiguity. From historical, behavioral, and sociological points of view, the *Wehrmacht* will always resist a simple explanation. There were committed Nazis in every corner of the institution, and they wielded great influence. But there were also practical men who thought of soldiering in more or less vocational, not ideological, terms. For many people interested in the *Wehrmacht* and its history, this ambiguity is discomforting, which has led to a variety of hurried conclusions that deliver simplicity but not fullness. It really is distressing when the whole situation feels so unresolvable, as if "the average *Wehrmacht* soldier" is stuck in some perpetual ideological limbo. The problem, you could say, is the presumption that there's much value in talking about something called "the average soldier" in the first place.

An especially important point from the above analyses is that any given soldier didn't have to be a card-carrying Nazi or a racist to meaningfully aid the Nazis and the racists. He only had to carry out his appointed duty. This was a war of extermination, both in purpose and effect, but it never relied on 100 per cent conversion among the soldiers. There were many pockets of fanaticism, and they make us shudder to this day, but in general, the *Wehrmacht* relied on the labor and expertise of millions of participants whose personal philosophies were all but irrelevant once the country took up its arms. By the time they were trained and ready, these men, the children who'd been ripped out of childhood for the sake of this dark service, were responsive to a single law, articulated bluntly by Meinecke: "Win power at any price!"[16]

## Frames of Reference

One of the best ways to understand the experience of camaraderie and cohesion in Hartmann's various units was introduced in *Soldiers*, a book about secretly recorded German POW conversations during the war. The book, which came about when Neitzel and Welzer—one a social psychologist and the other a historian, both German—unearthed a trove of old transcripts, finally lets the German soldiers speak for themselves during the time of the war experience and not after the fact. These intimate conversations between peers took place at the height of their combat experience, rather than 30 years later in an interview among friends. Perhaps the most powerful concept explored by the authors is frame of reference. Here is where German soldiers' conformity starts to make sense, and where Hartmann's penchant for clearheaded analysis in the air is finally reconcilable with his apparent non-reflectiveness on the ground.

Frame of reference has a specific meaning to psychologists. It describes the experiential and ideological contexts that shape how people see the world and act in it. People are products of their environments, the concept tells us, and our frames of reference impact our relationship to change, to family, to belief, and to difference, among other things.

The authors explain:

> To understand and explain why German soldiers waged war for five years with a ferocity still unparalleled today, we have to see the war, their war, through their eyes.
>
> In reality, people act as they think is expected of them. Such perceived expectations have a lot less to do with abstract "views of the world" than with concrete places, purposes, and functions—and above all with the groups of which individual people are a part.[17]

In other words, Erich Hartmann and many of the others didn't fly in the *Luftwaffe* with grandiose long-term political aims in mind, even if they had been conditioned by the Nazis and furthered the Nazi cause in any number of ways, from Hitler Youth onward. They were reared to accept Hitler's caustic beliefs and plans, but they pursued their jobs because they seemed sensible, and it's what was expected of them. Although *Soldiers* points out that many members of the *Wehrmacht* did exhibit a complicated amalgam of anti-Semitism and Nazi sympathies, few were motivated to do their job on the warfront by these ideologies. They were compliant agents of the emerging system of order, and in the intellectual bubble of their upbringing and training, that order was what was most important.

The language of work or jobs is important, too. "Most of the soldiers," Neitzel and Welzer write, "wage war not out of conviction, but because they are soldiers, and fighting is their job."[18] This is how soldiers from many cultures and wars describe their duty, and it applied to Hartmann as well. His recollections of his own leadership on the Eastern Front suggests a vocational understanding of purpose:

> I would say that in our group, there were the majority of us who found all the National Socialist idiocy a little sickening. We used to make jokes about Hitler, Göring, Göbbels, and the rest. They were just too comical in many ways to be taken seriously. Colonel Dieter Hrabak made it a special point to explain to the new young pilots that if they thought they were fighting for National Socialism and the *Führer* they needed to transfer to the *Waffen SS* or something. He had no time for political types. He was fighting a war against a superb enemy, not holding a political rally.[19]

This was one of the only times Hartmann ever mentioned National Socialism in published works, and it came at a time (decades after the war) when anything other than an unequivocal disavowal of it would have been unacceptable in public discussions. But it is consistent with what other German pilots said and reasonable in the context of Neitzel and Welzer's work. It could be that, despite the urgency we might feel in locating whatever fragments of National Socialism were hiding in Hartmann's world view, the most useful thing is to acknowledge that National Socialism was one among many complicated, even contradictory, ingredients to his frame of reference.

That doesn't mean he didn't help push National Socialism farther into the remote Eastern Front. Regardless of his convictions, his effects were clear.

# Part Two

Hartmann's Wars

## CHAPTER 6

# Kills

If your opponent dives on you, do not try to evade his onslaught, but fly to meet it.

—OSWALD BÖLKE

On October 14, 1942, a German convoy jostled along a rutted roadway a few miles from Soldatskaya, in the Russian south. Fall had come but the roads were still dry enough that the truck threw up a trail of dust visible from the air for miles. Not far above the horizon, the speck of an aircraft approached the snaking train of vehicles. It was a single-engine fighter, maybe an Il-2 *Sturmovik*. Probably agile and armed. The truck drivers couldn't quite tell its intentions at first.

At some point, the lead truck's occupants could see (probably with relief) that the aircraft was a Messerschmitt fighter—one of their own—and not Soviet. But this Bf 109, in its shadowy mottles of gray, was descending closer toward the German soldiers. Still heading toward them. Something was wrong.

In the cockpit sat Hartmann, in his very first mission, and at this moment he was wrestling with an impotent aircraft. His propeller, powerless, whirled lazily around, moved only by the rush of oncoming wind against the cocked blades. He could see the truck out of his windscreen just as the others could see him—it was his own slowly approaching speck—and he was equally glad to discern its nationality. But at this moment there was no time to reflect, because he was preparing for a treacherous belly landing.

Five hundred meters, reported his altimeter.

Hartmann's predicament had come about quickly. He had entered his first real dogfight just minutes before and was completely outmatched. A swarm of Soviet fighters had spooked him, causing him to lose his orientation and focus. He responded by using every bit of power his Messerschmitt could provide to run away from the scene. Even his wingman, whom Hartmann had mistaken for another enemy pilot, couldn't catch him. Edmund "Paule" Rossmann was his name, and he screamed over the radio trying to corral Hartmann, who escaped the battle only to have a fuel warning light remind him of his impulsiveness.

On it went, a little red flood on the corner of the instrument panel in front of him, and a few minutes later the last drop of gasoline was extracted from the tanks inside the 109's slender fuselage. The massive Daimler-Benz engine in front of him, starved of combustion, now became a weight dragging him toward the earth. The Messerschmitt always lacked range, but Hartmann's gas-guzzling sprint away from the battle had made it even shorter, and there was no way he was going to make it back to his base. There were two options: bail out dangerously close to the ground, or find a spot closer to safety for a controlled crash.

By the time the bone-colored altimeter needle unwound past the 100-meter mark, Hartmann would have already gone through a mental checklist: shoulder harnesses tight, flaps down, landing gear up and locked, situation announced over the radio. If he felt any consolation at this point, it might be that this sort of dead-stick flying, the intuitive calculus of trading altitude for distance, was exactly what he had been practicing over those hills near his

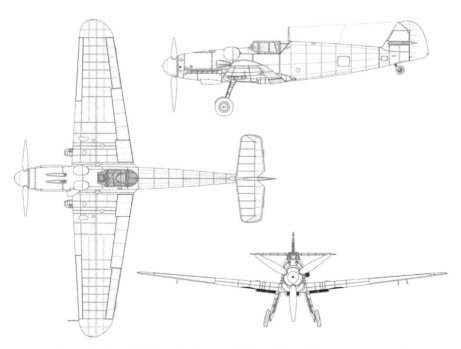

Messerschmitt Bf 109G—the "Gustav." (Björn Huber, Wikimedia Commons)

hometown back when he was a boy. Back then, he had set his glider down gently and precisely, and with no more of a jolt than a man stepping off a train.

The Messerschmitt sailed across the threshold of a sunflower field at just shy of 100 miles per hour. With the slightest force on the stick, Hartmann tugged the nose into a gentle flare—his last exertion of control over the aircraft—and the ground, for an instant, stayed an arm's reach away. Sunflower stalks whipped by the wings.

Maybe for this suspended heartbeat, Hartmann thought about the dangers of his new job, or whether he would see Ursula again. Or maybe it was the Soviets, the adversaries he'd been instructed to loathe, who had defeated him on his first combat engagement.

Then again, maybe he thought about nothing at all. It didn't matter. The altimeter unwound to zero.

# JG-52

Hartmann had learned in the spring of 1942 that he would be joining *Jagdgeschwader (JG) 52*, though at the time he didn't know how fortunate that was going to be. *JG-52* was on its way to becoming the most dominant fighter wing in the history of warfare; by the end of the war, its pilots collected more than 10,000 kills between them. The wing became a storied collection of personalities whose appetite for the aerial fight matched their tolerance for the cold.

It hadn't started out that way, and it was only after Hartmann arrived that *JG-52* started to perform so well. Formed in 1938 with Bf 109Ds, *JG-52* spent the first years of the war on the Western Front, where it operated in fits and starts. *JG-52* was comprised of three *Gruppe*, each designated by a numeral before the wing's name. Hartmann was initially assigned to *III./JG-52*.

*Luftwaffe* organization warrants some clarification here. In order of large to small, the organization broke down like this:

*Fliegerkorps* (air corps)
*(Jagd)Geschwader* (fighter wing)
*Gruppe* (group)
*Staffel* (squadron)
*Schwarm* (flight)

Hartmann's post to *III./JG-52* meant that he was part of the third group of *Jagdgeschwader 52*.

Initially used as a "'filler-in-of-gaps' for other units," *JG-52* played a modest role in the Battle of Britain, by which point it had upgraded to Bf 109Es.[1] It wasn't until Operation *Barbarossa* that the squadron more or less congealed into its famous form. For the first 18 months of *Barbarossa*, *JG-52* occupied an area of operations that stretched roughly from Ploesti in Romania in the west to Stalingrad and the Caspian Sea in the east. Scattered throughout were bases near Kiev, Kharkov, and Rostov.[2] After Hartmann's arrival, the fortunes of war turned and the lines began to constrict back toward Germany, forcing *JG-52* to move about frequently and at times operate from rudimentary airstrips or fields not far from the advancing Red Army. The units of the wing eventually retracted up through Hungary and what was then Czechoslovakia toward Germany. By 1945, what was left of the famed wing was charged with defending areas the Germans never thought they would have to defend.

Hartmann's time on the warfront, and his entrance into *JG-52*, began with a close call. He was ordered to ferry a Ju 87 *Stuka* to Mariopol, but he either didn't know how to operate the old-school dive-bomber, whose quirks were much different to those of the 109, or the *Stuka's* brakes malfunctioned before Hartmann ever got it off the ground. The scene of his attempted take-off—unlike that of his first engagement with the enemy—is almost comical. Hartmann fired up the engine and began to taxi out toward the runway, but ran straight into a wooden shack, watching as his propeller shredded the little building into splinters. The commanding officer at the scene had watched, helplessly, while the ungainly Ju 87 rambled in slow motion toward the building. A soldier who was in the shack at the time fled for his life just before Hartmann got there.

Once the dust settled, Hartmann clambered out "red-eared and awkward" and watched as yet another green pilot, over on the runway, buried his *Stuka's* nose in the ground while trying to land.[3] It wasn't a good day for the dive-bomber inventory, and the pair of would-be fighter pilots were shipped to their new base aboard a Ju-52 transport plane, safely away from the controls.

By October 1942, *III./JG-52's* base at Maykop was freezing over. Hartmann arrived to find accommodation that amounted to dull green tents dug halfway into the ground. The aircraft rested on tires caked with mud from the typical Russian fall season and, as winter approached, ground crews covered them with tarpaulins overnight to keep the wings from freezing too badly. (*JG-52* had developed a nasty relationship with the cold early on: *I./JG-52* once had

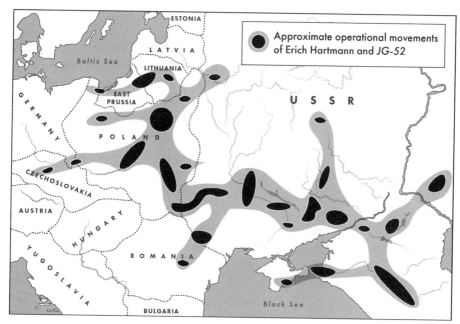

Range of *III./JG-52* movements, August 1942 to May 1945. The highlighted regions account for a full 50 separate *Gruppe* headquarters—a remarkable frequency of movement throughout the latter part of the war—and show us why Hartmann was so well-known and feared in the Caucasus and Ukrainian regions. This map is an approximation because there are problems with precisely plotting and showing every headquarters location. This is due to the variability of available records and the difficulty in translating wartime Germanized location names into contemporary ones on today's maps. On this map, the darkest regions are areas of concentration of bases, while the medium-gray areas are moderate concentrations and give a general picture of *III./JG-52* and Hartmann's range of movement.

almost every one of its aircraft suffer from cracked carburetor casings after a hard freeze.)[4]

You can imagine Hartmann staring eastward on those first bone-cold mornings, looking through his own silvery breath, aware that he had entered real war. These were harsh conditions and even harsher missions.

Later on, he recalled the experience living in the dirt: "The lice were the worst, and there was little you could do but hold your clothes to a fire and listen to them pop. We had DDT and bathed when we could. Illness, especially pneumonia and trench foot, were bad, especially among the ground crews."[5]

## Trial by Fire

Hartmann was lucky that he walked away from his first encounter with the Soviets in one piece. After he brought his gliding 109 down in the sunflowers, he connected with the group of German soldiers in the trucks, who drove him the 30 kilometers back to his airfield. But his punishment once he returned was severe. He was reprimanded for seven specific infractions during the mission, not the least of which were leaving Rossmann, his leader, and losing a fighter without inflicting any damage on an enemy plane. He was taken off the flight schedule and had to help the ground crews for three days.[6]

Fellow pilot Alfred Grislawski later recalled Rossmann's frustrated assessment. "That Hartmann," said Rossmann, "thinks he can behave in just any way because he is an officer ... I refuse to fly with him again until he has learned to behave decently."[7] He did learn, apparently, because he flew even more with Rossmann, who by all accounts was a demanding but skilled teacher.

Hartmann scored his first victory on his 19th mission, a free-hunt scramble on November 5. Above the river town of Digora he spotted the lumpy profile of an Il-2 *Sturmovik*, the armor-plated Soviet workhorse that was becoming all too familiar to Eastern Front pilots. It seemed like such an easy target: the *Sturmovik* was slow, heavy, and not very maneuverable. But there was a reason people called it the Flying Tank. It was armored to the gills, and later versions had two crew members, one of whom could return fire on an advancing predator using a machine gun mounted on the upper fuselage. The *Sturmovik* was celebrated in the Soviet Union as the bomber that helped to beat back the German *Panzer* tanks that had been so relentless in their early advances. It was, in fact, indispensable, and it became the most mass-produced military aircraft in history. The Soviets built more than 36,000 of them.

Once he had a visual on the *Sturmovik*, Hartmann did what any excitable pilot would do at the sight of a good target: he hit the throttle, reeled his 109 into a six-o'clock firing position, then fired and fired again—only to see the rounds from his guns either fly off into empty space or patter off the *Sturmovik*'s rugged fuselage. So he took another approach, this time flying in from slightly below. He let his crosshairs settle over the *Sturmovik*'s unarmored, grease-stained belly and chin-mounted oil cooler. He let go with another burst when the Soviet machine was fewer than 50 meters away, and it bellowed black, dirty smoke. Hartmann had his first kill.

But then his 109 started shuddering violently. It was the engine. Shrapnel from the Sturmovik had exploded toward Hartmann and hit his aircraft before he could get out of the way, and the damage was severe enough that he was going to have to either bail out or make yet another belly landing. He chose to stay with the aircraft and set it down, once again, in a field. He hit the dirt in another violent skid, fishtailing to a stop after plowing a couple of hundred yards. Another crash-landing and another 109 scratched off the inventory list—but this time he had at least done some good with it.

He heard another Daimler-Benz engine overhead and looked up to see his wingman, who had witnessed the whole event, circling overhead. His partner wagged his wings, a sign of acknowledgement that he saw the wreck and that Hartmann was alive, and before long Hartmann, again in German-held territory, was picked up and sent on his way back to debrief.

He returned having learned a lesson: although point-blank shooting had been the key to his success, it was also dangerous. He knew that his likelihood of scoring hits increased with proximity to the enemy, but so did the prospect that his plane would take damage from the wreckage. To Hartmann, the benefits of the approach always outweighed the costs, and this informed the strategy that would serve him extraordinarily well over the next couple of years on the front. Though occasionally rattled as the fighting picked up (Grislawski also recalled Hartmann being sent on leave so he could clear his head after an airborne collision and resulting crash), Hartmann made it through those harrowing first months that seem to test almost any fighter pilot.[8] With experience came confidence, clout in the squadron, and kills. Many, many kills.

## Kills in the Hundreds

If you were to plot Hartmann's earliest aerial victories on a graph, you'd see that his pace was gradual at first and then accelerated, with some wobbles, around his 15th kill. This was when he really developed his confidence and effectiveness, and the pace only accelerated from there. By this point in the war, roughly seven months into his deployment, he had seen the range of what the Soviets had to throw at him: everything from nimble MiG-1 and Lagg-3 fighters to the tank-like *Sturmovik* and larger, lumbering bombers like the twin-prop Boston, an American design.[9] He had subsequently conceived, tested, and optimized his preferred attack style over a suitably large sample size of airborne encounters.

In a sense, this sort of analysis is exactly how Hartmann would have assessed his own performance. Where there was information and experience available, he consulted it before acting.

Hartmann's formula for achieving kills, which he expressed frequently as "see, decide, attack," was tailored to fit the Eastern Front air war, and it wasn't really a dogfighting strategy *per se*. It was more of an anti-dogfighting strategy. Hartmann's Soviet enemies were, generally, less capable than the British and American pilots on the Western Front, which meant not only that they were easier to shoot down, but also that they were easier to evade and disengage from if the odds weren't right. Furthermore, Hartmann's most common mission type was the "free hunt," in which he was untethered to other ground or air units and could simply go find the enemy planes, engage them, and return to base. This contrasts with a typical bomber escort mission, for example, which limits fighter planes' movements and initiative, as well as the fuel available for tangling with enemies. Hartmann fought unshackled.

Soviet aircraft, for much of the war, lagged behind German and other Allied designs. Even when better fighters arrived, Hartmann retained the crucial advantage of experience. The *Luftwaffe* had already had the Spanish Civil War to practice using the Bf 109 to its greatest effect, and Hartmann exploited its strengths relative to his Soviet adversaries (small size, good low-altitude performance, high degree of automation, armament, climb rate) while minimizing its weaknesses (turn rate, endurance, high wing loading). For example, Hartmann could depend on the 109's relative superiority in the dive to get away from any engagements that weren't optimal for him. In dogfighting (as in any fight) it is an enormous luxury to disengage at will, and Hartmann almost always resisted the temptation for "just one more." Better to live and fight another day, he would say.

## 352?

During the war, a few pilots questioned Hartmann's dramatic kill totals, including some Germans. The most notable objections came from Carl Junger and Friedrich Obleser, both of whom eventually flew with Hartmann. In Obleser's case, Hartmann challenged him to see for himself and requested that Obleser be transferred from 8. *Staffel* to 9. *Staffel* (both were part of *JG-52*) so Obleser could fly on his wing. Hartmann said that Obleser "became a believer after a few missions and signed off on some kills as a witness."[10]

There are, naturally, lingering questions about the kill totals claimed by Hartmann and other German aces on the Eastern Front, 16 of whom claimed more than 200 victories. Most defenders of these aces are quick to cite the *Luftwaffe's* strict requirements for making a kill official, so it bears summarizing here.

As Hartmann described it:

> Having a kill confirmed was not an easy thing. If you did not have a witness in the air, then you had to have one on the ground; if not a witness, then you had to have a crash site. We hardly ever had gun cameras in Russia, and that would have helped many men confirm kills that crashed on the enemy side of the line when there was no air witness. You also had to have the altitude of the attack, aircraft type, time, and location all in your *Abschuss* [flight log].[11]

What Hartmann is describing here is the *policy* for crediting kills, not necessarily the *practice*. It is widely known that all air forces over-claimed, sometimes drastically, and that the records of opposing forces frequently do not line up. On one day during the Battle of Britain, for example, the British claimed 185 *Luftwaffe* aircraft shot down, but the German losses were apparently only 60. There are countless similar examples from every corner of the warfront.

The freshest criticisms of Hartmann's kill claims came in 2005 from the Russian historian Dimitri Khazanov, who published an article in French aviation magazine *Le Fana de l'Aviation* explaining various discrepancies between Hartmann's claims and the numbers of planes downed according to Soviet archives. Khazanov tracks Hartmann throughout several operational sectors and observes that, for example, the aircraft Hartmann claimed to have shot down sometimes exceeded the number of Soviet planes that were known to be in the air at the time.[12] Khazanov's reporting has been criticized for relying on questionable data (Soviet archives) and drawing stark conclusions from limited information. His guess that Hartmann probably shot down at most 70–80 aircraft is as difficult to substantiate as the supposedly spurious kill totals he was trying to discredit.

So, here's what we actually know.

1. Hartmann's biography, the original chronicle of kills, was partially substantiated by Hartmann's first logbook, which he retained after the war. It breaks down the 352 kills individually but relies on Hartmann's personal testimonies and has missing data from kills 151 onward. Those were the kills recorded in Hartmann's second logbook, which went missing after the war. The authors note that it was confiscated by an American or Czech captor, and they say they pieced together the missing information from old *JG-52* records and letters Hartmann wrote home. But those details are still sparse: you see, for example, that on March 2, 1944, Hartmann claimed 10 victories in one day but reported no other details.[13]

2. In 2015, researchers Johannes Mathews and John Foreman published what appears to be the most comprehensive analysis of kills and verifications ever made—examining every *Luftwaffe* ace with five or more kills, presenting brief biographies and detailed kill charts for all of them over the course of a huge, four-volume set. According to their data, which was apparently derived from research at the German Federal Archives, Hartmann's 352 claims can be accounted for with virtually complete detail.[14]

3. The Khazanov research is certainly suggestive and has provoked debate among *Luftwaffe* fans. This debate, however, usually takes place within the convoluted threads of internet forums, making it hard to discern who really knows what. Often, one portion of the readership roundly dismisses Khazanov's research as faulty, partisan, and rooted in bad data. Other contributors stress that pilots routinely exaggerated their claims, that there are, in fact, identifiable contradictions in Hartmann's records and kill credits, and that shooting down 352 aircraft would be an almost superhuman feat.

In a 2006 *Flight Journal* article, author Barrett Tillman provides a window into the sheer complexity of tracking and validating fighter pilots' scores and day-to-day exploits. The article compares the testimony of American ace Robert Goebel with what's in *The Blond Knight of Germany* to determine if it was Hartmann whom Goebel nearly shot down in July 1944. This concerns one specific engagement, which the opposing pilots later described independently and without knowledge of each other's recollections. Goebel, Tillman concludes, very likely engaged Hartmann, failed to shoot him down, but nevertheless caused Hartmann to run out of fuel and bail out. Hartmann and his interviewers independently came to a similar conclusion, and Hartmann was always content thinking that it was, in fact, Goebel who forced him to bail out on the one occasion he had to open his parachute.

During his research, however, Tillman discovered interesting discrepancies between Goebel and Hartmann's accounting of the air battles during that time period: "[Hartmann's] biography ... says that Hartmann claimed four P-51s on June 23, but *JG-52* records show his first Mustang kill occurred the next day." Elsewhere, Tillman describes an engagement where Hartmann said he saw what must have been Goebel and his flight, but he reported seeing eight enemy planes when Tillman and his fellow Mustang pilots only numbered four. *The Blond Knight of Germany*'s description of *JG-52* attacking B-17s also conflicts with the fact that Goebel's 31st Fighter Group actually escorted B-24s, which were quite distinguishable from B-17s unless they were far away.[15]

None of this suggests systematic lying on Hartmann's part, and it's safe to say that Hartmann was spectacularly successful against his Soviet enemies. Regardless of the grand-total debate, it's not as if many of Hartmann's actual

A wrecked IL-2 *Sturmovik* is inspected by onlookers, c. 1942. This particular *Sturmovik* has seen a fair amount of action, as evidenced by the paint worn off at the wing roots, where boots scuffed the area over time. (Fortepan, Wikimedia Commons)

kills were gifts—you don't shoot down enemy aircraft by the dozens or hundreds because you're lucky. That takes skill, physical and mental endurance, and a viable strategy. Hartmann had all of those things.

## Shoot When They Fill Your Windscreen

As the beneficiary of early-war *Luftwaffe* training, Hartmann had learned about his aircraft and the principles of physics it was subject to. He was wiry and strong, and even into his later years stayed physically fit enough to manage the strains of high-performance aircraft. Alongside his fortunate tactical situation on the Eastern Front, it was his strategy that served him best and gave him his reputation as a patient, cunning, ruthlessly efficient combatant.

Alongside his mantra "see, decide, attack," Hartmann would always say he liked to wait "until the enemy fills your windscreen." He was in good company: the Red Baron, we hear, sometimes got so close to his victims that his plane flew through spatters of their blood.[16] There were plenty of benefits to the approach, one of which was that it saved precious ammunition. (After one mission, Hartmann's crew chief reportedly came up to him looking perplexed. He had counted the rounds left in the ammunition belts and seen that Hartmann had managed to score three kills on that mission while expending only 120 rounds.) This philosophy of patience also gave Hartmann the element of surprise, since he rarely sprayed premature tracer rounds into the air. Ground crews loaded luminescent tracers every so often into ammunition belts to help pilots see the real path of their bullets, but the glowing tracers could also alert unwitting enemy pilots of an attack when they flashed by in front of them.

If all of this makes you think of Bölcke, it should. On the Eastern Front, several of Bölcke's dicta were especially valid:

> Try to secure advantages before attacking.
> Fire only at close range and only when your opponent is properly in your sights.
> Always keep your eyes on your opponent, and never let yourself be deceived by ruses.
> When over the enemy's lines, never forget your own line of retreat.

There were, of course, those times when the dicta didn't protect Hartmann as planned and he found himself on the defensive. In these situations, Hartmann liked to imagine the view from his attacker's windscreen and take actions that would foul up the enemy's learned tactics. One method of evasion he used frequently was to radically reorient his plane at just the right moment—that crucial instant when, while trying to pull enough lead to deflection-shoot Hartmann's 109, the attacking pilot could lose sight of Hartmann as he dipped below the nose of his plane. Hartmann knew that part of the trouble with deflection shooting is that if the angle of deflection is severe enough—if the turn is sharp enough—the long noses of contemporary fighters got in the way of the attacker's view. So he would guess when he would be "invisible" in this way and jam his stick forward, which took him suddenly from positive Gs to negative Gs and violently aborted his turn. He would simultaneously kick the inside rudder pedal (if he was turning sharp right he would lean into the right rudder), which, because of his high bank angle, would act like an elevator, forcing his nose down toward the ground, which promoted good airflow over the wings and a gain in airspeed. This combination of control inputs meant that, without being seen doing it, he could reorient himself into a protective dive at least 45 degrees divergent from the attacker's heading. It gave him airspeed, an unknown direction from the perspective of his shooter, and the time to either flee or seize the offensive.

Probably dozens of times, this approach left Hartmann's kill-hungry attackers pulling hard Gs somewhere above, straining their aircraft and shooting blind, thinking that Hartmann had maintained his original turn.

This scenario highlights the severity of the physics involved in air-to-air combat. Maneuvers like this could throw Hartmann around his own cockpit and subject him to substantial G-loads, both positive and negative—in the most drastic cases, the blood would start to drain from his brain and settle in his legs, causing his vision to gray or black out. These maneuvers could also stress the structure of his Bf 109 to the limit, causing it to creak and shudder in protest.

Amazingly, the whole dance of a dogfight could take place over the course of just a few seconds. The famed American pilot Robin Olds, who flew P-38s and P-51s in World War II and F-4 Phantoms in Vietnam, said: "Usually in the first five seconds of a dogfight, somebody dies. Somebody goes down. You want to make sure it's the other guy."[17]

## His Best Acting

The first 20 days of August 1943 were some of Hartmann's most productive of the war. On the 1st of the month, his kill tally stood at 42; not three weeks later it had risen to 90. In these intense late-summer days he flew 53 missions, giving him an average of roughly a kill per mission.

It would have been even better if not for one mission, an early-morning scramble on the 20th. Rousted from sleep, Hartmann scrambled into his 109 without breakfast and was told that his job was to take out an advancing Soviet airborne attack group, with focus on the bombers. He and his squadronmates intercepted a mix of Soviet bombers and their fighter escorts, and without any drama he downed one *Sturmovik* from close up, got out of the way of the wreckage, and looked down to search out the next opportunity. There was another one waiting for him, so he rolled in to take it out, too. A punch of the trigger and the second bomber was done with.

But then, suddenly, his engine cowl panels blew off their piano hinges and flew back in the slipstream. Hartmann, shocked, wheeled his 109 to a westerly heading toward the German side of the front, shut off his stricken engine, and checked for a place to set the plane down. He didn't know what had hit him—maybe shrapnel from the bomber, or perhaps it was ground fire. Now it was once again a field of sunflowers that filled his windscreen, so he focused on that, and into it his powerless 109 went.

He skidded to a stop and opened the canopy to take a breath. This time, with the war a little further along than before, he had to remember a new standing order among 109 pilots and remove the clock from his instrument panel to bring with him. Clocks, among other precision instruments, were in short wartime supply. As he bent down to unfasten the four metal retaining screws that held the small clock in place, he noticed a truck approaching. He paused. It was German. Back to the instrument panel he went, but when the truck arrived, several Soviets stepped out. Thinking quickly, Hartmann decided to stay in the cockpit and fake an internal injury with the hope that it might buy him some time and a way to think up an escape later on. He slumped over his instrument panel and cried in agony as soon as his captors tried to pull him out. When they heaved him out, one of them spat to Hartmann, "Hitler *kaput!*"[18] Another fake cry.

After a haphazard medical exam, which was crude enough that Hartmann's cries and gestures toward his abdomen convinced his captors that he was really hurt, he was thrown into another truck and driven somewhere vaguely eastward. Rumbling along, he noticed that a flight of *Stukas* was overhead, their trademark sirens screaming in the air. The truck slowed. This was all the distraction Hartmann could hope for, he figured, so in that moment he lunged into the precarious and frustrated guard and bolted past him out of the truck and into the brush. In a scene that has since become a movie cliché, Hartmann ran as the bullets thumped into the trees and dirt around him, never quite catching him. When the shooting stopped and he had the time to figure his position, Hartmann confirmed that he was in fine physical shape and that he had wandered even deeper into Soviet-held territory. He guessed at the time of day (he never did get the damned clock) and headed westward into the afternoon.

To gain concealment, he holed up to wait for darkness. The sun went down and Hartmann now had to use his basic navigation training (or, as *The Blond Knight of Germany* puts it, "the icy coolness of his combat head") to make his way back toward the front line.[19] If he could find that, he thought, he could find Germans.

He crunched along through wooded valleys and over hills, stopping here and there to check for any other movements around him. For a while he followed a Soviet column of infantrymen at a safe distance, thinking that they might lead him to fellow Germans. His hunch turned out to be right. After some time trailing the group, they became agitated and hustled over a knoll. Then came gunfire and grenade bursts. For an hour or two after the skirmish, Hartmann waited and observed from under a nearby house; then he walked cautiously into where it had taken place. Was this the front line, or just an unfortunate meeting of German and Soviet foot patrols? He saw shell casings stamped into the ground by a variety of boots. The combatants had dissipated into the night somewhere.[20]

After a couple more hours of cautious hiking, Hartmann was startled by the shout of a soldier's voice behind him, and then a rifle shot. A bullet tore through his pant leg and Hartmann froze. He listened for the next shot to come, but it never did. The soldier's voice rang out in German, and Hartmann yelled that he was a *Luftwaffe* pilot. He turned to find a young infantryman, who, in Hartmann's estimation, was even more petrified than he was. He had found his countrymen, even though he had almost been shot by one. Although Hartmann lacked any identification because it had been taken by the Soviets, he described his predicament and the German troops shoved him into a foxhole. He noted that this was a *Waffen-SS* platoon. For the time being, Hartmann was going to have to join them.

It turned out to be a hard reckoning—never before had he witnessed what the ground forces experienced every day. Hartmann was struck when the *SS* men told him about a recent Soviet ambush, in which several enemy soldiers had posed as escaped German POWs only to whip out machine guns and mow down some of the Germans who'd just taken them in. The lieutenant who had interrogated Hartmann told him this was why he had insisted on being so thorough in his questioning.[21]

Then he saw reality first-hand. Perched next to an MG-42 position (a spectacularly powerful machine gun nicknamed "Hitler's Zipper"), Hartmann watched as a group of about 200 Soviet soldiers meandered closer, unaware of the German position they were walking into. (Hartmann thought many of them were drunk.) The Germans waited, silently, until the Soviets were only 20 yards away. Then came the order to fire, and the enemies were completely shredded. With shattering cracks of firearms at close range, bodies and parts were strewn everywhere. The shooting lasted 30 minutes, Hartmann said, and mounds of the dead littered the forest floor afterward. It was the kind of carnage he and his fellow pilots had always been sheltered from.

"They finished the killing and then sat down and ate," Hartmann recalled. "I thought to myself, these *SS* men are tough, nothing fazed them … they were of a different mindset. I think all the hard ground fighting created a different kind of human being."

After this event, Hartmann's understanding of his war was different, even if his actions weren't. He had already heard of the futility of its destruction, as described by his war-weary father at home, and now he had seen it up close: "So this is the infantry. You can have it."[22]

Later, Hartmann said, he asked the *SS* officer in command why his men had killed wounded Soviets and left them on the ground rather than taking them in as prisoners (as dictated by the Geneva Conventions). The officer said

The MG-42 machine gun was nicknamed "Hitler's Zipper" for its sound and its effect. This was the weapon the *Waffen-SS* used to massacre dozens of Soviet soldiers while Hartmann watched on after he'd been forced to ditch in a field. (Hohum, Wikimedia Commons)

it was because all that took resources, and it would have exposed his men to other advancing Red Army divisions. Hartmann was dumbfounded. He and the flyers sometimes gave captured aviators hot cups of coffee.

Meanwhile, back at base, Hartmann's crew chief had become restless. Bimmel Mertens had grown close to Hartmann over the course of the conflict thus far—the pair had worked together constantly in preparing for so many missions—and when he learned about Hartmann's crash and failure to return, he set off after him. The realization that Hartmann had gone down must have been wrenching for Mertens, who was the one most directly responsible for the mechanical health of the airplane that was supposed to bring him back. It isn't clear what the crew chief saw or did during his foray into the wild, but when he wandered back onto the field and saw that Hartmann had returned on his own, the pair exchanged exasperated handshakes and chuckles of relief.

Maybe Hartmann told him about the massacre, or maybe he kept it to himself. Either way, the pair went right back to work.

CHAPTER 7

# Against Stalin's Falcons

We have only to kick in the door and the whole rotten structure will come crashing down.

—HITLER, PRIOR TO OPERATION BARBAROSSA

Blood-soaked snow. That's what many people remember about the Eastern Front, where, most notably at Moscow and Stalingrad, the German invasion stalled and then crumbled. It was supposed to be a lightning campaign, like France, but Hitler underestimated the hardiness and quantity of the Soviet people, not to mention the vastness of their territory. At Stalingrad, tens of thousands of attackers and defenders fell in a week's time, and the Germans were never able to recover. This truly was a frozen hell: along deserted, rubble-strewn streets, smoke still wafting into the sky, civilians and soldiers alike scoured dead bodies for dry boots, coats, food, or unspent ammunition. Anything they could use.

Because of this dreadful imagery, people forget that the Soviet campaign started, and was almost immediately won, in the air.

On the very first day of the preemptive invasion—the early morning hours, before daybreak, of June 22, 1941—the *Luftwaffe* sent a handful of its best bomber pilots to strike key Soviet airfields. They hit them ruthlessly, wrecking much of the Soviet air force before breakfast. This air force (*Voyenno-vozdushnyye sily*, or *VVS* from here on) was poorly dispersed throughout the territory it was responsible for protecting, so the damage from this initial raid was concentrated and catastrophic. *Luftwaffe* crews were delighted to find rows of *VVS* aircraft arranged neatly, unconcealed, and in tight bunches—just waiting to be strafed or bombed. This initial assault seemed to confirm the (over-)celebrated *Luftwaffe Blitzkrieg* model: hit them hard, hit them early, and cripple them before they can mount a significant response.[1]

The initial attack was a humiliation for an air force that was still dragging itself out of an earlier era. If there's a positive way to look at this from the

The first aggressions of Operation *Barbarossa*, beginning in June 1941. Erich Hartmann joined the southern portion of the campaign as it advanced into the Caucasus, north of the Georgian border, and retracted toward Germany as the invasion failed. The plane icon indicates the site of Hartmann's first combat mission, near Soldatskaya, October 14, 1942.

Soviet perspective, it could be that the beginning of Operation *Barbarossa* purged the *VVS* of technology that wouldn't have helped it much anyway. But that's a hard way to scrape together optimism in such a disastrous start to a campaign the Soviets saw coming ahead of time.

Just as the Bf 109 was a metaphor for the nimble, incisive *Luftwaffe* fighter squadrons, the malnourished Polikarpov I-16 fighter was representative of the *VVS* during the early months of the campaign. Here was a design that had raised hopes when it came off the drawing board but completely failed to deliver on them and was kept in service much longer than it should have been. The I-16 first flew in 1933, two years before the Bf 109, and featured a single metal wing, retractable landing gear, fast-firing machine guns in the wings, and outstanding maneuverability—all signs of modernity for a fighter plane. But it was also underpowered, technically crude, hampered by an old-fashioned open-air cockpit, and, if an airplane can rightly be called such a thing, generally frumpy in its appearance and behavior. At the start of hostilities, the I-16 was the most numerous fighter in the Soviet inventory, but it couldn't compete with the 109 in anything other than roll rate. German pilots could pick when they wanted to engage it and disengage at will. The Soviets nicknamed the I-16 "the Burro"; Finns who flew it called it "the Flying Squirrel."

Adolf Galland, fighter general of the *Luftwaffe*, was characteristically concise (and correct) in his assessment of the *VVS* at this point in the war: "The Red air force was numerically strong but, from a point of machines and personnel, hopelessly inferior."[2] This was one reason why the U.S., after the 1941 passage of the Lend-Lease Act, shipped so many of its own second-tier fighters to the

Soviet I-16, early-war workhorse of the *VVS*, 1939. Nicknamed the "the Burro" and "the Flying Squirrel," it was obviously outclassed by the Bf 109 and other fighters. (Public domain)

Soviets. The un-supercharged P-39 Airacobra and the old-when-it-was-born P-40 Warhawk both wore winter camouflage and red stars; these fighters were obsolescent but still fairly well-suited to the low-altitude fighting characteristic of the Eastern Front. It's a testament to the Soviet pilots that they used these second-hand planes as effectively, and for as long, as they did. Hartmann's logbook is littered with Airacobra kills alongside La-5s and Yaks.

The airborne clashes above the Eastern Front were influenced by the fact that both Germany and the Soviet Union had built their air forces to be essentially tactical. They were mostly deployed in service of the ground forces, unlike the American Army Air Corps, which was not subservient in the same way. The U.S. strategic bombing campaigns had no equivalent in the *Luftwaffe* or the *VVS*, nor did the American heavy bomber aircraft themselves. (After the war, the Soviets had to copy, nearly bolt-for-bolt, an American B-29 Superfortress in order to hurriedly put together a strategic bomber force for the Cold War. Their rampant plagiarism continued for decades.) The Germans never produced a successful four-engined bomber, which exasperates today's military historians and yesterday's unit commanders. Hitler's misplaced confidence in his small tactical bombers was rooted, in part, in the dubious assumption that Germany would always be on the offensive, hungrily consuming enemy territory theater by theater.

Those few German heavy bombers, mostly prototypes, are interesting for their failings. Many were essentially moonshot designs that either never made it off the drawing board or were so deficient that they never made a difference. The evocative "*Amerika* Bombers," supposedly able to cross the Atlantic to strike the East Coast of the U.S., were little more than figments of Hitler's imagination. The ungainly, technically ridiculous Heinkel He 177—with four engines, only two propellers, and no redeeming qualities—never captured the leadership's interest or confidence. Its propensity for bursting into flames in the air earned it the nickname *Luftwaffenfeuerzeug*, or "*Luftwaffe*'s Lighter."

In their book on the Soviet air force, historians Von Hardesty and Ilya Grinberg describe the early phases of *Barbarossa* as an "air debacle of unprecedented scope" brought on by failures in Soviet leadership and production, and this gives us a full and useful preface to Hartmann's career in the East.[3] In the years before the war, they say, Stalin claimed to prioritize modernization, but the Communist state economy took too long to get up to speed. The *VVS* also suffered from a decentralized organizational structure that was inadequate for marshaling coordinated attacks across a vast front with many points of weakness.[4] Even the Soviets' extended network of airfields conspired against them, since most of the best-equipped ones were in the far west, where they could be taken out by the earliest German raids.[5] A striking confirmation of this comes from the fact that the *Luftwaffe* destroyed 4,000 Soviet aircraft within the first week of Operation *Barbarossa* while losing only a few dozen of its own.

There are a few practical factors that made the *VVS* more resilient than it might have seemed in the summer of 1941. One of these was the Soviet Union's ability to evacuate much of its industry far to the east, beyond the Ural Mountains, beginning in the early months of the invasion. This was a spectacular technical feat—more than 1,500 factories and other heavy installations were picked up and moved beyond the Germans' aerial reach in order to protect production capacity. Had the *Luftwaffe* built a reasonable number of long-range strategic bombers, these factories, and Moscow, might have been more vulnerable. These installations, quickly restarted, were soon producing much more effective machines and equipment.[6]

As the weather turned toward the end of 1941 and the Soviets started to mount effective counter-offensives, the *Wehrmacht* was already showing signs of fatigue. The final, concerted assault on Moscow, Operation *Typhoon*, began on October 2. The first snow came four days later, worsening the existing slurry of mud along the roadways. Life-draining cold came soon after, paralyzing many of the German ground units. Temperatures soon dipped below -30 degrees Fahrenheit. The Germans recorded 100,000 cases of frostbite, and thousands of amputation procedures were performed.[7] Amazingly, this was in part their own doing: the *Wehrmacht* actually *withheld* winter clothing from its ground troops because issuing it would have conflicted with the earlier promise to Hitler that the Soviet Union would be crushed before winter.[8]

On November 7, Revolution Day in the Soviet Union, Stalin declined to cancel the normal military parade through Red Square, despite the ongoing German assault. He simply ordered the troops to keep marching once they completed their parade route—all the way out to the front lines to fight back the Germans.

All this was a year before Hartmann even made it to the front. You can see not just what a tragedy the Eastern Front was, but also how long it took to run its course.

## Hartmann, Meet Kozhedub

In our historical memory, Soviet pilots are supposed to be the antitheses to Hartmann: unskilled, robbed of initiative, technologically backward. That's one of the common explanations for the Germans' dominance over them, and there's some truth to it. But it's a limited way to look at Hartmann's enemies. It's surprising, actually, how many similarities *VVS* pilots shared with their *Luftwaffe* brethren. One teaches us interesting things about the other.

Most obviously, the Soviet state and its propaganda arms also created near-worship of aviators, and for many of the same purposes. In both countries, national leadership assigned individual pilots a set of ironclad ideological convictions, which they might not have ever claimed on their own but never dared to disavow. The Soviet pilots, Stalin believed, were evidence of Communism's historical inevitability and the Communist ruler's brilliance as a national father figure. Recall that paternalism was a theme that also served Hitler, and that National Socialism was supposed to be the great corrector of history's wrongs.

In both countries, the pilots also represented both the past and the future—pasts defined by honor and great victories, and futures made winnable through the exploits of ideologically pure, hardy, skilled men. In the Soviet Union, Aryan purity and physicality were replaced by notions of the "New Soviet Man"—another concocted archetype that Stalin was convinced would rescue his country from predatory capitalism and the nefarious West. This heroic persona fought in service of national solidarity (which was again placed above individual achievement), progress toward a utopian vision of Europe, and glorious victory at any cost.

Under different circumstances, Hartmann might have gotten along with Ivan Kozhedub, the top Allied ace of the war. Kozhedub is often left out of conversations about the World War II air war, but he was renowned in his own country, highly skilled, and enormously successful. He was also, like Hartmann, more than a little brash: In one interview he argued that "the Yak-3, La-7 and La-9 fighters were indisputably superior to the Bf 109s and Fw 190s." This claim would get scoffs from many pilots and aviation fans, but Kozhedub, let there be no doubt about it, would have challenged anyone to prove it. He also claimed to have taken the La-7 to more than 700km/h (434mph).[9] This assertion is within the realm of plausibility—barely—but it's probably an example of the "rounding up" enthusiastic pilots of all nationalities do when they're talking about their war experience. The La-7 was the last in the line of Lavochkin's wooden fighters, and it's true that it was an excellent design. Westerners who flew it after the war praised its raw performance and speed, even though they criticized its rudimentary instrumentation, dodgy systems, and frail construction.

Kozhedub grew up in a poor family in a Ukrainian village called Obrazheyevska. Later in life he recalled a drab childhood filled with constant work and little play. He said he only had three toys as a boy: a pair of handmade stilts, a rag ball, and a pair of skis made from barrel planks.[10] He managed to finish studies at the Shostka chemical technical school en route to an arduous career in Soviet industry.

From the beginning, Kozhedub shared Hartmann's lust for flight, and, like thousands of Soviet boys, he marveled at the exploits of famed Russian pilot Valery Chkalov. Chkalov was best known for several harrowing long-distance flights over the Arctic in primitive aircraft and under horrendous flying conditions. His signature accomplishment was a nonstop, 63-hour, 5,475-mile flight from Moscow to the U.S. city of Vancouver, Washington. And his death, like Manfred von Richthofen's before, was dramatic: He died in December 1938 on the maiden test flight of a Polikarpov fighter—a flight he wasn't actually approved to be making. After breaking allowable altitude limits, he crashed the plane short of the runway, presumably after his engine cut out. As a result of this national tragedy, several officials connected to the test program and one of the plane's designers were made scapegoats and promptly arrested. Chkalov was immortalized by the state.

In recalling Chkalov's influence on his own career, Kozhedub described a moment in school when his teacher advised him to "choose the life of an outstanding man as a model, and try to follow his example in everything."[11] For a 16-year-old Kozhedub, learning to fly in the Communist-funded flying clubs was a mission of emulating Chkalov and the other leading pilots. These aviators, collectively, were being advertised as "Stalin's falcons" who flew "steel birds" straight into the heart of danger. The rhetoric and imagery here were intentional because, as historian Jay Bergman notes, "Kievan and Muscovite princes were often described in Russian folklore as falcons, and some of the heroes in these tales miraculously transformed themselves into birds."[12] These pilots weren't just aviators, in other words. They were connections to the mythical Russian past.

Like Hartmann, Kozhedub's wartime career started disappointingly. His raw flying skills were apparently so good that his leaders held him back as an instructor early on; he didn't get into a dogfight until the second year of the war in the East, even though he had received his pilot's license in 1940.[13] He flew his first real mission during the intense air battle above Kursk, which ended up being a decisive blow to the *Luftwaffe* and a key sign of the *VVS's* resurgence.

Kozhedub's first brush with the enemy—again, like Hartmann—almost got him killed. On a flight over Kursk in an La-5, he lost contact with his leader and ended up alone among Bf 109s and Bf 110 twin-engined fighters.

When he spotted a formation of 109s, he lunged in for a kill, doing little more than irritating the formation and alerting two 109 pilots, who happily followed him and peppered him with hits as he tried to escape. Kozhedub's evasive panic took him to treetop level, where he zigzagged toward the front line in search of something Soviet. His misfortunes multiplied from there. As soon as he made it to the line and the 109s gave up (we assume they did, since Kozhedub never claimed shooting them down), Soviet anti-aircraft artillery started firing at him, apparently confusing his aircraft for the aesthetically similar Fw 190. By the time he landed, Kozhedub had almost been blasted out of the sky by two countries. He was missing a wingtip and a bunch of random shards from his fighter.[14] Years later, he remembered the event as "a bitter experience and a serious lesson."[15]

One benefit of wooden and fabric-covered aircraft such as the La-7 was their durability. Compared to all-metal aircraft, they were easier to repair, and bullets would often go right through them without creating much structural damage. They were also lighter and used noncritical war materials: in Britain, piano makers famously helped build the "wooden wonder" DeHavilland Mosquito, which was a front-line fighter-bomber design through to the end of the war.

Kozhedub eventually claimed 63 kills, and no British or American ace came within 20 of that figure. Maybe it's unsurprising that he was never hailed as the top-scorer in the West—the Cold War precluded it—but he was certainly celebrated at home. He was named Hero of the Soviet Union, the country's highest distinction, three times.

He was, of course, a perfect fit for his nation's propagandizing and mor-alizing, the heir apparent to Chkalov. Stalinism, like Nazism, was a swamp of ideals, many of which were inconsistent or contradictory, and one of the more interesting conflicts within Stalin's totalitarianism was that between his paranoid protection of self-image—his fanatical cultivation of power and violent smothering of any competition—and his gleeful elevation of Soviet aviators as the new national heroes. Their exploits, even in peacetime, were assigned almost deistic weight by the state-run media, and a generation of soon-to-be soldiers idolized the fliers as evidence that Communism was working, and that Stalin really was the engine of the Soviet rebirth. That he held onto that role, even longer than Hitler managed to hold onto his, is another of the 20th century's glaring tragedies.

CHAPTER 8

# Recognition and Attrition

This was insane. I told Hitler so, and I even told him that the best veteran pilots were being lost.

—Erich Hartmann[1]

Somewhere, a Soviet pilot, new to the cockpit, cruises above the summery fields of the Ukrainian east. He has no kills to his name, not many landings. He only becomes aware of the Messerschmitt behind him when cannon shells start shredding his smooth, wooden wings, throwing clouds of debris into the slipstream. A heartbeat later, more shells have hit his oil cooler and his engine. At this point he is only just beginning to take evasive action.

Sticky smoke belches into the cockpit, and when the first red-starred wing is sheared off, the lift from the other one throws the aircraft into a spiral no one could recover from. Aerodynamics wins, the aircraft disintegrates, and the pilot stays conscious just long enough to see those green fields rushing toward him. His last sensory experiences are of the airstream tearing at his limbs, and of the scenery below fading to grayscale. A few heartbeats later, he is dead.

It's impossible, of course, to tell exactly what it's really like to be killed this way, as countless men were during World War II. Many of the pilots (probably a smaller proportion than we're comfortable admitting) managed to escape their stricken planes, take to their parachute, and fly and fight again. But many thousands perished in the rarified air, isolated, unbelievably out of their element—neither their bodies nor their stories to be recovered by anyone.

When they do survive, their memories are often fogged. They describe the disorientation, the chaos, the pain—occasionally the rage—that gripped them in these tense moments. When you bail out at 250 miles per hour, the wind hits you like a sack of gravel, assuming you get out of the cockpit conscious. At 20,000 feet, you can't take a full breath, and any air you manage to inhale is well below zero degrees Fahrenheit. At most coordinates throughout the Soviet territory, making it safely to the ground doesn't offer much solace: help might be so hopelessly distant that your parachute just delays the inevitable.

Our nameless Soviet pilot, like many thousands of real ones, has completed a brief and uncelebrated career, but he has added luster to the career of the German who caught him by surprise. The ultimate gift of Soviet lives, or at least Soviet war materiel, is what made Hartmann and the other *Luftwaffe* men renowned in their own country, celebrated as heroes, and rewarded with honors.

They wore their rewards. The *Wehrmacht*, like most militaries, used a progressive award system, and these awards commanded the attention of almost everyone, announcing the identity, status, and skill set of the wearer before any formal introductions were made. The most recognized symbol, familiar even to people who had no interest in flying or fighting, was the Knight's Cross of the Iron Cross.

The Knight's Cross, as it was usually known, was a pendant worn at the neck, about two inches square but obviously with some mass to it. Deep black and lacquered, it rested just over soldiers' top shirt button so that you couldn't miss it if you met them. Its four flared arms, edged in silver, are still the classic, predominant national marking for the German military. Today it can be seen stenciled in low-visibility gray on Eurofighter Typhoons, and a version of it was painted much more glaringly on the Red Baron's Fokker all those years ago.

The wartime pendant came in several different versions with increasingly prestigious adornments. Unlike the swastika, it wasn't weighed down with any particular ideology—to soldiers it carried a more general connotation of bravery in the line of duty—though the Nazis were happy to appropriate it into their symbolic scenery. Just over 7,000 soldiers on all fronts received the Knight's Cross in World War II, and Hartmann received his in October 1943—just after his foray behind enemy lines—when his kill tally was approaching 150. By March 1944 he had surpassed 200 victories and received the Knight's Cross with Oak Leaves, the first graduation in the sequence. From there, if you were among the best of the best, you received the Knight's Cross with Oak Leaves and Swords, and then the Knight's Cross with Oak Leaves, Swords, and Diamonds. Only one person, Hans-Ulrich Rudel (a fantastic *Stuka* pilot and unrepentant Nazi ally, as we will see later), received the highest grade—the Knight's Cross with Golden Oak Leaves, Swords, and Diamonds.

Starting at the level of Oak Leaves, the Knight's Cross was typically awarded by Hitler in person. Because of this, the benefits of the award included a brief leave (Hartmann recalled 10 days' worth) and a trip from the warfront for the ceremony. When it was time to receive his, on March 2, Hartmann hopped on an overnight train headed west, toward Hitler's Eagle's Nest. And for him, this brief vacation was one of the oddest experiences of the war.

It started with cognac. Hartmann traveled to the ceremony on a train with fellow fighter aces Gerhard Barkhorn, Walter Krupinski, and Johannes Wiese, and during their journey, they met some generous admirers who bought the pilots all the rounds of alcohol they could drink. There was one last leg of the trip that had to be made by car, Hartmann remembered, and their driver lowered the top of the convertible to wake up his drunken passengers. It was just 25 degrees Fahrenheit outside.[2]

Once inside the compound, Hartmann picked up a strangely large hat ("Oh yes, there's my hat!" he remembered exclaiming) and sauntered around wearing it until someone told him that it belonged to Hitler. He also recalled mocking Hitler's gesticulations and hand movements from his emotional speeches as the still-drunk quartet made their way toward their ceremony.[3]

This first meeting with Hitler—Hartmann met him several times to receive awards—was the most positive one from Hartmann's point of view. The war was already lost, and somewhere in his mind Hartmann probably knew it, but there was still a sense of momentum and possibility in Hitler's demeanor. Hartmann sobered up enough to remember most of the details, as well as his impressions of the dictator.

"Hitler had a weak handshake, almost like a woman really—not very manly," Hartmann told his interviewers decades later. "We chatted about the war, mostly light conversation … Hitler then spoke about the new jets and rockets, and all sorts of great wonder weapons that we would soon have. He had this great vision about our ultimate victory." Hartmann recalled being unimpressed with the man, who "rambled about how we were defeating the Soviets, which was news to us, I can say."[4]

Hartmann was awarded the Swords to the Knight's Cross in July that year, and this time the conversation was a little more personal. Again at the Eagle's Nest, Hitler and the pilots discussed the steady American bombings of German cities, and Hartmann was well aware that Ursula was employed at the time by the Heinkel Company, which made aircraft and engines—a prominent target. It turns out that she left the job just in time. "Right after she left, the factory was bombed," he pointed out later.[5]

On August 24, Hartmann scored his 300th victory. After that mission, he was called into the operations center and informed that he was going to meet Hitler once more to receive the Diamonds to the Knight's Cross. By this point, Hitler, famously, was losing his grip on reality and his own conduct. When Hartmann arrived, he saw that fanatical suspicion had replaced the fanatical conviction Hitler had shown earlier. "You had to enter three areas of security," Hartmann said, "and no one was allowed to carry a weapon into the last section."

Hartmann was incensed by this, apparently. He informed the *SS* commander assisting him that he wasn't about to relinquish his Walther, and would not stick around if he wasn't trusted with it. "The guy looked like I had just married his mother," Hartmann told his biographers later. "Hitler came to me [after he heard of this] and said, 'I wish we had more like you and Rudel.'"

That final meeting came immediately after the failed assassination attempt on Hitler. As Hartmann described it, Hitler was a completely different man: "His right arm was shaking, and he looked exhausted. He walked bent over and had to turn to his left ear to hear anyone speak because he was deaf in the other one from the blast. Hitler discussed the cowardly act to kill him and attacked the quality of his generals, with a few exceptions."

Hartmann then gave Hitler his frank assessment of the war—unvarnished and somewhat negative, as Hartmann recalled later. He corrected the dictator about the resourcefulness of the Soviets and described the widespread supply deficiencies he saw at the front. Hartmann didn't remember anyone at the meeting acknowledging the impending loss of the war, but he said there was a shared sense that such a thing was at least plausible. He left the meeting thinking Hitler had become "isolated and disturbed."[6]

Long after the war, Hartmann implied that he had always found Hitler to be a bit of a clown: "I told him that the propaganda we kept hearing was ridiculous—claiming that all the new, young pilots needed was greater National Socialist spirit to win … This was insane."[7]

Threaded through Hartmann's stories of these meetings is a certain level of passive aggression—messing with the hat in Hitler's lair, showing up drunk, telling the *Führer* about his tactical misunderstandings—and this is actually a predictable behavior for someone in Hartmann's position. The same pilots who devoted themselves meaningfully to National Socialism, or at least the military that propped it up, could also—and often did—assert some level of rebellion against the oppressiveness and belligerence of Hitler and the Reich. Naturally they couldn't do it too loudly, but passive aggression is a well-studied way of protesting against power structures that don't allow active dissent.

The term actually originated in a military context and describes behavior that is, in fact, a "rational response when individuals are deprived of their autonomy—that is, in an authoritarian system shaping all their overt actions."[8] According to Mosier, passive aggression helped German combatants maintain a feeling of independence—something especially important to fighter pilots—without actually doing anything that would create too much confrontation with authority or put themselves at risk (or alter the course of the war). Passive aggression can also help the soldiers feel like they're not at fault for whatever larger situation they're a part of. They protest within the limits available to them, enabling what Mosier calls "seductive behavioral rationalization."[9]

Recall that Hartmann described it perfectly himself earlier: "We [pilots] used to make jokes about Hitler, Göring, Göbbels, and the rest. They were just too comical in many ways to be taken seriously."

We don't know exactly what Hartmann meant by "comical," but it is plausible that these responses were subtle demonstrations of frustration or disregard during the time of the combat (not just decades later in interviews with a bunch of Americans). Of course, it could also have been Hartmann's immature way of dealing with the weight of confronting Hitler himself, the father figure he had been reared to depend on and, very likely, celebrated throughout his earlier leadership positions in the Hitler Youth or elsewhere. Or it might have just been the cognac.

Whatever views were really rattling around Hartmann's head after that final meeting, he spent most of the personal leave that followed focused not on the war, but on Ursula. During these precious few weeks off, he decided that he and Ursula should get married, accelerating earlier plans that called for a ceremony around Christmas 1944. He made arrangements for the wedding and honeymoon to take place at Bad Weissee, a popular spa town 180 miles east of Weil, on the shores of Tegernsee Lake. Bad Weissee was also the location of the *Luftwaffe's Jagdfliegerheim* (Fighter Pilots' Home), a sprawling compound for rest and relaxation where he had been granted a luxurious vacation stay, so the location was convenient as well as idyllic.

The wedding was a stressful adventure of its own. The date was September 10, 1944. Ursula lagged behind Hartmann in getting to the resort from Weil because the German rail network had been bombed and thrown off its regular service. The day before the wedding, while he waited for her to come, Hartmann enjoyed a continuous flow of champagne and cognac provided by visiting pilot peers. He showed up at the train station for each posted arrival time, only to find that Ursula wasn't there. Finally, on the last train of the night, after midnight, she appeared.[10]

The solemn, traditional ceremony was punctuated by a festive march through the town afterward, and the couple began their honeymoon right away. There is a discrepancy in Hartmann's story at this point, however, at least as recorded by his biographers. *The Blond Knight of Germany* says that he and Ursula were still at the *Jagdfliegerheim* when they received exciting (and illusory) early news about the German Ardennes offensive; they even suggest that the positive news put Hartmann in the mood to start a family. (Ursula left the trip pregnant; her views on the matter are not recorded.) However, the Ardennes offensive began with a surprise attack in mid-December 1944, not mid-September, so it doesn't make sense that it would have been the inspiring news Hartmann received.[11] Regardless, with news of the battles taking place in his absence, Hartmann decided to cut his leave two weeks short and return to the front. Back to *JG-52* he went.

## Hartmann's Chronology: World War II Operations and Commands

| Date | Status | Location |
|---|---|---|
| Mar-41 | Air War School | Berlin-Gatow |
| Nov-41 | Pre-fighter School | Lachon Speyerdorf |
| Mar-42 | Fighter School | Zerbst-Anhalt |
| Aug-42 | Fighter Supply Group | East Gleiwitz/ Oberschleissen |
| Oct-42 | 7 Sqn. / III Group / *JG-52* | Eastern Front |
| Sep-43 | 9 Sqn. / III Group / *JG-52* (Squadron Commander) | Eastern Front |
| Oct-44 | 4 (7?) Sqn. / III Group / *JG-52* (Squadron Commander)* | Eastern Front |
| Jan-45 | I Group / *JG-53* (Group Commander, Temporary Posting)** | Eastern Front |
| Feb-45 | I Group / *JG-52* (Group Commander) | Eastern Front |
| Mar-45 | Me-262 training for *JV-44* | Lechfeld |
| Mar-45 | I Group / *JG-52* (Group Commander) | Eastern Front |

* There are disagreements among available records about which unit Hartmann moved to after his long stint with 9 Sqn. *The Blond Knight of Germany* lists this unit as 6 Sqn., and other sources, including Weal's *Bf 109 Aces of the Russian Front* say it was 4 Sqn. This chart consolidates several sources, with deference given to the more recent of them, Matthews and Foreman's *Luftwaffe Aces: Biographies and Victory Claims*, which purports to have been derived to official German archival records. But even it is inconsistent, listing both 4 and 7 Sqn.

** Similarly, Hartmann's movements in early 1945 are less than clear. He most likely took a temporary posting with *JG-53*, during which he scored just one kill (the only one of the war not with *JG-52*). After his brief transfer to the Me-262 training group, he returned to finish the war as the C.O. of I/*JG-52*.

## Wonder Weapons, Almost

In March 1945, Hartmann received a telegram at the front:

CEASE OPERATIONAL FLYING IMMEDIATELY REPORT LECHFELD FOR CONVERSION TRAINING ON Me 262 TURBO[12]

This was *the* Me 262, the world's first operational jet fighter. Hartmann was being pulled away (with just two months of war left, unbeknownst to him) to train for the only one of Hitler's wonder weapons that would make much of an impact on the air battle. This logically could have been cause for celebration—it was a prestigious assignment and an acknowledgment of his skill and leadership—but he didn't want anything to do with it. He said he had seen the "Russian hordes swarming into the fatherland" and was distracted, above all else, by thoughts of Ursula and their soon-to-be-born baby's safety. He followed his orders to report to Lechfeld, but recalled later that this was a deflating experience and the point when he really knew the war was lost.[13]

His destination jet unit was *JV-44*, which some have called the Squadron of Experts. Hartmann, Galland, Steinhof, Krupinski—the famous German pilots present accounted for many hundreds of kills between them, and suddenly Hartmann was among the finest group of peers he would encounter during the war. He wanted out immediately. This, he said, was because he didn't relish the idea of being someone else's wingman in the company of these senior aviators.[14] He wanted to get back to *JG-52*, and a timely telegram from his *JG-52* commanding officer, Hermann Graf, made that possible.

So he skirted around the jet squadron and headed back to the front, where the full strength of the Soviet war machine awaited him.

By this point, German pilots in every theater were falling out of the sky faster than new ones could be shuttled in to replace them. For the younger men moving quickly up the ranks and toward the action, entering the fray was a heavy prospect to bear. Hitler's delusions and Nazi propagandizing notwithstanding, the airmen knew they were going to lose. And they knew it wasn't going to take long.

One of these young men was Kurt Fengler. Fengler joined the *Luftwaffe* by direct conscription in early 1945 when several soldiers entered his high school classroom and coolly informed him that he was now a member of the *Wehrmacht*, and his time in the classroom was up. He was just 15 years old. He got up and left with them.

His assignment was to fly the rocket-powered Messerschmitt Me 163 *Komet*. The *Komet* was among the few rocket-powered vehicles that made it into combat, but it didn't accomplish much other than confusing and frightening a few bomber crews who glimpsed it.

The aircraft was, in fact, a horrible death trap. Its pilot sat in what amounted to a swept-wing, flying fuel tank. The sidewalls of the cockpit were formed by the flat sheet-metal tanks of *E-Stoff* and *C-Stoff* rocket fuels—substances that were fiercely hypergolic, meaning that they would spontaneously ignite if they came into contact with each other. The *Komet* randomly exploded on the ground because of tiny leaks in the fuel system's poorly made metal fittings.

On takeoff, the aircraft had so much thrust that it shot almost straight up to 39,000 feet. It was also ferociously fast: the *Komet* was the first aircraft to exceed 1,000km/hr (621mph) flying straight and level. This was far beyond any performance profile Hartmann would have ever experienced, even had he stayed with the jet squadron. The *Komet*'s mission was to intercept the ceaseless Allied bomber formations before they could drop even more tonnage on the German cities (cities that, as Hartmann noted nervously, now included Stuttgart and nearby Böblingen, a university town just 4 miles from Weil).[15] And while the *Komet*'s rocket motor was theoretically capable of throttling, pilots had little control over the level of thrust it produced—they lit it and held on, basically. After the war, a British test pilot tried out a preserved *Komet* and remarked that it was the only aircraft he ever flew that always seemed to be just beyond his control. It used a harrowing flight profile and was extremely hard on those subjected to it. Aside from sitting on an unproven rocket engine and its caustic fuels, *Komet* pilots ate preflight meals low in fiber because the rapid climbs to high altitude in an unpressurized cockpit had a tendency to rupture their intestines.

The Me 163 burned so much fuel that it always had to return to base unpowered, and this made it vulnerable to enemy fighters. Without a source of thrust, dogfighting or even basic evasive maneuvering was hopeless. The best the pilots could do was dive away as fast as they could. To their good fortune, the aircraft glided like a brick and dived to earth even faster.

To simulate flying a *Komet* during training, Fengler's cohort experimented with weighted-down gliders that could at least reproduce the high-speed, high-inertia landings they would have to make if they made it back from their missions. The 163's lack of wheeled landing gear (scratched during design because it was too heavy) meant that pilots had just an extendable skid mounted at the aircraft's centerline for cushioning and stability on the ground. It was essentially useless for both, and pilots sometimes broke their backs when they got their descent rate wrong. There is understandable speculation that

*Luftwaffe* designers and commanders—after a delayed, problem-filled design and development phase—didn't actually expect many 163 pilots to make it back to have to worry about a landing anyway.

Fengler was among the lucky ones who managed to survive the war and a handful of missions in the *Komet*. He never scored an aerial kill, partly because his guns malfunctioned so often. This made perfect sense, as he put it years later, because by that point the guns were being manufactured in underground tunnels by slave labor.[16]

The tactical futility of the Me 163 was unsurprising considering the condition of the late-war *Luftwaffe*. As imaginative and promising as it and other new weapons were, a combination of poor strategic planning and destroyed infrastructure delayed their implementation and precluded any real hopes of a Nazi revival. Hitler's senseless, years-long insistence that the Me 262 should be used as a bomber rather than a fighter robbed him of whatever tactical and propaganda benefits the aircraft could have produced, and the *Komets* often lay empty on the ground because there was no rocket fuel to put in them. The Allies didn't need to destroy all the secret weapons if those weapons had no means of getting in the air.

When the war's end came, Fengler was briefly captured by the advancing Soviets and locked in a Berlin basement. He escaped from it and located the American 82nd Airborne Division, got his discharge papers, and, after being grilled for a while about the mysterious *Komet*, walked away from the war carrying a duffel bag and not much else. He emigrated to the U.S. shortly after.

In the eyes of those *Luftwaffe* men left standing in 1945—from youngsters like Fengler to veterans such as Hartmann—the grand, chivalrous dogfight, for so long the emotional propellant that took them into war and helped them enjoy it so much, had not endured. But nor had it ended in some dramatic final combustion. The realities of the war and aggressive modernization—culminating, of course, with nuclear weaponry—had threatened to make it obsolete once again. Still, some of the pilots stayed until the very final hours, holding onto their vision for how an air war should be fought, until they could feel the Soviet, American, or British tanks getting closer through the rumbles in their boots.

Hartmann's last mission—on May 8, 1945—was not the hunt-and-kill sortie that had served him so well over the past several years, but a scouting flight to see how long the fast-moving Soviet units would take to get to his base in Czechoslovakia. He took off at 0800 hours, as he had done hundreds of times before, and flew toward the smoke. His recollections of the mission convey an eerie sense of calm as he and his wingman kept formation and followed their last waypoints. They spotted several Soviet fighters over Brno, their reconnaissance target. The fighters were doing celebratory aerobatics, completely unaware of who or what was nearby in the air. They zigzagged around Brno at low altitude so they could watch their comrades on the ground do their work and follow the steady push westward.

Hartmann saw an opportunity with a Yak-7 that was nearing the apex of a lazy loop. He gave a wag of the wing to signal to his wingman that the fight was on, and dove down to take out the fighter with a point-blank shot. A burst from his cannon and the clueless Yak was aflame and heading to the ground. It was Hartmann's 352nd and final kill, a perfect pounce-and-dash engagement, and he dove out of the way of the wreckage and sought the concealment of the smoke near the ground to avoid a lengthier, obviously pointless, engagement with any others. For the sake of completing his mission, he documented that the town was, in fact, burning hopelessly and the Germans had lost all control of the fight.

A glance backward after he and his wingman had emerged from the smoke showed that the Americans were arriving over Brno in their glistening P-51s and had begun tangling with the Soviets, who they apparently mistook for enemies.[17]

## No Man's Kill

"I was never shot down by an enemy plane," Hartmann said in his lengthy interview with American historian Colin Heaton. "I had to crash land fourteen times due to damage from my victories or mechanical failure, but I never took to the parachute but one time. I never became another pilot's victory."[18] Elsewhere in the same interview he estimates that his crashes numbered 16, noting that he was occasionally damaged by flak. Other sources on Hartmann say he was shot down plenty of times, but they're probably equating damage from victories as shoot-downs, which pilots probably wouldn't appreciate.

Hartmann always said that his proudest accomplishment was that no wingman of his was ever killed. One wingman of his was shot down, but he survived. His name was Günther Capito, and Hartmann described this event in great detail because it lingered as a failure in his mind, long after the war. Capito was an older pilot who had earlier flown bombers, and Hartmann said he was ill-trained to be transferring to a fighter squadron. "A peacetime-trained professional and an older man to boot," Hartmann's biographers write, "Capito was not at home with a fighter unit. The freewheeling informality of the front-line fighter pilot's life, which Erich had found so much to his liking and so suited to his temperament, tended to jar on Guenther Capito."[19]

As a result, the two didn't get along so well. Capito described Hartmann as "a gangling baby-faced, sloppy young man. He wore a crushed cap pulled down tightly over a mass of matted, unmanageable hair. He slouched in his chair and talked with a maddeningly slow drawl. He was unkempt and appeared to have nothing to say, unless the talk turned to flying combat. Then he came alive."[20]

On one mission, Hartmann and Capito were bounced by several Soviet Airacobra fighters, and the Airacobras came in hard with altitude advantage. Hartmann, as per custom, waited until the they were in firing range—this helped him judge their methods and made it harder for the Soviet pilots to follow the Bf 109's sharp evasive turn—but when he banked and started his maneuver, Capito made a turn more characteristic of a lazy bomber, which put him in the Airacobras' crosshairs. Hartmann, who had easily disengaged and could now observe from afar, watched Capito get further tangled among the enemies and tried to rush back in to down the Soviets before they could get to his wayward wingman. But after further lackluster maneuvering, Capito's 109 was hit and headed to the earth.

Hartmann yelled over the radio for Capito to bail out, which he did safely. Then Hartmann found the Airacobra that had shot his wingman, soared in to get it, and blasted it to pieces. The plane supposedly spun earthward and crashed in a huge explosion.

Hartmann recalls that, after the mission, he and Capito (who had been safely picked up, given that they were on the German side of the line) drove out to the crash site to take a look. They saw that the dead Soviet pilot, whose charred uniform showed that he was a captain, had been thrown from the plane and had been carrying a strangely large amount of German money on him—almost 20,000 *Deutschmarks* ($8,000 at the time). Hartmann and Capito never did figure out what that was about.

Historian Edward Sims, who wrote several popular books about the World War II air war, once met with Hartmann to try to figure out what was so special about him—what, in other words, enabled him to have such consistent command of the air battles he was involved in, protecting not just his own hide but his wingmen's as well. "In our meeting I was seeking to discern superior talents, a will, or nature, or whatever, in this remarkable pilot," he writes. His assessment? "His most signature talent might have been a unique ability to size up a situation carefully and coolly in all its dimensions before acting, thus avoiding mistakes."[21]

His gravest mistakes, as would become more apparent with time, usually took place outside the cockpit. Hartmann later listed his decision to leave *JV-44* as one of them—because, he said, it had resulted in the worst hardship of his life: more than 10 years of suffering at the hands of war-weary and begrudged Soviet captors.

Captors who knew very well what the Black Devil had done to their air force.

## CHAPTER 9

# Into Captivity

In the pockets of the dead, we found bread and sugar, and we ate our fill. We weren't fastidious anymore.

—WILLY REESE[1]

Landing his Bf 109, call sign Karaya One, even after 1,400 flights, took care. This landing, after the Brno mission, was the last Hartmann would ever make in that aircraft. He probably knew it at the time.

It would have gone like this: airspeed falling toward 150 miles per hour, Hartmann presses the blue button above his left knee for lowering the landing gear. On the Bf 109G, the two main landing gear legs drop out of their wells at uneven speeds and make slow hydraulic creeps down to the locked position. It takes surprisingly long for the gear to cycle. The tailwheel, meanwhile, is fixed at the rear fuselage—it's been out there spinning in the open the whole time. Flaps are lowered incrementally until, lined up on final approach, they extend to their full 40-degree angle. These large-area flaps, coupled with the leading edge slats that have fallen automatically at the slower speed, massively increase the volume of air the wings are pushing down to keep the plane aloft. A familiar buffet tells Hartmann, without a single glance at a cockpit gauge, where the flaps are in their travel and what his airspeed is.

Once across the threshold of the airstrip, Hartmann cuts the throttle, allowing the 109 to settle down to a 110mph landing speed. This is a makeshift runway, so it deserves a careful flare to pause, briefly, with the wheels just above the earth. They make contact and the suspension gives its stiff jiggle as it takes on the weight of the aircraft. But here Hartmann's job has only started: it takes constant adjustments of every control surface to keep the aircraft straight and level while it slows. Finally, after a few seconds, the wings have lost their airflow, the tail is securely down, and the aircraft now behaves like a precariously balanced ground vehicle. Three streams of dust waft in its wake.

Hartmann taxies in, bumpily on the uneven ground, leaning into the rudder pedals to swing the nose around and park the plane. Shutdown procedure quickly taken care of, the propeller shivers to a stop, the hot engine gets its rest, and all's quiet. It's done.

As per usual, Bimmel Mertens hustled up to begin the routine of refueling and rearmament for a midday mission. But Hartmann waved him off. The ace walked to the *Kommodore*'s tent to pass on the report everyone around the place could have predicted: the Soviets were assaulting Brno and closing in. Hermann Graf, fellow ace and commander of the unit, was unsurprised.

In fact, Graf had already received surrender orders. The directive, which had been transcribed from a radio message earlier, was short and unconventional. It came from General Seidemann, air fleet commander:

> Graf and Hartmann are to fly to Dortmund immediately and surrender to English forces there. Remaining *JG 52* personnel will surrender to Russian forces in *Deutsch Brod*.[2]

Graf, who received the message in the commander's tent while Hartmann was still out on his mission over Brno, grasped the dilemma the message presented. Hartmann got it after a moment's thought.[3] It made strategic sense, from the top brass's point of view, to separate the two most famous members from the wing and have them surrender to the British—that way they would be less likely to fall into the hands of the Soviets, who would want to exploit them and press them for intelligence. On the other hand, the scheme smelled of abandonment. Hartmann and Graf looked at each other there in the tent, and Graf suggested that they disobey the message and stick with the rest of the group to the end, whatever that end turned out to be. Hartmann agreed, and he said later that this was the only time in the war that he disobeyed an order.

The pair decided that it was most important to them to maintain the integrity of the unit and not desert the others, so they made plans to mobilize a convoy and surrender to the Americans at Pisek, another small Czech town. The message went out to the men and women who still occupied the doomed airbase—these included soldiers as well as some family members and German-friendly refugees—and the group prepared to move out.

It seemed reasonable to Hartmann that he should destroy the remaining aircraft and equipment before the Soviets could claim them. The Messerschmitts that remained on base were valuable war prizes, as were the ammunition, various supplies, and fuel stockpiles. His first move was to douse his own aircraft in 100-octane gasoline and shoot out the unused ammunition. Karaya One sat tail-down with its nose pointed somewhere over the trees, so when he dispersed his ammunition from the cockpit, he could see the tracers arcing high into the air. He also noticed the intense flashes from the gun barrels—the shots were oddly bright and loud now that the aircraft was stationary on the ground. The 109 vibrated and leaned back on its landing gear with the powerful recoil, and while Hartmann was fixated on what he was doing, the aircraft caught fire. There was gasoline vapor everywhere and there he was, shooting flames out of his gun muzzles. He managed to scramble out of the cockpit in time, much to the relief of the ground crew members who had been watching him, and he only burned some hair and the skin of his hands. (What a cruel twist it would have been if the top ace of the war had shot himself down sitting on the ground.)

This was a huge moment in Hartmann's life. You can imagine him, heart still racing, watching his beloved plane burn. Who knows whether this was a moment of reflection or one of frenzy—Hartmann and Graf had a small population to mobilize—but the weight of the scene exists anyway. You can imagine the mottled paint bubbling off here and there; the rubber tires smoking; the panes of the canopy blackening with the swirling soot; the flames lapping at the national markings on the fuselage and the swastika on the tail. This was the fiery end of the war, the end of Karaya One, and the beginning of a horrible new chapter in Hartmann's life.

## Horrors

The trouble with Graf and Hartmann's surrender plan was that the Americans were just going to hand them over to the Soviets anyway. According to the end-of-war arrangements among the Allies, captured German combatants in the region were to be transferred to the Soviets, regardless of whose military they surrendered to.

Here begins what is probably the most wretched scene of Hartmann's life. When the Americans dropped off the Germans, they stayed around to watch a while as eager Soviet infantrymen began to corral the men and women into separate areas and hold them in place with rifle barrels. Some of the Soviet soldiers, as Hartmann would describe with hesitation and disgust later in life, began to beat and rape the women out in the open. Hartmann said they did it with a level of violence and savagery he had never seen; the madness went on throughout the night. It was exactly the kind of desperate and vicious scene that had already created the legend of Soviet barbarism on the Eastern

Front (and which Hartmann, of course, had been trained to expect since he was a youngster). The German males were helpless and likely to be shot if they made any moves; the Americans were held back by their orders and the same rifle barrels, and they eventually left. And still the Soviet soldiers battered their captives, taking turns with some of the women until they were dead. Hartmann and the others at least tried to bury the victims, but they lacked the right tools.

The next morning, Hartmann awoke on the ground alongside a German sergeant who had cut his wife's and daughter's wrists, and then his own, so that his family would escape the carnage.[4]

A Soviet general arrived at the makeshift camp, surveyed the scene, listened to the captives tell him what had happened, and had three offending soldiers hanged immediately on the spot. There was no court-martial, no deliberation, no formality. Hartmann kept his parched mouth shut.

Hartmann said later that he was aware of no German rapes of Soviet women. Of course, this was due in part to the *Rassenfeind* order—Germans were aggressively prohibited from making any advances on "racial enemies"—but it's also true that these actions would not have been tolerated in the traditional *Wehrmacht* ethos.[5] This is not to say that they didn't occur. We should, at this point, remember how pervasive this kind of activity was in the war, and that it was the Germans who initiated the barbaric, explicitly racist and inhuman war against "Jewish-Bolshevik" systems and influences.[6] Men and women of many nationalities suffered from it. Hartmann's experience on the ground was scarring, damaging, corrupting—but so was the one that he had earlier sitting alongside his *Waffen-SS* countrymen, which, to be sure, showed only a sliver of the carnage of which that organization was capable.

All of this highlights the fact that Hartmann always, essentially, had the privilege of flying above the nastiest behaviors—a generosity of circumstance, you might say—and the millions of families harmed by German aggression, equal to or greater than what Hartmann witnessed in those horrid few days after the war ended, would be unimpressed by his emotional difficulty in recounting the scenes. War is hell, yes. But this war was not merely imposed on the Germans like Hartmann: it was their handiwork.

Years later, Hartmann would advise his wife on how to cope if put into the kind of situation the captured German women faced back on the front in 1945. His advice demonstrated fear—the first taste of hatred he ever felt toward others, he later told his biographers—as well as his latent beliefs about Soviets. "Never hesitate," he told her. "Go to the highest ranked officer and do your charming with him … in this way, you have to suffer only one man and you can avoid the brutality and dehumanization of belonging to every man.

"In the kind of age in which we are living, where civilization might well be overturned at a maniac's touch, every Western wife should be aware of this approach when dealing with people of Eastern mentality."[7]

Hartmann's judgment about "Eastern mentality" sits uneasily with a footnote that Toliver and Constable added to the page on which it appears in *The Blond Knight of Germany*. Perhaps written as an editorial counterbalance, the note nevertheless clarifies that these stories of Soviet aggression are "not for the purpose of fomenting hatred of the Russian people." This is, at the very least, a focused and important call for reason amid passages that might otherwise have been allowed to fertilize stereotypes and old biases.

## Pens and Peat Bogs

Soviet soldiers soon shepherded the prisoners toward a station at Neubistritz, 60 miles east of Pisek. This wasn't so much a permanent camp as a crowded, disease-infested transfer point—the beginning of a long introduction to the Soviet prison bureaucracy. They entered chain-link corridors on the way toward a disorganized documentation process. Hartmann, in the human traffic jam, occasionally overheard encouraging talk filtering through the lines—one Soviet official said that the group was headed to Austria and would simply return home from there. But he was skeptical, and later described pangs of fear as the superficially encouraging Soviets' fakery became obvious.[8]

Then it was on to Budweis and another transfer point. Most of the captives had to walk the roads to get there, but Hartmann remembers befriending a Soviet soldier who let him ride on a horse-drawn cart part of the way.

There are photos of similar caravans moving among the fields and war-scuffed roadways. You can't help but look at the prisoners' faces for some kind of emotion, urgency, or message. What on earth would a person be feeling at these moments? Strangely (or maybe not), their expressions are often just blank. No anguish, no agitation, no activity at all. Probably just fatigue and hurt. This blankness, this apparent resignation, lingers.

From Budweis, Hartmann and Graf left for another pen farther away, this time run by a group of Romanian Communists who had their own methods for dealing with the prisoners. There was apparently some heated conflict between the captives and the captors this time, and Hartmann later told the story of when two guards clubbed a German pilot senseless one night for leaving his assigned area to go and relieve himself. This enraged Hartmann and several others, so they staged a trap for the aggressive pair of Romanians. Hartmann and his posse went out after nightfall the next day, baiting the guards, and then sprang from the shadows to beat them when they arrived. They left the Romanian soldiers, in their characteristic bright-red trousers, lying at the bottom of a well-used latrine. The odd part—and this speaks to the illogic of these environments—is that the avenging Germans received no punishment afterward. Hartmann said that the guards even stopped carrying sticks from then on.

After a week of standing in the dirt and dealing with debilitating pangs of hunger, the next train came. This one had machine guns and searchlights attached to it, and guards packed the prisoners into rail cars, stuffed in randomly and without any chance to move, stretch, or relieve themselves in private. There was no thought given to military rank or expertise at this point, so Hartmann and Graf, who were still together, faced the same conditions as everyone else. Hartmann said the mass of captives took turns standing and lying down on shifts of several hours, never knowing when the routine would end.[9]

They headed eastward, rocking along the rail lines past the Russian cities of Kiev, Moscow, and Vologda.[10] Nobody, by this point, had any delusions about a quick release, and when the train finally shuddered to a stop, the prisoners emerged into the cold air and a scene of heart-wrenching desolation. Watery turf and canals stretched out in all directions, and Hartmann recognized the terrain as a massive network of peat bogs. Peat was an important natural resource in Russia's cold climate because it could be harvested and used for heating no matter the weather or season (peat can be dried easily by compression and burns well). This was a work camp, and Hartmann understood right away why there were hardly any Soviet guards present. Prisoners might as well have walked right out of the place and into the impenetrable wilderness. The Soviets probably would have loved to watch.

All work would be done hurriedly and by hand, and after the prisoners dug their daily quota of peat, they had to dig their accommodations for the night. By now, the toll of captivity had become obvious. It had been weeks since the surrender, and Hartmann was already thinner than usual and had trouble finding the endurance to keep working. Others started dying. The prevailing strategy in the peat bogs was to work slowly enough that you wouldn't work yourself to death or create high expectations from the guards, but also work fast enough to make your quota and avoid drawing attention.

Hartmann dug through the organic patches and helped pile the peat clumps into bundles that were picked up each morning by a single train that came through the camp. He lost skin off his hands from the constant digging and gained rows of bruises on his undernourished muscles. When each day's work was done, the prisoners retreated to their improvised shelters, which could only partially shield them from the rain and the wind, both of which were constant. Hartmann spent a month in this situation.[11]

By this point, he was resigned to the fact that his rank would do him no good in the work camp environment. Clearly nobody was interested in talking about the awards he had received or the status he had attained as an officer. He might have been able to apply some of his learned skills in organizing or leading groups of prisoners, but the usefulness of that was unknown. This experience was looking more and more like an endurance race to the calm of death.

Then his fortunes changed abruptly.

Soviet officials showed up and told the prisoners that officers of the rank of major or above would be moving to a different camp, Camp No. 150, at the small Russian town of Gryazovets, 200 miles north of Moscow. Hartmann was a major and Graf was his senior officer; they would be making the move together. (Hartmann is said to have ended the war a major, though his date of promotion is unclear: *The Blond Knight of Germany* is inconsistent on the issue, stating at one point that he had been a major for almost two months before the end of the war, and elsewhere listing his date of promotion as May 8, the last day of the war and an odd date for a promotion. There would be further complications related to Hartmann's rank later on.)[12]

When Hartmann and Graf arrived at Gryazovets, they found accommodation that was startlingly different than what the others endured in the bogs. There were actual buildings scattered about a compound that had a small, quiet stream running through it, in which they could bathe when they wanted. They found hot food and even employment opportunities—Hartmann secured a job working in the kitchen, which gave him easy access to all the food he wanted and allowed him to heal and gain some weight back. He could buy a morning coffee for a ruble.

Hartmann was heartened to meet up with another fellow ace, whose performance during the Battle of Britain he had admired. Assi Hahn had been at Gryazovets since 1943, Hartmann learned; he'd been shot down over Russia after transferring from the Western Front.

Hahn later wrote about the camp's conditions: "One could hardly have wanted anything better ... if it hadn't been for the fact that everything was merely a front."[13] Hahn, with characteristic wryness, said Gryazovets was "like a home for convalescents."[14]

The relative luxury of Gryazovets was part of a strategy on the part of the Soviets to turn desirable members of the German leadership to their side. They hoped these captives would join the Soviet air force, provide useful military or technical intelligence, or even serve as moles when they returned home. Nothing made the Soviet leaders happier than the thought of ex-*Wehrmacht* luminaries defecting to serve the Communist state, and they got what they wanted some of the time.

There was already a large faction of Germans at the camp who were aligned with the People's Commissariat for Internal Affairs—better known as the NKVD. The NKVD housed the Soviet secret police and, like the German *SS*, was responsible for mass executions and various other brands of repression and violence. Some members of this camp group were former German Communists who already shared the ideology, while others were defectors. The group's existence created an environment of widespread doubt and suspicion among the captives, and Hartmann, Hahn, and the others found this difficult to navigate. By Hartmann's account, the camp turned into something resembling a high school lunchroom: everybody had to pick a side, and Hartmann later recalled that even the way you wore your clothes said something about your allegiance. The Gryazovets leadership encouraged this political organizing because of the discord it created. Vocal, conflicting Germans shared more information and exposed more about their loyalties.

There seem to have been three primary factions to choose from at Gryazovets: the National Committee for a Free Germany, the League of German Officers, and the Antifascists (or Antifa). You could call the National Committee the most neutral of the groups, but "neutral" is relative. Much of its leadership was comprised of German Communists, and, during the war, it had simultaneously advocated for the removal of Nazi leaders from Germany and an affirmation of Germany's strong military heritage. Its symbology relied on the emotive colors from old Imperial Germany, not the new flag. The second group, the League of German Officers, was closely related to the Committee for a Free Germany and was created as an offshoot so officers wouldn't have to associate so directly with Communists and enlisted men. It's hard to say why Hartmann never (apparently) joined this group. The Antifa were a far-left-wing group that, with the NKVD, was unleashing the most heavy-handed pro-Soviet propaganda.

Hartmann's allegiances are just as hard to pin down as the groups themselves. According to Graf, Hartmann joined the National Committee for a Free

Germany, but in a letter Hartmann got smuggled out of camp for him, he says he was briefly enticed by the Antifa before abandoning them for so-called fascists (possibly an umbrella term under which the National Committee for a Free Germany fell).[15] In *The Blond Knight of Germany*, Toliver and Constable write that the Antifa "seemed to do best in a material sense" but stop short of confirming that Hartmann ever had any association with them.[16] Only his letter, reprinted a few pages later, does that.

You can tell, reading that letter, that his flirtations with the Antifa were brief and disappointing:

> The [Gryazovets] camp is administered by the NKVD, the Russian secret police, aided by renegade Germans. Among these is a German military judge who is mightily afraid of the Russians, but does his share organization-wise. The others are mostly political swine and traitors and similar types in charge of the camps. They call themselves the "Antifa." Looked at closer they are former *SS* medics, Hitler Youth leaders, *SA* commanders and similar trash. I don't know what the Russians mean to do with them[;] yesterday they betrayed us and tomorrow they will change flags again. Such people make imprisonment hell for us.[17]

This passage is fascinating. Hartmann had earlier climbed the ranks of the Hitler Youth, but here he shows disgust toward its leaders; are we to take him at his word that he was a frustrated anti-Nazi amid fascist betrayers? Or were all these declaratives part of a self-protective ruse? Remember that captives often used encoded meanings buried in seemingly innocuous letters, and they were always aware that their correspondence was likely to be read by captors one way or another. No Soviet censor would have been pleased to hear Hartmann praising German nationalists.

The confusion around these groups today probably echoes that which the prisoners faced while navigating them at the time. This was an entirely deliberate, and strategic, context of disarray and pressure. Every man had to deal with it in his own way—sometimes successfully and sometimes tragically.

Hartmann and the millions of internal Soviet prisoners were unified in at least one thing, and that was their fear of the camps' lawlessness and violence. A former gulag prisoner once reported seeing two *urkas* (professional criminals, usually feared and accommodated within the gulag system) playing cards one day. It dawned on him that they were literally betting on the life of another prisoner.[18] This episode would not have surprised Hartmann. The West Germans in the 1970s calculated that just over 3 million *Wehrmacht* members had been taken to Soviet prisoner of war camps, and a third of them died in captivity.[19] The Soviets did their own studies and, unsurprisingly, came up with different numbers. One reported that 2.7 million

*Wehrmacht* members were taken into camps, and about 400,000 died there.[20] The numbers are staggering either way (and they vary slightly by study, owing to faulty and inconsistent records), but it's also true that far more Soviet POWs ended up in German hands than the other way around. At the end of the war, Germany had taken in 5.7 million Soviet POWs; nearly 58 per cent of them died.[21]

This doesn't invalidate the hardships of the captured Germans, but does provide a little more context that is usually absent from their stories.

## Defector

The Soviets, at this point, were scrambling to put together an infrastructure for the Cold War. Just as teams of German rocket scientists were being snatched up by the United States and the Soviet Union to continue their leading-edge work, *Wehrmacht* officers like Hartmann were desirable for their experiences at the front, the successes they had orchestrated, and their talents. Turning Hartmann and his fellow officers into Soviet spies, advisors, or even soldiers would have been of incalculable value for the NKVD and the Soviet propaganda machine. To this end, his captors used every tactic they could muster.

Hartmann was profoundly disappointed when their efforts worked on Hermann Graf, who was, up to this point, his most dependable partner in the camps. When he heard that Graf had endorsed the Soviets in an effort to secure a better future (it worked—he was released in 1949), he and many of the others were incredulous.

There are, however, contradictions and confusion in people's accounts of Graf's change of allegiance. Hartmann remembered Graf lobbying him to defect while both pilots were housed together at Gryazovets; Graf, however, claimed later that he hadn't become intertwined with the Soviets until after he had been moved to a different camp, near Moscow. There, Graf said, he had been mistakenly labeled a Soviet sympathizer after a journalistic report he wrote about an airshow was edited into a gushing propaganda piece about the greatness of the Soviet air force.[22] Either way, Graf's reputation among the surviving German pilots was forever tarnished. He was informally disinvited from the fraternity and spent his post-captivity life pursuing other talents and interests.

After Graf gave up, the emboldened Soviets switched to Hartmann. They brought him into their offices for periodic visits, each one meant to wear him down a little more. The routine was usually the same: the leader of the day would sit Hartmann down on the other side of a heavy desk, offer him some paltry gesture of goodwill—a cigarette or a shot of vodka—and shove paperwork in his face. This paperwork, usually written in Russian, might amount to an admission of guilt for crimes against the Soviet Union or describe how Hartmann could commit himself to the Communist cause. Hartmann never signed anything. Occasionally, tempers flared and leaders dismissed Hartmann to solitary confinement when he refused to budge. This back-and-forth psychological combat proved very clearly that Hartmann was no longer fighting World War II—he was playing a small part in the Cold War.

One interrogation scene stands out. A Soviet lieutenant working for the NKVD became enraged one day when Hartmann sarcastically responded to questioning about the Me 262. Hartmann knew little about the technical workings of the jet to begin with, since he had flown it only a handful of times and wasn't fluent with its design principles or systems. But the NKVD man had orders to get information, whatever the means required. He got out of his chair and hit Hartmann across the face with a cane, at which point Hartmann said he got up to face him, grabbed a wooden chair, and smashed it over the Soviet's head. Hartmann's permanent prisoner's dossier later supposedly read: "Be careful how you handle this man—he hits."[23]

A year went by, the only bright spot for Hartmann being the mail. German officers were allowed to send and receive periodic correspondence, but the postcards Hartmann sent (mostly to Ursula, probably) were limited in word count, censored, and handled carelessly. Hartmann only squeezed a handful of lengthy letters to family out of camp, often hidden with people who were being repatriated. Most of the time, Hartmann was allowed to send out just 25 words a month, or even nothing at all.

Hartmann's first Christmas postcard gave a cursory update of conditions:

> My Usch-
>
> I can tell you that I am alive. I wish you a nice Christmas and a good new year. Fear not for me [...] All my thoughts are with you. With a lot of kisses.
>
> Your Erich[24]

Ursula, getting by in Stuttgart as a postal worker, wrote Hartmann hundreds of letters over the years, addressed to whatever camp she was most recently aware of. Throughout his time of imprisonment, Hartmann received about 40 of them, and Soviet officers used many of those as bait for more of their little chats.

The drastic length of Hartmann's term as a prisoner was predicated on a 1947 verdict, concocted by a Soviet court, that defined him not merely as a POW but as a war criminal. This was his handlers' greatest coup and a tactic the Soviets used frequently: By asserting that Hartmann had deliberately bombed a food factory, taken part in rash obliteration of civilian targets, and randomly strafed unarmed Soviets (all laughable fabrications, according to Hartmann), they changed the rationale for his imprisonment. The Soviet Union hadn't signed the Geneva Conventions, but any international standards for prisoners they might have acknowledged essentially went out the window.[25]

Hartmann protested the verdict bitterly and demanded a fair and reasonable court proceeding, but it got him nowhere. Even as the Soviets were beginning to send some other German prisoners home, his outlook worsened. The local newspaper back in Stuttgart printed news of the war criminal decision, which Ursula and her mother must have read with horror: the sentence was for 25 years of hard labor. There was a wartime picture of Hartmann, his Diamonds airbrushed away under his chin. It was the grimmest bit of news about her husband that Ursula would ever have to bear.

There is a strange levity to Hartmann's recollections of these events. Discussing the various war-crimes charges leveled against him, he said:

> Then they said that I destroyed a factory making corn meal, or something. That was considered sabotage. I asked where this place was, and they told me and even showed me on a map. I started laughing until I cried, because it was farther east than any German I knew of had ever been ... They laughed also and said that it was just a political charge against me.[26]

Discussing one Soviet officer's attempt to get him to sign documents in Russian, which he had no ability to read or understand, he recalled:

> I looked at this man and laughed. I told him that, under the Geneva Convention, I could not be forced to sign anything, and as a senior officer, I could not be forced to work ...
>
> Then he laughed at me and said, through an interpreter, that the Soviet Union never signed the Geneva Convention. I then reminded him that, under both the Geneva and Hague conventions ... open belligerents did not have to sign them to be held accountable for their actions ... Then he reminded me that we invaded his nation, not the other way around. Then I told him that he was correct, but I was still not signing his damned paper.[27]

These passages seem to encapsulate Hartmann's persona as a prisoner: feisty, defiant, and at times combative. He seems to have leveraged his rank fairly well, too—he got away with things that would probably have been life-threatening offenses for other captives. While it would be natural for him to exaggerate his defiance and combativeness to his interviewers after the fact, there is nothing to suggest he ever withered under the pressure. That pressure was constant, potent, and expertly applied. Captivity, whatever confusion remains in the story, was a war of its own.

And the war occasionally turned hot.

## The Revolt

Packed off onto another train, Hartmann rumbled southward toward an infamous labor camp called Shakhty. He could tell the place wasn't going to be like Gryazovets. A sign hung near the camp gates read, "Our labor makes the Soviet Union strong." (He might not have known about the sign above Dachau that read "Work makes you free," but it's hard not to notice the parallel.)

Shakhty provided the most cinematic scene in Hartmann's story of imprisonment. A full-on revolt bubbled up when Hartmann refused to do any work in the nearby mines, again citing what he believed to be his rights as a prisoner. His protest method was to go on a hunger strike, which got him thrown into solitary confinement until the Soviets forced a tube down his throat and fed him some vile liquid blend. The surprising protest, and Hartmann's subsequent treatment, was enough to inspire a group of fellow prisoners to take action and attempt to break him out of solitary.

There was a numerical imbalance at the camp that made this possible—more than a hundred prisoners were being managed by no more than a couple of dozen Soviet soldiers—and the prisoners managed to retrieve Hartmann from his confinement in a violent ambush. Hartmann remembered the event:

> Soon the door crashed open, and this guy had an axe that he had used to tear down the door, and more than a dozen prisoners ran in and grabbed the guards. It was quite violent; I mean, a piece of wood the size of my arm flew right past me—a part of the door, such was the force. They then took the camp commander, a Soviet colonel, and the two majors hostage, [plus] a woman doctor, and then also rounded up eighteen of the guards, as the men had weapons, and locked them in the cellar.[28]

Hartmann urged his fellow prisoners to stay put and not try to escape the compound. He reminded them that fleeing would put them more clearly at fault, and he decided that the best outcome of the revolt would be to use it to shed light on the awful camp conditions—instead of fleeing and getting shot by snipers. He earned some respect from the locals, who were within earshot of the events and witnessed what they perceived to be an exercise in sound judgment and leadership. The camp commander, through whom Hartmann and the others relayed their demands of food and better treatment up the Soviet hierarchy, pleaded with them to not release him outside the camp to the villagers. Locals had been gathering, throwing food over the fence to the German captives, and were violently agitated at the camp leadership.

When reinforcements arrived at the camp gates, Hartmann and his fellow revolutionaries went outside to meet them. By now Hartmann's command of Russian was (apparently) strong enough to interact with the villagers and soldiers:

> "You Russian soldiers!" Erich shouted. "We are on this side of the wire because we were once soldiers, just like you are today. We fought a war under orders, and we lost. We are soldier prisoners." ... "Shoot!" he yelled. "I can't shoot back."[29]

Shortly after, all hard labor was suspended at Shakhty for five days to ease the mood at the camp. When an official from Rostov arrived, Hartmann was called in to receive his instructions. For their revolt and defiance, Hartmann and a few of the others were being sent off to a camp at Novocherkassk near the Sea of Azov, where Hartmann was promised a new solitary cell—"the bunker," he called it—far away from his comrades at Shakhty. He says he spent five of the next nine months in that cell.[30]

At some point, the Soviets brought him out of the bunker and, in response to his constant demands, put him before a tribunal so he could air his grievances. Maybe this was a rare concession on their part, but it was more likely an opportunity to reaffirm the war-criminal charge he had received earlier. Hartmann scolded the Soviets once again for ignoring the Geneva Conventions, informing them of their own "inferiority complexes and stupidity." An endearing interaction it was not, and his 25-year sentence was affirmed.

Back home, Elisabeth Hartmann received word of the proceedings and her son's continued trek through the Soviet Union as an official war criminal. In a letter she directed to Stalin himself in April 1951, she implored the dictator to soften his methods and see Hartmann not as an enemy agitator, but as someone's son: "My son is said to have been condemned ... because he had been a staff officer. I cannot believe this condemnation, for my son has, like every Russian, done nothing but his duty of soldier toward his country, did he not?"[31]

Perhaps the most telling parts of the letter are the commitments to Stalin that Elisabeth was willing to make on her son's behalf:

> I herewith assure you that my son, when again at home, will never again participate in activities against you and your nation, but will quite peacefully and in entire neutrality lead his further life. I promise you this, and as his mother I shall cause him to do so. I shall exact the promise from my son immediately after his return, and I know that he keeps unconditionally what he promises.[32]

Elisabeth, like all of those who loved Erich, had endured her own ordeal for the previous six years. Her evident desperation and protective will are something other parents might recognize. While it did not do her son any good, Elisabeth at least felt she was trying to help him.

From Novocherkassk, Hartmann moved to a camp called Diaterka, where he occupied a specially designed maximum-security pen set within the broader camp. Roughly 45 prisoners lived in the pen, some of the big names in the German military. They were mostly former servants to Hitler and prisoners whose family names made them automatic villains to the Soviet leadership. One of them was Otto Günsche, former adjutant to Hitler, whose last job in the war had been to burn Hitler's body. He told Hartmann how he'd done it: rolling Hitler's body in a rug, dousing it with gallons of gasoline, and setting it on fire to let it burn out behind Hitler's Berlin bunker.

Hartmann's biographers describe the maximum-security pen as a bastion of infighting. They detail the fighting skills of some of Hartmann's fellow prisoners—never going into what Hartmann's approach might have been, other than to say that he allied himself with Günsche and a couple others.

In July 1954, Hartmann was transferred for the last time—back to the camp at Novocherkassk. Hartmann later recalled that camp conditions had generally improved after Stalin's death in March 1953. Here he was once again pressured to serve the Soviets and adopt Communism—his handlers even desperately threatened to harm his family and drag them to the Soviet Union—but he also had the vague sense that things might be improving and that he might soon be allowed to return home. He and the other prisoners were allowed to go to see a movie and were issued new clothes. They also had hot showers, with soap. It all felt different. Something was going on.

All of this might have been caused, in a small way, by Elisabeth Hartmann, but not because she had written to the Kremlin. In 1955, she wrote to a more interested head of state—Konrad Adenauer, Chancellor of West Germany—pleading again for the release of her son. The young West German government was still finding its way onto the world stage, and Adenauer was eager to be a change agent and be seen as a man of action. Surprisingly, he replied personally, giving Elisabeth great hope. Adenauer restated the West German government's concern for the remaining few thousand prisoners held by the Soviets and offered optimism for Hartmann's quick release.

At about the same time, he orchestrated a diplomatic reckoning between his own government and Moscow. At the Soviets' invitation, he made one of his most important excursions and visited Moscow to talk policy. West Germany, Adenauer said, demanded the immediate release of the remaining prisoners of war and an end to the stalemate; the USSR, in turn, demanded diplomatic recognition of East Germany as an autonomous government. Both sides got what they wanted, and Hartmann and the others were released.

## Assessing the Camp Experience

Today, it's hard to imagine, much less interpret, these experiences in Soviet prison camps. If a writer's job is to occupy the lives of those they write about, it's an unrealistic expectation here. We can recall how frigid it was in these camps during the long winters, and how poorly clothed the prisoners were (Hartmann was stripped of his heavy coat and the warm boots he had obtained during the war; his time in solitary confinement was often spent in a shirt and trousers, no matter what the season). We can imagine the weakest, wateriest soup in giant vats and marvel at the idea that such a thing could seem luxurious to someone lacking sufficient calories. We can listen carefully, when we're in a situation of silence, and shudder at the thought that a person's life would ever be diminished to total, wretched, forced solitude for months on end.

We do know that these POW camp environments incorporated some consistent and illustrative features. Rudimentary barracks usually housed dozens or hundreds of prisoners at a time, who slept on bunks of varying height and construction. Showers were usually unheard of, as were private restrooms (recall the relative luxury of being able to bathe in a frigid stream). Although some camps sported haphazard security because of their surrounding geography or other factors, many had concentric rows of barbed wire, electrified fencing, wooden walls, and sniper posts, making escape all but impossible. Commanders and interrogators ushered prisoners into ramshackle offices, where they sat on hard chairs, often tied up, waiting to see what kind of manipulative game or accusation was coming. Stench, death, sickness, and the bone-chilling filth of the northern Soviet Union were the default.

And yet we're still some distance from Hartmann's actual experience in the camps. He shared this wretched decade with countless others—many of whom died just as anonymously and agonizingly as infantrymen in World War I trenches—but detailed testimonies from the camps are few and fragmented. The only closeness we're afforded today comes almost exclusively from Hartmann's personal recollections, many of which we only encounter after they were shaped and packaged by his adoring early biographers. While this is a harrowing picture, it is also an incomplete one.

You can't help but imagine the most awful parts: the untold horrors that occupied prisoners' private thoughts. Suicide attempts, violence, and every imaginable variety of despair were parts of the experience from which many returnees would never escape, no matter how distant they grew after the fact. Hartmann talked about occasionally losing his will, about succumbing to hate in the face of so much of it coming from others. There is, undoubtedly, an entire story from those months alone that he never told us about.

But remember: the reason Erich Hartmann suffered through the Soviet prison system was the hate and villainy of his own regime. He was a prisoner of war, to be sure—but that war was caused by the vile instigators who wore swastikas, not red stars.

## CHAPTER 10

# The East and the West

We all live under the same sky, but we don't all have the same horizon.

—Konrad Adenauer

It was October 1955, 13 autumns since Hartmann had arrived on the Eastern Front.

When he rolled through the border stop at Herleshausen, a junction between the East and the West, the first free German he met was a young woman at the counter of the border authority. She was attractive and warm. She smiled at him, demanding nothing more than his service request. He hadn't met anyone like her in a decade.

He asked to send a telegram:

ARRIVED THIS EVENING. PLEASE DON'T PICK UP, TOO DIFFICULT, WAIT AT HOME. KISSES ERICH[1]

For Ursula, it was a moment she had waited a decade for. That yellowed telegram paper must have arrived as a miracle. And she was one of the lucky ones.

German POWs had been trickling back to West Germany for years, but their arrival was disorderly. As a result, some wives waited dutifully for partners who they knew, in some corner of their mind, might never come back; others moved on. Many a soldier stuck in the camps received notification of his wife's divorce proceedings without ever exchanging a word, and countless family units were broken by the lack of hope. It was yet another cost of the war.

Ursula had always waited, and she and Erich would always say that there had never really been any choice in the matter. Telegram in hand, she called Elisabeth Hartmann to share the news. They had been encouraged by Adenauer's responsiveness earlier, and now everything was real. Erich Hartmann was free and coming home.

It was a bittersweet time, too. Elisabeth couldn't share her relief with Alfred Sr., who had passed away of heart disease while Hartmann was still being held captive. Worse, Ursula had earlier given birth to a son, conceived while Erich was home on leave during the last months of the war, but the youngster had died at the age of 2, well into Hartmann's tenure in the camps.

Hartmann didn't hear of his father's death until months after the fact, and he hadn't known about his son's death for a year. He never met him.

The triumph of Hartmann's return was further dampened by the fact that so many other German families were still incomplete, never to be repaired. He talked about this later on. It was shocking, he said, to arrive at a West German train station on the way toward Stuttgart and meet all the welcoming committees. Throngs of people greeted the trains, and they included dozens of women—desperate, hopeful, and scared—who waved photographs of their husbands aimlessly and frantically in the air as if the returnees would be examining them to give updates on those they recognized. In many cases, those husbands had died in the camps years earlier, yet nobody in West Germany knew.

On arrival, Hartmann's physical condition was just as bad as you'd expect. He was seriously underweight, even for such a lanky frame, and the skin of his face, normally toned and taut, hung loose. He had gained a foggy distance in his eyes that his characteristic smiles couldn't quite conceal. Behind those smiles you can perceive fatigue, bewilderment.

He made one unexpected move on the way to Stuttgart. Possibly out of delirious enthusiasm, he made an extra stop that took him out of his way and delayed his arrival overnight. Assi Hahn had approached him out of the blue at one of the train stops and asked him to visit his house. Hahn offered Hartmann a brief rest and a more comfortable car ride back to Ursula the next day. Years earlier, Hahn had managed to get out of Gryazovets; by the time of their meeting at the train station, he had filled out amply and was enjoying a prosperous postwar life.

Although the meeting slowed his travel, seeing Hahn would have been a special experience. It also afforded Hartmann some rest and a couple shots of coffee before making the final leg of the journey. The next day promised a more refreshed, early-morning reunion in Stuttgart.

Hartmann remembered it as something out of a fairy tale. Ursula (who forgave him the detour) was trying to use the extra time for sleep. A noise woke her from a light doze, and she scrambled to her top-story window to see a shadowy figure, draped in an oversized coat, standing at the front door. Looking down, her heart must have surged in her chest.

He knocked. Of course he wouldn't have had the key. Ursula rushed down to her husband and finally, after almost 11 years, they touched each other again. Hartmann had no grandiose speech to recite and his initial words were confused, showing his exhaustion. But he had achieved his goal, and Ursula had kept her word to him. That's what mattered to the pair at that moment. She broke down in tears when she saw how thin he was. He'd lost a full third of his body weight.[2]

They went inside and, after spending some initial precious time together, they welcomed family and friends for more reunion festivities. Hartmann said he declined a big party because so many other soldiers were still missing or had died in the camps—this didn't strike him as a cause for celebration.

Soon after his return, he was called to Berlin to be interrogated by West German officials about his experience. The officials were collaborating with the CIA: "I was [for] three days in Berlin being asked about everything, like names of anyone still missing, conditions, interrogation methods, locations of camps, all of this."[3] This must have added stress to what was already a fatiguing experience.

It was, of course, a long road to physical and mental recovery. Hartmann's first priorities were rest and good meals, and slowly he began to understand his new home situation. He could tell right away that the physical and mental recovery process would bring their own challenges. He was severely undernourished (so said his brother-turned-doctor, Alfred Jr., who gave him his check-ups), and although his state of mind was good relative to many other returnees, there would be plenty of social and cognitive challenges. Not only was he returning home after a decade of estrangement, but home itself had become a completely different kind of thing. "I ... could not believe the rebuilt areas and numbers of new cars, cars without clutches, the airplanes in the peaceful sky. Stores full of food, clothes, even car dealerships," he said.[4] In a surprisingly complete way, West Germany had been created without him.

He and Ursula walked in Stuttgart one night and drifted past a dance hall, but Hartmann couldn't go in. He stood frozen on the sidewalk, daunted by the choice he faced. The music teased him and he wanted to dance as he had done with Ursula years before, but he felt "physically blocked ... awkward, silly and hung up."[5] This was a manifestation of habit. He had been under surveillance for so long in Russia that the notion of dancing—of public physical expression, of not watching his back—seemed as foreign as the new cars that rolled by on the freshly paved streets. It took him weeks, in fact, before he could carry on normal interactions with the West Germans around him. These Germans were enjoying modernity and the fruits of a functional democracy, both of which were confusing to Hartmann. Even shopping for food, where he had to make multiple independent decisions at once, was a trial after so many years of having his decision-making curtailed and his options stripped down to the essentials of staying alive. It wasn't just captivity, either. His wartime and pre-war life had been defined by such a different conception of order and responsibility that this new-found flexibility was as overwhelming as it was empowering.

Wisely, he avoided idleness. He had no work, of course: his only occupational skills had to do with flying and fighting, both of which were curtailed in West Germany, and it would have been next to impossible for him to take another job so soon after his release. So he filled the hours with whatever else he could think of doing. He read ragged old magazines, which were all new to him, and pieced together an understanding of his country's recent history and the complicated terms of West Germany's occupation. He learned what the partition of Berlin meant, how it had come about, and about the blockade of 1948–49 that had resulted in the Berlin Airlift. There was plenty to know about Adenauer and the government, the return of viable political parties, and newly defined international alliances. When he wasn't trying to soak up his own missed history, he worked on the house. In search of occupation and routine, he took to managing the chores.

"Every morning I would get up and fix the breakfast," he said. "After Usch left for work on the 8 a.m. commuter train, I would wash the dishes, sweep the floor, make the beds, do the laundry and generally straighten up the house. All of this I did just like a girl!"[6]

Having been removed for so long, Hartmann had an interesting perspective on fellow West Germans. He saw them as nimble, audacious, and modern, as if there had been some strange, clean break with recent history. With the new democracy providing such a capable economic (and by extension, social and cultural) engine, West Germans seemed unencumbered by any longing for the past—even for Bismarck's historic Reich. It was, thoroughly and irrevocably, a new Germany. How disorienting it must have been.

As far as we can tell today, Hartmann's struggles during this time were typical in type but only moderate in severity. In any system of captivity, POWs often experience similar kinds of mental damage; back then, doctors called it dystrophy, which resembles today's diagnosis of post-traumatic stress disorder. Dystrophy was characterized by a potpourri of physical and psychological deficiencies. Physically, returnees often showed malnourishment, water edema, heart disease, and liver and kidney damage. Psychologically, their ailments included depression, apathy, irritability, and a diminished ability to perform tasks.[7]

"In postwar Germany," writes historian Frank Biess, "dystrophy was defined as an insufficient functioning, narrowing, and 'dedifferentiation' of returnees' personalities resulting from deprivation and starvation in Soviet captivity."[8] In other words, they were unable to differentiate themselves as individual agents in the society—they had essentially ceased to be themselves.

Any present-day psychologist would gain much from studying a man like Hartmann. Unfortunately, with only brief recollections from the time period to go on, we're left staring aghast into the history. We can wonder how Hartmann must have felt, or where his mind went when he was alone with his own thoughts. It's a scary exercise. We know he had dreams that wouldn't stop for years, but there would have been innumerable private questions and concerns. *What can my role in this country even be? What will I do with myself? Where can I find meaning again? How must I start? Has the hardest phase of my marriage even taken place?*

## Incentives

Ludwig Erhard, economic advisor to Chancellor Adenauer, was not an outwardly endearing man. He was of imposing size, wore a draping, dark suit, and had a continually downturned mouth that he tended to pinch over the stem of a cigar. He would replace Adenauer as Chancellor in 1963 and serve a satisfyingly unremarkable tenure. But in the early postwar years, he was the right man for a job of enormous breadth and urgency.

Erhard knew capitalism better than his boss did, and he wielded it to orchestrate a comprehensive postwar economic strategy for the young Federal Republic of Germany, which in 1949 had gained official status as an independent government. Just four years after Hitler had killed himself in a bunker, Erhard and his team were orchestrating the thorough and headlong transition into democracy, just as East German leaders, on leashes strung from Moscow, were lunging in the opposite direction. From 1949 to 1963, Erhard presided over the so-called economic miracle that would provide jobs, build modern infrastructures, and bring dozens of destroyed cities back to life ahead of all forecasts. The completeness of this recovery, not merely the philosophy behind it, fortified West Germany's stance against the Communist bloc, where collectivism and state-owned means of production were becoming further entrenched. The country's second glimpse of democracy, to the credit of its leaders and to the benefit of all the Western powers, took hold and sustained itself.

Some historians, aware of Germany's checkered relationship with democratic rule, have called the recovery "the catastrophe that never happened."[9] This was undoubtedly a precarious time for all involved, and everyone knew how slippery the slide into authoritarianism can be. But thinking of it this way makes it sound a little bit like a happy accident, which it definitely was not.

In Erhard's world, innovation was the tool of healing. His policies married individualist, free-market competition and property exchange with an active social welfare infrastructure and regulations meant to protect fair markets. This came to be called the "social market economy," and economists have described it as a strategic compromise between right-wing *laissez faire* economics and left-wing social policy. Germany has more or less stuck with it to the current day, and with continued prosperity.

The West German economic system took hold in part because it brought social benefits along with the financial ones. The idea of entrepreneurship helped many West Germans come to see themselves as active participants in a way that they hadn't for at least half a century. Hitler's notion of the national community had meant that individual citizens' value was minimized and could only be determined by their contributions to the Nazi-inspired solidarity. Before Hitler had come to power, leaders had introduced an economic system that resembled Erhard's, but they had failed to make it meaningful to ordinary Germans. In the minds of post-World War I Germans, the Weimar government had always appeared foreign, external, and imposed—but the post-World War II government seemed, incredibly quickly, to belong to the people.

Hartmann experienced a concurrent revival, largely because he had a built-in network in the old fighter pilots. This was a tightly connected, conversant, insulated group of men—they talked all the time, visited each other, offered all kinds of council—and the mutual support was crucial for most of them as they regained their sense of self and oriented themselves with all the newness. And because of his local fame and other past connections, Hartmann's network extended to several barons of industry.

He once described the excitement of the time with an anecdote about one of Germany's most famous postwar innovators, Ferry Porsche. Porsche had inherited his father's automotive business, which during the war had built tanks, and he now was ready to show off his centerpiece car, the 901. (This was the car that would evolve into the legendary Porche 911.) It was fast, powerful, and confidently impractical. Hartmann was acquainted with Porsche and was privy to some of the early design drawings for the 901, which fascinated him. Eventually, he got to test drive the vehicle, which he adored. "I took it on the *Nurburgring* [racetrack], and it was excellent," he said. "Like a 109 with a steering wheel!"[10]

You can see, even in this short anecdote, the process in which Hartmann found himself again: explorations with close confidants, with new chances to test his mettle. He always needed that. The question was whether he would find that kind of satisfaction anywhere but in a warplane.

## Overwriting the Past

Aside from obvious civic and industrial progress, what is remarkable about the first several peacetime decades in West Germany is how devoid they were of national navel-gazing related to the war, guilt for Germany's manifold atrocities, and how something like Hitler had managed to happen. These were, definitively, years of progress and action. There was a short-lived program of denazification organized with help from the Western Allies, but in West Germany it basically amounted to a purge of obviously tainted public officials whose past ties to the Nazi Party made them so conspicuous that reintegration was impossible. West German citizens, eager to forget and move on, didn't have much patience for it, either. In March 1946, 57 per cent of Germans approved of denazification programs; by May 1949, just 17 percent did.[11] Historian Richard Evans notes also that, on a practical level, the "superficiality of the denazification process failed to change many of the Nazi views held by those it affected."[12]

It was about mathematics and practicality: given the many millions of Germans who had become entangled in *some* element of the Nazi state, it would have been impossible to identify the guilty party agents and separate them from the innocents. (How do you find them? What do you do with them? Who decides who is guilty? How long would it take?) Moreover, the new country needed to mobilize as many people with as many talents as soon as possible if it was going to rebuild and sustain itself as a democracy.

As Kurt Schumacher, leader of the Social Democratic Party from 1945–52 (and a political rival of Adenauer's) put it, leaving thousands or even millions of Germans out of the rebuilding effort would have been "numerically not a good thing for a young democracy."[13]

Kristina Tonn of the present-day (2019) German Center for Ethical Education in the Armed Forces echoes this idea: "The focus was on getting the system up and running again. In retrospect, Germany was not given a favor. Many things [were] overlooked during the reconstruction."[14]

These things undoubtedly included public servants who really should have had no right to their roles anymore, and begrudged, tainted militarists hiding in the weeds of the new bureaucracy. Chancellor Adenauer was no Nazi sympathizer, but he was criticized for his leniency with other officials who had been. He once said: "You don't throw away dirty water for as long as you haven't got any clean."[15]

John le Carré, the famed spy novelist (who was, in fact, a Cold War spy himself) supposes that Adenauer's remark might have been a sneaky reference to Hans Globke, an anti-Semite and Nazi colluder who nonetheless won an important position in the postwar government. Globke had helped draft the Nuremberg Laws, which stripped German Jews of their citizenship, but he still kept up a reputation as a stable Catholic whom even anti-Nazi groups tolerated. After the war, he spearheaded legislation that provided back pay and other dispensations to Hitler's civil servants (including himself) "whose careers had been curtailed by circumstances beyond their control."[16]

In other words, not only were relics of the Nazi regime tolerated despite their dubious pasts; many of them were literally paid for the professional disruption of losing the war. Le Carré summarizes as only he would: "Former Nazis with attractive qualifications weren't just tolerated by the Allies; they were positively mollycoddled for their anti-communist credentials."[17]

## Return of the POWs

One of the most crucial parts of reintegration was the return of the West German POWs, and this impacted Hartmann's stakes directly. "Their delayed homecoming," writes Biess, "literally transported these experiences of violence back into postwar society and ensured the presence of the war's consequences."[18] And what were those consequences? Widespread destruction; dismantled infrastructure; broken families; food and job shortages; loss of standing in the world.

This gave rise to what Beiss says is one of the most consequential phenomena in West Germany: the portrayal of the Germans as victims of their own war.

In one sense it's not a huge leap to portray Germans as victims of World War II's destruction—especially if you can quarantine the racist madness within Hitler's inner circle, leaving ordinary Germans guiltless. Look at postwar photos of these citizens putting their country back together, wading through the rubble, and it's clear that there is an element of truth in this victim narrative.

Even some of the policies of the faltering denazification program contributed to this: in some cases, German civilians were forced to tour the mass graves and walk among the dead bodies strewn in the fields. Elsewhere, posters showed pictures of dead victims and instructed entire towns that they were responsible for the atrocities. As valid as it was to remind Germans, as a moral matter, of their complicity and support for the regime (which is inarguable and deep), the practical impact of this campaign was that it created revulsion and engendered sympathy for Germans as a whole.

But Biess pulls us back before we go too far down the sympathetic path:

> It cannot be emphasized strongly enough that the violence that Germans had to endure during the final stages of the war was a direct consequence of the unprecedented violence that Germans had previously inflicted all over the European continent. Any moral equation between German losses and German violence is misleading and necessarily obscures the relationship between cause and effect.[19]

"In both postwar [German] societies," he continues, "the return of the POWs prompted social and discursive strategies that sought to erase the consequences of German violence and of violence against Germans."[20] Former German combatants were identified most of all as victims of imprisonment, not as Hitler's former fighters. Commentators claimed here and there that the Germans' treatment under the Soviets in the POW camps was on par with what Jews had experienced in the Nazi concentration camps. They also invoked a more vague, but familiar, sentiment: that Germany was an injured, beaten-down country as a result of deceit and external punishment. This never quite developed into the "stabbed in the back" mentality from World War I, but it echoed the themes.

These rhetorical and social shifts were steered by several important groups within West Germany. The strongest influence in the immediate postwar period was arguably the Church, which had weathered Nazism with comparatively little disruption (recall that Hitler viewed the Church with animosity but had deferred its destruction on practical grounds) and was palatable to the occupying powers after the war. Church leaders quickly pivoted away from a discourse of German guilt and toward one that focused on the suffering and healing of their own. Hans Asmussen, a leader of the German Evangelical Church, circulated a widely read memo in 1946 called "The Guilt of Others," affirming the widespread focus on the violence Germany had *received*, rather than that it had plotted and dished out.[21]

Elsewhere, leaders welcomed POWs home by describing how "injustice that has originated from our people … falls back upon us and we are suffering much injustice ourselves."[22] These Church leaders wielded great power, since the Church was widely viewed by Germans as the only intact moral authority that made it through Nazism.

Subsequently, key thinkers and public figures amplified the victim narrative. Kurt Schumacher, observing from the political left, introduced as official policy the idea that the German soldiers had been the real victims from the beginning. There is a grain of truth to this, too, if you think about the theft of German childhood during the war build-up—the victimization of indoctrination and militarism is real, especially when it impacts the young—but as a blanketing generalization, it's shallow and insufficient.

The POWs' reintegration was also aided by the German cultural concept of *Heimat*, a term without a very precise English equivalent. Roughly, *Heimat* represents the attachment to a specific home community and to the land itself (particularly the idyllic rural farmlands that had survived more or less unscarred by wartime bombings). It invokes the ultimate form of harmony, where Germans' attachment to the land is combined with traditional societal roles and notions of communal well-being. It is a gendered concept in which the women, who were left at home waiting for their captive partners following the war, were the dutiful protectors of moral codes and the health of the family unit. By associating homecoming soldiers with this powerful concept, German leaders further reinforced the idea that the soldiers' return was essentially a reclamation of social cohesion, a cleansing return to moral equilibrium, and that it was permissible—indeed desirable—for them to disengage from the war and its consequences.[23]

Let's be clear: Erich Hartmann was unambiguously a victim of Soviet punishment, lawlessness, and bureaucratic machinations. Likewise, the millions of German mothers, sons and daughters, and others were unambiguously victims of bombings, terror acts, and coercive violence over which they had no control. No serious observer would think otherwise. But using these realities to buttress a victim narrative that seeks to wipe away the realities of German aggression does us no good. It might have been at least palliative in 1950; it's transparently inadequate today.

Hartmann's return to West Germany also coincided with one of Adenauer's riskier and more lasting expressions of unity with the West: rearmament. In 1955, West Germany was getting closer to asserting its autonomy on the world stage, just as Hartmann was beginning to find his autonomy at home.

Erich Hartmann was about to find a mission again.

## CHAPTER II

# Old Gray Ghosts

> During the Nazi years I sometimes despaired of my people. But afterwards, I realized
> that much decency had survived. Something good can and must be made of the
> Germans.
>
> —Konrad Adenauer

German rearmament was bound to be difficult. It's true that in the years after 1945 Germany was never fully without a military presence—each of its partitioned zones had been controlled militarily one way or another—but the new question in West Germany was how and whether to build up an indigenous military to augment or relieve the Allied forces. Rearmament made sense to Adenauer on a practical level (he was no militarist), but nobody seemed exuberant about it. The French were especially worried about the prospect of a newly armed Germany, since the Germans had invaded their country three times in the previous century. As late as the mid-1950s, much of the Western world didn't quite know what to think about this strange, cleaved country, and it was an uncertain period even for those within its newly drawn borders. After all, the basic governmental systems of the Federal Republic and the GDR were both fewer than 10 years old; so was the fragile postwar peace.

Adenauer's encouragement filtered down to a justifiably wary populace. Many rejected the notion outright, but an armed West Germany, as a bulwark against a Soviet incursion, was deemed a strategic necessity. And it was the veterans of the last war, irrespective of their Nazi ties, who were most prepared to join the new *Bundeswehr* ("civil defense") and provide its first skilled and experienced leaders.

At the time, no German men under 30 years old had any viable combat experience. Responding to lingering questions of Nazi allegiance, the government set up a vetting system by which former *Wehrmacht* soldiers could be incorporated only if they were sufficiently clear of damaging ties to the Nazi Party. Questionable volunteers could be dismissed without any option for appeal.

It was also important to the West German and Allied leaders that the *Bundeswehr* be meaningfully accountable to the government and comprised of ordinary Germans, rather than a born-and-bred military class. When Defense Minister Josef Strauss was showing off the new military uniforms, people noted that they looked strikingly similar to what the Germans had worn in World War II. He reassured his audience that "these boots are fitted with democratic civilian rubber soles."[1]

The tradeoff, as Hartmann would lament continually, was that it made the *Bundeswehr* seem like a bureaucratic mess run by politicians. "Citizens in uniform" was the line in 1955, and the government meant it. The rationale was preventative, of course: giving any German military too much power felt dangerous to everyone. It also reflected Adenauer's skepticism of the Prussian culture that had dominated the military for decades.

The first *Bundeswehr* volunteers reported for duty at almost exactly the same time that Hartmann was sitting through the train ride home, late in 1955. Their experience was very different from what his had been in the old system, however. They were paid poorly and used sub-par equipment. The opening ceremony for the new armed forces, at which Chancellor Adenauer spoke and reminded attendees of the pivotal role West Germany was to play in keeping the Soviets behind their Iron Curtain, took place on a grim, rainy day in November and lacked any meaningful sense of ceremony or rebirth. It sparked intense, visceral reactions among onlookers, too. One point of controversy was that the new military volunteers all sang together that day, which was not altogether unconventional for a German group but still reminiscent of those not-so-old days of the Hitler Youth, the *SS*, and paramilitary terrorizing. As a visiting French reporter put it: "The singing suffices to evoke old ghosts in me: the memory of the days in June 1940, when the sweat-covered German infantry, with fur-covered knapsacks on their backs, surrounded by the smells of leather and rancid fat, entered our villages … I am not certain whether the Germans understand that even a song with its 'Halli and Hallo' awakens anxiety."[2]

## Hartmann Enlists

As the West German military was being reconstituted, Hartmann was continuing his own revival. He and Ursula had taken care of the business of a real church wedding (which they had missed, despite completing the civic ceremony at the *Jagdfliegerheim* in 1944) and were doing what they could to catch up on a relationship that had been severed by a 10-year break. Their commitment to each other had never wavered, but their familiarity with each other had. And Hartmann still had no vocational training to speak of other than soldiering; the secondary profession he had grown up considering, becoming a doctor like his father and younger brother, was far out of reach for a man of his age who had been intellectually detached for at least a decade.

That's why the emergence of the new *Bundeswehr* was so timely. It gave Hartmann, who otherwise might have gotten lost in modernity, a new mission when he needed it the most.

It took some encouragement from his peers. Less than a month after Hartmann returned from the Soviet Union, fellow ace Walter Krupinski called Hartmann at his home and urged him to go to England for a refresher flying course. "You'll feel better when you fly again," he said, bubbling with an energy that took a reticent Hartmann by surprise. "Like the old days."[3] Hartmann refused, reminding his enthusiastic peer that he hadn't even had time to adjust to eating dinner in public yet.

Then Dieter Hrabak, long-time mentor and highly regarded commander of Hartmann's on the Eastern Front, came by for a visit. He had been part of the planning process for the new German air force back when Adenauer had started the work in the early 1950s, and he made sure to tell Hartmann about the financial security the military would offer if he rejoined. Ursula had kept her job with the post office, but the financial situation was getting difficult.

And so the seed was planted. Flying was what Hartmann was good at, and people certainly expected it of him. Ursula wasn't going to stand in the way of the decision, whichever way it went. If Hartmann was struggling to reacclimatize to life after imprisonment, a cockpit would be a familiar thing—a means of taking to the air to help himself stand on the ground.

So he joined, and trouble began almost immediately. Hartmann's incoming rank was an issue of some debate, his promotion to major toward the end of the war having only been brief. As mentioned earlier, there is some ambiguity about when Hartmann actually attained that rank. Sometimes you hear that he was promoted weeks or months before the end of the war; other times the date of promotion is listed, somewhat confusingly, as the last day of the war, May 8, 1945.

There is even a suggestion that he was still referring to himself—in writing, no less—as a captain as late as May 16, 1945, injecting still more ambiguity into the question of when, or even whether, he was officially promoted to major during the war.[4] *The Blond Knight of Germany* confuses this, since it says in one place that Hartmann was still a captive of the U.S. military on May 16 and had not yet been handed over to the Soviets—but in another place Hartmann himself states that he was handed to the Soviets on May 14.[5]

Whatever details were available to the *Bundeswehr* brass at the time, someone suggested that he should come in initially at the lower rank of captain. Maybe there was some personal animosity involved, or it was an awkward attempt at being politically sensible, or there was empirical information to support it. Whichever, Hartmann's biographers use the saga to frame the *Bundeswehr* as an insufferable bureaucracy run by a bunch of hand-wringing politicians rather than real military men, which, strictly speaking—and by full intention—it was. They say that there was a person or multiple people in the leadership whose intent, from the very beginning, was to make life hard on Hartmann. They don't mention who, but they do assert that "[j] ealousy and pettiness are natural attributes of the incompetent and fearful … often [Hartmann] was the victim to his own frustrated reaction to the machinations of nasty little men."[6]

These "nasty little men" were his superiors, but, fortunately for him, the U.S. Air Force ran much of the new German *Luftwaffe*'s airborne training program. For a time, therefore, he evaded the *Bundeswehr*'s leadership by plunging into a much more palatable military environment: the American one.

## Sorties in the Southwest Desert

As far as Hartmann was concerned, the Americans shared a military culture that was much less tentative and bureaucratic than the newly concocted West German version. The U.S. had won of the war, after all, and the stories of the Eighth Air Force and other groups had an emboldening effect as the Americans pivoted to the Cold War. This resonated with Hartmann and undoubtedly reminded him of the pomp and excitement that had enticed him into military service in 1940.

Enlistment as a squadron leader had to begin with flight retraining. Hartmann started in the small seat of a Piper Cub, that ubiquitous high-wing light plane that can still be seen in every corner of the U.S. backcountry in the early 21st century. Often painted yellow, the cub has given thousands of budding pilots their first turn on the stick and rudder. It's the Matchbox car of the aviation world—small, cheap, you could even say adorable—and it has always been endearing for its simplicity and frugality. It's covered in fabric, and the fuel gauge is a piece of bent wire on a floater that sticks up out of the engine cowling. The flying experience resembles what Hartmann would have recalled from his time in the Fieseler Storch during the war: docile, light, and elemental.

Aside from the thrill of flying again, the best part of retraining for Hartmann was that it allowed him to spend time in the American Southwest. The first West German jet trainees flew to the U.S. to be where the instructors, the aircraft, and the good weather were. By all accounts, Hartmann loved every moment of it.

In some ways it resembled the family odyssey to China 30 years earlier. Here, Hartmann sought the right mix of stability and adventure. There would be professionals and friends who valued his expertise and assigned him a fitting level of clout and authority within the community. And as he oriented himself within a new dominant culture—one that was familiar for its sense of military rigor but otherwise new—he would gain exposure to new ideas, technologies, and adventures. If there was one place that could accelerate Hartmann's understanding of the Cold War and one of the superpowers, it was an American airbase.

Prior to his departure to Luke Air Force Base in Arizona, Hartmann and Ursula welcomed a daughter to the household. They named her Ursula, which quickly became "little Usch." The timing of his training meant that Hartmann had to leave her at home with Ursula almost immediately, but he apparently stayed happily distracted by the graduating complexity of the job. After the first flights in the Cubs, he was introduced to the rugged North American T-6 Texan, the prop-driven grandfather figure to the P-51 Mustang he had occasionally tangled with toward the end of the war. The American jet trainer at the time was another classic: Lockheed's T-33. Durable and simple, it had descended from the P-80 Shooting Star fighter that had nearly made it into service in time for World War II (Germany and Britain, with their Me 262 and Gloster Meteor, managed to press their first jets into service during the war, but the U.S. and Soviet Union did not). The T-33 was much more successful than its fighter predecessor: more than 40 air forces around the world would choose it as their primary jet trainer over the coming 60 years.

The T-33's size and weight were similar to World War II fighters (it had a wingspan of 39 feet compared to the P-51's 37 feet), and its handling was similarly sedate. Construction and materials were conventional. But managing a turbojet was a lot different than handling a piston engine. Jet pipe temperature had to be watched carefully, for example, as did fuel load, since these early jets were notoriously thirsty. The T-33 and most other jets also sported bubble canopies and tricycle landing gear, both of which were huge conveniences for the pilot and stark differences from the Bf 109. In the air, the clear bubble provided an unrestricted view in every direction, while on the ground, the T-33 taxied nose-level, unlike the old tail-draggers, and had none of the adverse handling characteristics of Hartmann's first fighter.

As the trainee, Hartmann sat up front in those early flights, his instructor behind. The T-33 provided Hartmann with the quintessential single-jet experience. Even with 1940s technology, it provided a rush.

On that very first flight, harnesses cinched, Hartmann rumbled into the wind, several tons of jet thrust spooling up behind him. The bleached runway, skidding by as a blur, was infinitely smoother and better maintained than the grass fields from World War II, and Hartmann would have quickly confronted the two most profound differences between flying the T-33 and a propeller-driven aircraft: the lack of sideways-tugging torque from a propeller and the near-silence of a jet engine buried in the fuselage behind the cockpit. At about 100 knots, a T-33 rotated back on its main gear easily, the tug of lift arriving a heartbeat later. The wings flexed up an invisible inch as they shouldered the weight of the jet and he was smoothly aloft. Hartmann understood that the landing gear must go up immediately after the plane left the runway because, in jets, there is always a danger of over-speeding and damaging the struts, wheels, or gear doors while they all still hang down.

Hartmann thus became enveloped in a new era of flight that not even he would have imagined a few years earlier.

The celebrated archetype for this first generation of jet planes is another American aircraft, and the one Hartmann would soon fly in the first West German jet fighter wing: the F-86 Sabre. It was a fitting choice for the Germans in both capability and imagery. A fast jet with no real vices, the Sabre represented the bristling, future-is-now era in aviation he joined in 1956. The Sabre was always as sensuous as it was menacing, with perfectly smooth lines and those gorgeous swept wings. Robert Coram, in his biography of USAF pilot John Boyd, enthusiastically describes the Sabre as "the most romanticized instrument of war in history, a flashing streak of silver whose guns spoke for America."[7] This might be an exaggeration, but the sentiment is shared by thousands of pilots and enthusiasts.

Interestingly, the Sabre might never have risen to fame without World War II German research. Its swept wings were the key that unlocked the airframe's potential and pushed it to higher airspeeds, but the aircraft had initially come off North American Aviation's drawing boards as a conventional, straight-winged design much like the F-80 and T-33. In an interesting bit of sharing, the North American engineers in charge of the initial design not only borrowed swept-wing research from late-war German work, but solved one of their main engineering puzzles—how to install automatically deploying leading-edge slats onto the wing to improve low-speed handling—by literally removing the slat mechanism from a captured Me 262 and using that as a template. It is well known that various Germans influenced rocketry and the space programs in the U.S. and the Soviet Union, but they also altered the course of fighter development and plenty of other fields.

After 10 cleansing years, there was little or no animosity toward Hartmann or other Germans who were going through the training at Luke. As much as West German leaders kept their eyes toward the future, so did the American military men. He was well-recognized as he shopped around the various units and tried out equipment that interested him. It helped that the American pilots were just as preoccupied by their distaste for the Communists as Hartmann was. In many ways, these officers were kindred spirits.

Hartmann reveled in it. In rooms filled with American pilots, he showed reels of gun camera footage from World War II, explaining his trademark strategy of getting up close before firing and then getting out of the way of the debris. The new generation of American pilots learned eagerly from Hartmann, itching to get into the air and try out his lessons in mock dogfights. He was never a commanding figure—even after he'd recovered the weight he'd lost in captivity, he was wiry, with a uniform that hung loosely from his shoulders—but his reputation gave him his size.[8]

Imagine him at the front of the screening room, film reels rattling on behind him, telling the U.S. flyers: "You can't shoot when you're too damn far out. You have to wait." And then, an on-screen Soviet fighter gets a little closer until it starts to shed crumbs of wing and fuselage as the assailant's bullets hit their mark. World War II gun camera footage, with its lack of sound, is strangely evocative. Tension builds as all those scattered tracer bullets narrow in on the victim and the first puffs of smoke emerge from cowlings and engines. Occasionally you can even watch an anonymous pilot bailing out of the cockpit in slow motion. Silent explosions captivate just like audible ones do. You can imagine the applause and hollers in those darkened rooms.

Hartmann made some important friends on his tour in the U.S. One was an Air Force major named Frank Buzze (probably the best name imaginable for an Air Force major), who offered to house Erich for as long as he would be staying. Most importantly, Buzze and his wife opened their home to Ursula as well. She came to the U.S., too, having left her new daughter in Germany with her parents. She always recalled the experience with wonder and gratitude. "It was the nicest time we ever had in our lives," she said years later. "There was not the slightest resentment of us as Germans, and everyone was kind and helpful. We felt completely at home, and it is the only country outside Germany where I would like to live."[9]

The pair returned home in 1958. Hartmann, arguably the most accomplished officer in the new *Luftwaffe* (he was the only holder of the Knight's Cross with Oak Leaves, Swords, and Diamonds to re-enlist), was to command *Jagdgeschwader 71* (*JG-71*), the first West German jet fighter wing. *JG-71* was given the honorary name "Richthofen," which made it even more fitting that Hartmann—heir to Richthofen—should command it. (When *JG-71* was assigned the name, there had already been three German squadrons under Hitler named after Richthofen: *JG-132, JG-131,* and *JG-2.* Even the World War II German navy named one of its ships after the famous World War I ace.)

*JG-71* equipped with the first of its eventual 50 Sabre Mk.6s at Ahlhorn, its initial base of operations, which had previously been under British jurisdiction and was briefly home to RAF Meteor jet fighters and Canberra bombers.[10] The Mk.6 was arguably the best Sabre ever built: Its engine produced 23 per cent more power than the one that had powered the American Sabres that tangled with MiG-15s over Korea, and its rate of climb, speed, and survivability in a dogfight were enhanced accordingly. There was probably no single-jet fighter in the world that would have been a better fit and stronger asset for the upstart air force. Hartmann landed the wing's first Sabre on the newly lengthened runway on February 26, 1959.[11]

At the outset, he enjoyed substantial social and political capital, but he depleted it over time. One of Hartmann's first moves as leader of the fighter wing was to bring back the black tulip from his time flying Messerschmitts, despite the negative connotations of dredging up an old war symbol from the Nazi days. He later said that he had been aware of the risk involved, but disregarded it in favor of using the symbol to drum up morale and a sense of tradition in the wing.

He had ordered that his aircraft receive the tulip paint scheme during regular overhaul procedures; this was a paint-shop-level change rather than something a member of the ground crew would apply using a stencil, like they had done with kill markings during the war. These overhauls were regular parts of the service lives for any aircraft and included a strip-down and check for unseen corrosion, electrical faults, hydraulic leaks, etc. Their administration was part of Hartmann's job description, so he added the paint scheme to the checklist.

The black tulip as applied to the Sabres was even louder than it had been on the Messerschmitts. The gloss black paint, again with thin white outlines, was especially prominent on the Sabre's open snout air intake and was never obscured by a propeller. The petals reached back along the fuselage and over the machine-gun troughs, and now there was a tulip design adorning each side of the vertical tail as well. It ran up from the fuselage spine and just touched the rudder hinge line. In an era when gaudy nose art and flashes of paint were common on unpainted aluminum jets (subdued camouflage didn't return to most U.S. Air Force fighters until they were sent to Vietnam in green and tan; European fighters, forever in some combination of gray and green, went *au naturale* for a while, too), the black tulip scheme was still exceptional for its vibrant clashes of color. And it wasn't just the Sabres—eventually, even the wing's T-33s and a few tiny P.149D liaison aircraft received tulips.[12]

A general paid Hartmann a visit once he had brought *JG-71* up to speed. After one look at the Sabres, this general, whose name we do not know, pulled Hartmann aside to talk about those tulips. As Hartmann recalled:

> "That's *paint* on those aircraft?" sputtered the flak general.
> "Yes, *mein* General."
> "But only half the planes are painted, the wing looks a mess."
> "We paint them when they are in for overhaul, and that maintains our serviceability ratio. They'll all be painted soon."
> "Paint costs money, Major Hartmann."
> "That is perfectly all right, sir. I will pay for the paint myself. The paint marking makes for strong spirit in the wing."[13]

This was bureaucracy in action: a disorienting mix of politics, resource management, accountability measures, and interpretations of vague directives. It was also, probably, the wellspring of Hartmann's lasting irritation: he was in the West German military version of middle management.

He recalled:

> I ... did ... things that were considered criminal, such as having the unit's F-86s painted with my old tulip pattern, and then I created the squadron bars, like in the old days, and this raised eyebrows. We were told to take them off, but it is funny how now they are used again ... I did have supporters, such as *General* Josef Kammhuber, but he was a rare breed from the old days.[14]

Hartmann's longing for "the old days" was innocuous enough. The *Bundeswehr*, as anyone should have expected, had a rocky start and a confused organizational

Sabre Mk.6 on display at the Air Force Museum of the *Bundeswehr*, Berlin-Gatow. Marked as JA-111, this aircraft represents Hartmann's personal Sabre in *JG-71*. It features the later painted camouflage (not the earlier bare aluminum) and remnants of an updated Martin-Baker ejection seat. (Public domain)

identity. Hartmann saw it as a hamstrung scheme of appeasement and softness, while much of the populace saw it as dangerously close to the former *Wehrmacht*. With hindsight, it could only have ever been a confused institution: When it was created, most or all of the officer corps was comprised of ex-*Wehrmacht* men, basically by necessity. By the time of Hartmann's retirement in 1970, that portion had fallen to less than half.

These identity issues occasionally resulted in controversies that hurt the *Bundeswehr* in the public eye. One of these was the Rudel scandal, in which the famed *Stuka* pilot was invited to an official *Bundeswehr* event despite his obvious and continued association with the Nazis and contemporary neo-Nazi politics. Generals Walter Krupinski (Hartmann's confidant who had urged him to join the *Bundeswehr* when he returned from captivity) and Karl Heinz Franke excused Rudel's Nazism by essentially saying he was no worse than the politician Herbert Wehner, a former Communist who had lived in Moscow during the war, reportedly mingling with the NKVD. Unfortunately for them, the pair made their argument publicly in front of journalists, who pushed the issue and sought to clarify their thinking around arguing on behalf of an unambiguous Nazi sympathizer. To make matters worse, Rudel was there to sign copies of his book, which glorified Hitler and the Nazis—all under the auspices of the *Bundeswehr*. Defense Minister Georg Leber ordered Krupinski and Franke into early retirement over the affair.[15]

Today, the *Bundeswehr* has solidified its institutional identity, and it has veered with even more certitude into the citizen-soldier-with-a-conscience philosophy that never made total sense to Hartmann. It is well-known, for example, for its insistence on limiting soldiers' responsibility to comply with unethical orders. Thomas de Maiziere, Defense Minister under Angela Merkel from 2011–13, confidently described how each soldier "is not only allowed, but obliged, to disobey any order he or she feels might violate human dignity."[16] A Bismarckian culture this is not. One commentator described the *Bundeswehr*'s core philosophy as "ostentatious peacefulness."[17]

With such a transition taking place in the *Bundeswehr*, it isn't difficult to imagine why Hartmann would look, and feel, like a relic. His age and past service created preconceptions and judgments from many around him. And, probably frequently, his attitude toward change and his longing for the old days only confirmed those snap judgments.

Over the years, some members of the *Bundeswehr* came to see Hartmann as "a good pilot but not a good officer."[18] The opinion seems to have been in reasonably wide circulation when Hartmann's biography was published in 1970, since its authors were careful to dismiss it as uncharitable rumination. They gave few specifics, though they inserted some clues about Hartmann's reputation throughout their work. In a passage describing Gunther Capito's unfavorable impressions of Hartmann during the war—recall that Capito was the only wingman to be shot down under Hartmann's watch—they say that Capito's negative view of Hartmann "was to have many echoes in the new German air force in the 1950s and 1960s." Capito had described Hartmann as "sloppy" and "tedious," and wondered out loud: "This is supposed to be a commander?"[19]

There seem to have been three key conflicts during Hartmann's 15-year *Bundeswehr* career—actions of his own—that set him back. The first was his re-adoption of the black tulip marking, which was rooted in an earnest desire to promote morale but suggested a lack of foresight and sensitivity. The second, which was much more publicized and divisive, was his unvarnished (but correct) objection to the West German Sabre's wonder-plane replacement: the Lockheed F-104 Starfighter. And the third involved some very consequential paperwork.

# Ground Nails

Fighter pilots over Korea, including those flying the earlier Sabres, had lusted for more power. Fortunately for them, jet technology was developing rapidly, and as the Cold War progressed, many of the fastest fighters were built as interceptors capable of taking off and climbing extremely quickly to deploy air-to-air missiles against hypothetical waves of enemy bombers. This increasingly important mission profile deemphasized the twisting and turning of traditional dogfighting and prioritized brute force moving in a straight line.

The F-104 was the drastic embodiment of this new paradigm. Often called "the missile with a man in it," it could exceed Mach 2 on a single engine, which is a remarkable capability even in the early 21st century (no current American fighter can do such a thing). To facilitate this speed, however, designers gave it extremely small wings that only spanned 20 feet and were so thin that ground crews had to put protective bumpers on the leading edges so they didn't cut themselves. These wings were great for reducing drag, but they didn't provide much lift. Whereas a Sabre landed gingerly at about 100 knots, the F-104 landed as elegantly as a length of pipe at 170 knots—under the best of circumstances. If the plane's sophisticated flaps (which drew bleed air from the engine and forced it over the airfoil to add lift) failed, that landing speed rose to a ludicrous 240 knots. Pilots were sometimes told not to bother with a no-flap landing. Better to just eject from the airplane.

The U.S. Air Force didn't use the F-104 for very long, in part because of these shortcomings but also because it had a lot of other options in its arsenal. But Lockheed, which had invested mightily in the aircraft, marketed it shrewdly to NATO allies, who purchased upgraded versions of the Starfighter convinced that it would be a quantum leap and a good fit for their needs.

As soon as he heard that the Starfighter was the leading contender in the *Luftwaffe*'s evaluation for its new fighter, Hartmann voiced his concerns with Kammhuber, his general. "We should not buy an airplane we cannot handle," Hartmann remembered telling him.[20] His objection wasn't that the F-104 was a bad aircraft *per se,* but that it was a poor operational fit for West Germany, which was still flying jets designed in the 1940s. There were two other aircraft formally included in West Germany's fighter evaluation at the time—the French Mirage III, which served for many decades with various air forces around the world, and an upgraded version of the Grumman F-11 Tiger, a U.S. Navy fighter used by the Blue Angels demonstration team.[21] Other options, like the American F-100 and F-102, could have provided clear advancements and were also proven and available. The F-104 required a protracted redevelopment program to make it suitable for the West German geography and mission needs—which now included ground attack, something the aircraft was never designed for.

Kammhuber responded diplomatically and on-script, according to Hartmann's recollection: "Erich, *never talk about this*. We are happy to buy this aircraft. The political people have decided that we can buy this aircraft."[22]

So, beginning in January 1962, West Germany painted up the F-104s in its then-standard slate gray and green, and the pilots tried to tame the beast.

The accidents soon piled up. Often they took place during takeoff and landing, but pilots also flew the aircraft into mountains because of its difficult handling. Before long, the F-104 had earned a reputation as *Witwenmacher* (widowmaker), *Fliegender Sarg* (flying coffin), and—maybe the most illustrative—*Erdnagel* (ground nail). The failures hit their peak in 1965 and might have contributed to the change of leadership that put Johannes "Macky" Steinhoff in charge of the West German Air Force starting in 1966.

Steinhoff was an old Me 262 jet pilot from the war, and the politicians trusted him. When he assumed command, he immediately grounded the F-104 fleet until some of the problems could be worked out and training could be improved for pilots and ground crews alike. The loss rate for F-104s in the *Luftwaffe* dropped almost 75 per cent, from 41.9 aircraft per 100,000 flying hours in 1965 to an admirable 10.7 in 1967.[23] With this stability came more trust in the aircraft.

This drastic improvement points to something seldom acknowledged: The F-104's problems were sometimes dramatized, and they resulted, in large part, from factors beyond aircraft performance. A substantial problem was readiness: pilots and ground crews lacked the training and experience they needed to deal with the new technology, so when that technology arrived, it failed to deliver the performance and mission successes that had been promised. In this sense, Hartmann was spot on: West Germany wasn't ready for the aircraft, and lives were lost because of it.

Despite the safety improvements, the German F-104 program was plagued by other issues. Lockheed, maker of the jet, had earlier closed a series of lucrative deals with West Germany and other NATO allies during several years of fierce F-104 marketing, despite the obvious challenges of adopting the plane and a market filled with other good options. This massive buy-up was known among the media as Lockheed's "deal of the century," and it really was too good to be true. In 1976, a U.S. Senate subcommittee announced that Lockheed had paid off foreign governments to the tune of $22 million, motivating them to buy the plane.[24] The West German order had miraculously surged from 250 Starfighters to 900 right around the time Lockheed paid the Germans at least $10 million in bribes.[25]

Just five years earlier, the U.S. government had bailed out Lockheed because the company was on the edge of insolvency.

Several Lockheed executives admitted to paying the bribes, but a direct connection to West German Defense Minister Franz Josef Strauss was never established. During the West German election of 1976, renewed investigations showed that most of the paperwork from the F-104 deal had been destroyed back in 1962, when the ink was still wet. With no paper trail to follow, the exact depth and illegality of the scandal were never fully clarified. Oddly enough, as *Time* magazine noted, Lockheed's point of view (shared, apparently, by many large corporations that make such deals) was that paying potential customers is "a normal and necessary feature of doing business in certain parts of the world." Furthermore, so it goes, to punish large corporations for making them (and especially to make them disclose their various recipients) would cause substantial financial damage through canceled international procurements.

In the end, the scandal irreparably tarnished Lockheed and its customers. *Time* magazine writers mused after the fact that "the Lockheed scandal seems to have acquired a quality of indestructibility"—a quality that, unfortunately, eluded its prized fighter jet.[26]

## On His Way Out

Strike three in Hartmann's contest with the *Bundeswehr* came when he forgot to renew his pilot's license while still in command of *JG-71*. There was a basic form that he simply never filled out—it could have been lost in the shuffle precisely because it was so minor a task—but the *Bundeswehr* initiated a convoluted proceeding akin to a court-martial, draining Hartmann of whatever political clout he could still claim by the mid-1960s.[27] It was a serious and embarrassing infraction for the commander of a fighter wing to lose his flying credentials, of course. Although Hartmann was eventually held blameless by the military lawyers, he was relieved of his command of *JG-71* and transferred away from Ahlhorn to staff headquarters near Cologne. There he became that well-known cliché among military aviators: the flying officer reduced to pushing paper around a desk. He wrote tactical reports all day long.

Hartmann (far right) inspects a tarmac under construction in Zurich. Behind is a Douglas DC-9 short-haul airliner, which flew for Swissair until 1988. (Atrus Feist, Wikimedia Commons)

All along his path through the *Bundeswehr*, Hartmann had watched as younger officers, many of whom he had trained, were promoted to colonel over him—a rank he only attained in 1968, despite his obvious seniority and decorations. As his biographers say in *The Blond Knight of Germany*, spending eight years as a lieutenant colonel while being leapfrogged by officers who had never flown a single sortie in combat was "unseemly" for the aging ace.[28]

"They really forced me out," Hartmann said later. "Kammhuber told me that my promotion to *Brigadiergeneral* was killed for political reasons. It just would not seem politically appropriate to have a Diamonds holder in such a position. I said to hell with them."[29]

*The Blond Knight of Germany* assesses his retirement (which was recent at the time of its publication) with much more of a flourish. It says that Hartmann "has emerged the victor from his jousts in the tournament of life more often than not, but he also knows the experience of being knocked from the saddle, and of being trampled when prostrate by an unchivalrous foe."[30]

Meanwhile, the Starfighters were still blasting their afterburners overhead, and another, much more capable American design—the twin-engined F-4F Phantom II—was on its way to the Richthofen squadron. The Phantom was, finally, the ultimate combination of power, serviceability, and multi-role versatility. The Germans operated it expertly until 2013, finding utility in it decades after other air forces had moved on to more expensive, less durable jets. Hartmann never flew it.

Just as Erich Hartmann's career was suffering, so, too, was his legend. By the time he retired, many in the *Bundeswehr* leadership didn't know quite what to do with him, and his reputation and place in history were as out-of-focus as ever. Here was a decorated and experienced officer whose road to glory had been laid by the servants of the Third Reich; whose revived career had provided renewal but then led to unforeseen, conspicuous challenges; and whose importance to the nascent West Germany had once been clear but now, at the deflated end of it, felt overblown from the start. The biggest risk Hartmann faced at the time of his retirement, probably, was falling into obscurity as a burnt-out former *Wehrmacht* agent—whether or not that would have been the most accurate way to characterize him.

But here's when the new fraternity of writers, interviewers, and commentators coalesced, gathering in strength and number. They had already begun talking with Hartmann and his peers to capture their stories first-hand, just when these soldiers' legacies were most fragile and West Germany was pivoting away from them. They did this in person, at airshows, and at World War II reunions, and their purpose was to redeploy the old pilots to a new front: the war of popular opinion. Like a craftsman might restore an old piece of machinery, they sifted through the aces' stories, cleansed them, hammered them straight, and reassembled them, at each step renewing their glory and meaning. They moved beyond Hartmann's troubles with the *Bundeswehr* and focused on what, ironically, was a much more pleasing and marketable period of his life: his career under the Nazis.

## CHAPTER 12

# Last Missions

The various judgments are determined by the viewpoints of the judges. Mythology shows itself to be as amenable as life itself to the obsessions and requirements of the individual, the race, the age.

—JOSEPH CAMPBELL[1]

It usually went like this: several German, British, and American flying veterans gather on the tarmac at an airshow, each leaning against the wing of a warplane as they reminisce, sign books, or entertain questions from fans. They're older now, but you can see the youthful pleasure in their faces now that they're free of life's other matters and focused on flying. They'll pause their conversations abruptly every so often to look skyward, tracking the sound of a familiar engine—they recognize the planes by ear, easily distinguishing a Merlin from an Allison or a Daimler-Benz—and wave at the machines as they pass by. Then it's back to the conversation.

The fans clustered nearby treat them with a double helping of reverence: one for the fact that they are elder heroes, and the other for the fact that they are pilots. No other group you're likely to stumble into conducts such peaceful discussions about the most violent and horrid war humans have ever concocted for themselves.

For an aviation fan, these airshow events are heaven. And there are fewer of them these days, so they're precious. There's just a dwindling supply of people who can tell you first-hand what it was like to dogfight against an Fw 190 (utterly frustrating), whether a Spitfire could out-turn a Mustang down on the deck (likely, but don't brag about it around a bunch of Mustang pilots), or what it was like to fly the P-47 (you could practically get up and walk around the huge cockpit). These old soldiers harbor a wealth of knowledge, and seeing them relate so fluidly with one another, no matter their national allegiance—this seems inconsequential to them—is one of the most profound takeaways of these events. It can feel inspiring, exciting, unifying. These pilots, true to what we now know about their vocations, their bonds, and their shared hardships, are less interested in expired political schemes than the unifying experiences they endured.

Their charm is heightened, somehow, by the antique technology they stand next to on the pavement. Today, in the era of fly-by-wire and beyond-visual-range fighting, it's amusing to talk tactics with someone who just kicked an oil pan beneath a still-warm, still-leaking, radial engine.

At one event in Dayton, Ohio, in 1970 or 1971, Hartmann was filmed for an interview while leaning against a restored Bf 108 two-seater. Never one to ramble on with his responses, Hartmann still projected youthfulness, focus, and composure. He didn't look much different than he had in wartime, really—his hairline hadn't retreated, though his blonde hair had darkened with time. He wasn't wearing the glasses he did later in life, and only his sideburns, which had crept down a little with the styles of the time, gave away the period. The interviewer, an American pilot, was interested in Hartmann's time in captivity, and he asked what it was like spending 10 years away.

Hartmann replied: "It is a lost life. The only thing … that gets you through such times [is] that you have a good family at home, or that you … [believe in] God … or that you are fanatically nationalist, that you believe [in] your country."

The expression "fanatically nationalist" hits our ears strangely today, but to a German of Hartmann's age the words were probably synonymous with "patriotic." He was raised with "fanatic nationalism" being a normal and daily expression, and his English was never excellent. Still, the video's producers used it as their cue. Immediately after Hartmann finishes that sentence, the patriotic snare drums start up, without irony, and the video fades into its outro with footage of an aircraft climbing dramatically from a sun-drenched runway somewhere.[2]

We don't get many glimpses of Hartmann at these events, unfortunately. He seldom traveled after retirement and didn't care much for the limelight—a preference that was deepened by a 1980 bout with coronary heart disease, the condition that had killed his father. He heeded his brother's medical orders and laid low, eventually recovering enough to resume casual flying back at home. Later in the 1980s he went back to managing several flying schools and serving as the Federal Aviation Administration representative for Wurttemberg. His public presence, unfortunately for us, was limited.

One other preserved video interview of Hartmann warrants mention here, and this one appears to have been published online as recently as 2018. It takes place in a backyard between Hartmann and a young interviewer of uncertain background (not American—he appears to be a non-native English speaker). It is the most curious, and troubling, testimony Hartmann ever gave.

The video proceeds as the typical chronological discussion of Hartmann's life and career for about 20 minutes. Then, surprisingly, the interviewer asks Hartmann point-blank about his views about Jewish people and the German concentration camps. This is highly unusual and not done in the other video interviews you'll find out there.

Here is a transcription of the questions and answers:

Interviewer: "Have you ever been taught anything about hating anybody else? … When you were … training for pilot … Have you been trained to be against the Jews, for example?

Hartmann: "No. They made fun about the Jews, but you get no training against them."

I: "Now you say you've been informed. Have you passed through areas where concentration camps were? Like, say, Auschwitz, Birkenau, [garbled]."

H: "We heard, we sometime hear, our own people come through concentration camps who have stolen or so. But we didn't … very few about the concentration camps."

[Here Hartmann turns to near the camera and has a brief exchange in German with someone else, who summarizes in English: "He never flew over, he got this information all after the war."]

I: "Do you think it's possible that that happened over [at] the concentration camps, that they were killing Jews?"

H: "I don't know."

I: "Because Rudel himself, he said that when he flew over them, and he says the only thing he saw was when the German cities were destroyed [there were] piles of people, but he says actually that … he was surprised when he was interviewed by the British, [and he wondered] 'What are they talking about?' Because he never saw this mass of people being killed."

H: "Because during the war the young people [were] all at the front. Who works at home? … [If you] kill the people then they can't work more. The [key] factor is to build airplanes and tanks and cars and everything [that] you need."

I: "So were you aware for example that Auschwitz was a factory?"

H: "I think … They had to work."

[The interviewer mentions things that were supposedly manufactured there—planes, chemicals, and steel. Forced labor is ignored.]

I: "They heard rumors about some people going [missing] but the smell that they smelled was from the factory from the steel, but never from the people [after being exterminated] … nobody could ever see."

H: "It's the same as in Russia. Russia has concentration camps so much—so many—but they don't kill the people in the concentration camps because they are very cheap working people."

[The footage cuts away from the two men and to an image of a workshop, with the heading, "Workshops in Auschwitz."]

I: "You would think that would be the German idea."

H: "The first who had concentration camps was the English ... you had the people for working, not killing."

I: "Exactly."

H: "You had the people for working."

I: "Yes."

[Now the interviewer keeps talking but turns toward the camera.]

I: "So you gave me here a map."

[He holds up map of Russia with dots all over it, many of which are in the western territories. Presumably this is a map of Soviet camps. There are dozens of dots scattered around.]

H: "[There are] no people in Russia who don't have work ... We have now here in Germany two millions of people, no work."

[Hartmann points to the map. He appears to be arguing, with seriousness, for the economic efficacy of Soviet work camps. It's unclear whether he gave the interviewer the map midway through the interview off-camera, or if the whole thing was scripted ahead of time.]

H: "They put them in concentration camps. It's very easy."[3]

The footage then cuts to a different conversation about how Hartmann was never treated as a criminal in Germany after the war.

There are quite a few things to notice about this exchange. First, Hartmann's response that he heard jokes about Jews but didn't get any specific anti-Semitic training is wholly unreasonable—unless, maybe, he's thinking specifically and solely of pilot training, as opposed to the Hitler Youth, schooling, other military training, or the propagandizing that was everywhere when he was younger. This could have been the case, since he once acknowledged: "We as young people had been hit hard with this subhuman propaganda, such as Slavs, Jews, that sort of thing. I never really thought much about it. It was the same in America with the blacks. Some believed it while some did not."[4] (It wasn't, of course, the same in America, and his flippancy is unconvincing.)

Second, Hartmann's claim that he and the other soldiers knew little about the concentration camps until after the war is suspect. It's hard to say what he and the other aviators really understood about the exterminations, but the old theory of the members of the *Wehrmacht* as passive bystanders to the Holocaust is thoroughly worn out by now. Anyone who hadn't encountered Hitler's explicit plans for racial extermination by 1935 wasn't paying attention. Moreover, German soldiers frequently knew what was going on in regions and theaters other than their own, often in great detail. They relied on that intelligence to carry out their missions and retain a sense of cohesion and connection to their peers in such a vast and segmented theater of war. They certainly did not rely on other pilots' impromptu overflights of the territories for their intelligence. For Rudel, the virulent Nazi sympathizer, to be trusted as the carrier of the truth about the concentration camps is obviously inadequate.

It also helps to remember that racial extermination was explicitly a war function, not some tangential flourish to the conflict that only a few people cared about; it required integration, intelligence, systems, and manpower from all the branches of the German military.

From there, the interviewer gives away the most interesting thing about the discussion, which is that there is a shared agenda of Holocaust denial—or at least obfuscation—behind it. This is suggested by how easily the interviewer agrees with Hartmann's claim of ignorance at first, but when he mentions Rudel as the airborne authority on whether or not the killings were taking place and then pulls out a map of Soviet camps—which Hartmann had earlier given him—the blame-shifting begins and the illusion that this is a journalistic interview is out of the window.

In terms of his mannerisms, Hartmann doesn't give much away throughout this exchange. He's poker-faced, basically unsurprised, and shows occasional language confusion with phrasings. He never seems to gesture in a way that suggests agitation or discomfort, and the fact that this conversation was conducted in English, a language in which he wasn't fully comfortable, makes it harder to extract much from his speech patterns.

The problems with this interview deepen with a little background research. It turns out that the YouTube channel that posted it also posts content from the Institute For Historical Review, an upright-sounding organization that happens to harbor Holocaust-denial content. Other videos on the channel, which are often low-quality digitizations of decades-old speeches and interviews of lesser-known figures, include several talks by David Irving, probably the best-known Holocaust denier, who famously lost a libel suit against an American author and her British publisher when he objected to their negative characterization of his work. (The case was turned into a Hollywood film in 2016.) The written decision in the case stated: "Irving has for his own ideological reasons persistently and deliberately misrepresented and manipulated historical evidence."[5]

Although it would be presumptuous to assign Hartmann full-fledged complicity based on the conversation, he and his interviewer do demonstrate several tactics characteristic of Holocaust deniers and the most blatant Nazi apologists: (1) shifting or spreading blame (to the English or the

Soviets); (2) evading the real issue through distraction (it's all okay because the camps must only have been used for work; forced work is economically understandable); and (3) deferring to obviously compromised or biased sources (Rudel and his supposedly authoritative overflights). If you're a committed Holocaust denier, these tactics are key parts of your playbook.

Here I'm reminded of a lesson from some old college course: that the root of the word "sophistication" lies with the sophists of ancient Greece, who perfected the art of concealing their own faulty reasoning with specious arguments and distracting, irrelevant complexity.

The pretend sophistication of Hartmann and his interviewer's ramblings about the camps is part of what makes them so conspicuous. Hartmann, importantly, shows no reckoning with German responsibility, no particular interest in the Jews' (or anyone else's) victimization, and no notable personal reflection.

This conjures another memory, a conversation I once had with Rudi Florian, the Catholic Holocaust expert and advocate, during which I asked what he would say to Erich Hartmann if the two had ever sat at the same table. Florian replied with typical gentleness, peering into a dark beer at a restaurant, that he would simply ask if Hartmann had gathered the necessary facts over time and updated his views of what his country and his military had done. All Florian wanted, in other words, was a sign that Hartmann had progressed, sought the truth, and walked out of the swamp of denial and misrepresentation that people like Florian have been so diligently combating these last decades.

If this was indeed Hartmann's last English-language interview—if it came, as we assume, not long before his death—I'm not sure Hartmann would have cared to look Rudi Florian in the eye.

Hartmann died of unspecified natural causes at the age of 71 on September 20, 1993. One source suggests he died after complications from a fall at his home.[6] Several American newspapers printed an Associated Press-authored obituary describing Hartmann as "one of Germany's most daring World War II aces" and briefly detailing his aviation career.[7] His death was marked by little fanfare outside the fighter-pilot communities, which saw it as a significant loss of a feisty character and valuable institutional memory. It certainly was all of that, since he left behind just a handful of digitized video interviews, most filled with the same tales and tactics, along with a few interview transcripts from lengthier conversations he gave here and there, and of course the celebratory stories written about him by others. There were also many private memories shared by the people who knew him after he'd settled into retirement, but those will remain largely concealed until there isn't anyone left to convey them.

For Hartmann, *doing* always seemed more important than *remembering*, and people have allowed him that.

At Hartmann's grave in Weil im Schönbuch, a boulder serves as his headstone. It's a weighty thing, speckled slate gray. There's a carved eagle perched at the top, which makes plenty of sense to anyone who knows Hartmann's name, and down at the bottom, near the soil, is a phrase written in metal letters that have been drilled into the rock: *In Liebe für Immer* ("In love always"). To us and his early biographers, Erich Hartmann's life story is not primarily about romantic love—it's about flying and war and nations and heroes. It's about that eagle on top of the headstone, in other words. But isn't it interesting to wonder whether, to Hartmann, as his life waned, all that might have changed? Could it be (if we're feeling especially analytical) that there was a subtle meaning in putting the reference to Ursula down low, near the earth itself, such an important German cultural symbol of connection and stability?

There's a comfort—a sense of harmony—in thinking that Hartmann might have wanted his most eternal message to be not about temporary and complicated wars but about permanent love and the portion of his life that kept him most grounded.

How alluring it is, harmony.

# Part Three

## Stories Told

## CHAPTER 13

# Marketing the *Wehrmacht*

After all, if the Germans were not only to be our friends, but also our armed allies, it was important to erase at least some aspects of the recent war from the public memory and to revise the terms of discussion...

—RONALD SMELSER AND EDWARD J. DAVIES II[1]

In the fall of 1964, in front of a pair of burnished metal microphones and red, white, and blue drapery, Ronald Reagan gave a televised speech in support of Republican presidential candidate Barry Goldwater. This was an intimate venue—a small hall containing a few hundred people and a handful of modest rally signs—but he was also speaking to a huge televised audience. Already, hardly four years after John F. Kennedy and Richard Nixon had sparred in the first televised presidential debate, Reagan was using the medium as effectively as few have since. With forthrightness and flair, he pitched a political agenda whose central qualities were emotional richness and narrative drama. It would put him in the Oval Office twice, and lawmakers from both sides of the aisle have admired his tactics for decades. What Reagan was able to secure that evening was not the election of Goldwater but, instead, new momentum for his own national political career.

Reagan was a masterful storyteller who made Americans feel like the protagonists in their own story. A full 25 minutes into the Goldwater speech, his voice still buzzed with energy, and everyone watching could see the fervor building in his face. His sentences ran together, leaving few pauses for breath:

When Nikita Khrushchev has told his people ... that we are retreating under the pressure of the Cold War and someday, when the time comes to deliver the final ultimatum, our surrender will be voluntary—because, by that time, we will have been weakened from within spiritually, morally and economically—he believes this because from our side he's heard voices pleading for peace at any price.

This was a smart political statement because it located moral decay not just behind the Iron Curtain, but also—ominously—within America's borders in the hearts and minds of those unwilling to fight. Reagan was staying 30,000 feet above any policies that would undergird his administration, but he didn't need to get down to the details on this night. He was evoking in his audience's minds a powerful, mythical drama: the story of a vigorous, emboldened United States poised to extend its prosperity but threatened by the scourge of collectivism; of earnest, hard-working, heroic individuals who were being tamped down by their runaway government; of faraway, mischievous antagonists with fur hats, always plotting ways to subvert freedom at home and abroad. The "Great Communicator" was proving that the Cold War's contest of ideas could, at times, be about feelings first and details second.

He was also helping to deliver a modern brand of heroism. Heroic storytelling in the Cold War years diverged from traditional mythologies because of its focus on the individual rather than the group. Whereas the heroes of the old times—some of the ones Erich Hartmann might have remembered when he was young—were frequently working on behalf of social order and the expectations of the polity, Reagan's American heroes were their own bosses. This was in part a reaction to the collectivist theories that drove Communism, but it flowed in the same stream with many other hero narratives that celebrated the nobility and efficacy of people on their own. Think of the leading men (and women, occasionally) who became so popular throughout the 20th century: Superman, the ultimate strong individual; Indiana Jones, the rugged explorer-loner; and even the more recent anti-heroes and outcasts who amuse us precisely *because* of their alienation from society.

The way we understand Hartmann and his airborne peers doesn't reflect who they were intrinsically as much as how they've been portrayed by the first generation of writers and commentators who defined their heroism for us. The modernized, individualist conception that Reagan leveraged so well also helped Hartmann's first biographers make sense of and celebrate him during the Cold War. Just when the West was defining its heroic figureheads and launching ideological attacks against the Soviets, Hartmann was being molded into a great new case study in bristling individualism.

## Allies and Enemies

Immediately after World War II, after those first American and Soviet soldiers awkwardly shook hands at the River Elbe near Torgau at the confluence of the Western and Eastern Fronts, there was a rapid change in the way Americans viewed Germans and Soviets. On the surface, the Soviets were still America's allies. The Germans, tainted by Hitler, militarily defeated, and politically unmoored, were the vanquished enemies and builders of the concentration camps. But even before most people were talking about anything called the Cold War, those roles began to flip.

This was due in part to the experiences of occupying forces at the end of the war and immediately after surrender. While they were trying to figure out what to do with Germany and the other war-torn territories that had to be sewn back into a European map, the victors spent a great deal of time interacting with the citizens of those areas. An American officer named John Maginnis, who was stationed in Berlin, described his own creeping animosity toward the Soviets, as compared to the Germans he was surrounded by. He described the Soviets as having "a baffling combination of childishness, hard realism, irresponsibility, churlishness, amiability, slovenliness, and callousness." He was self-aware of the mental switch taking place, too: "It became a continuing problem to remind myself that the Russians, who were giving us trouble, were our friends, and the Germans, who were giving us cooperation, were our enemies."[2]

Maginnis's experience wasn't unique. Historians Ronald Smelser and Edward Davies studied this widespread rise in sympathy toward embattled German citizens and the corresponding decline of people's views of the "callous" Soviets. The more time Allied occupying soldiers and public officials spent in Germany, the more they sympathized with the German mothers who were scrambling for food scraps in the alleyways, the children who were missing their fathers, or the doctors who were sacrificing everything they had for their neighbors. "The myriad contacts between Americans and Germans from 1945," Smelser and Davies write, "not only created a growing sympathy, respect, and even kinship between the two peoples ... they also created a vital opportunity for the Germans to educate [Americans] at the grass roots military (and civilian) level about the Russians."[3] Numerous articles from major American magazines told readers "Why So Many GIs Like the Germans Best," for example, which "caused many to reject or deny stories they read in the press about Nazi atrocities during the recent war."[4]

As you would imagine, the Germans had well-developed views of the Soviets—most Germans could describe the rapes and the unbelievable violence suffered by friends and family at the hands of Soviet combatants or captors, and even Erich Hartmann had already had his memory stained by that gruesomeness. So to the degree that the German atrocities were hidden or minimized, tales of Soviet atrocities were available and accentuated. We know today, of course, that countless Soviet families had their own horrific stories to tell about the German aggressors; SS and *Wehrmacht* members, by formal decree, were permitted to execute Soviet citizens as they saw fit. But the postwar Allied occupation was centered in Berlin, not Moscow. The Germans were the ones doing the public remembering.

Importantly, this remembering was conducted at the most official levels. With sanctioning from the U.S. military, *Wehrmacht* veterans of great authority and influence were put in charge of recording, evaluating, and disseminating the official historical record of the war effort. What was intended to be an empirical, analytical process of documenting how to do battle with the Soviets became infused with the German military worldview. It steered American understanding of the war, Germans, and Russians for decades.

In 1946, the U.S. Army established the Operational History (German) Section of the Historical Division. Its purpose was to record and distribute intelligence from German leaders, especially as it related to fighting the Soviet military. This intelligence, American leaders figured, would be valuable as historiography and as training material for the conflict ahead. In a sense, they were correct. Useful intelligence did flow into U.S. training programs, and the German generals doing the writing were forthcoming and detailed about German successes and failures; our understanding of World War II would be shallower today if not for this work. But they apparently never reckoned with an important side effect of the program, which was that scores of former *Wehrmacht* officers were being empowered, often through advisory roles, direct authorship, and fraternization with American officials, as the enthusiastic carriers of this *Wehrmacht*-centric narrative. They initiated the now-familiar pattern of normalizing and glorifying German soldiers' professionalism, celebrating the German military's institutional pride, and focusing on the notable victories enjoyed by the *Wehrmacht* during all stages of the conflict—all while ignoring the gristlier parts.

They also inserted racism and bigoted generalizations about the Soviets that supported Americans' realignment with the Germans, and in various places you see traces of the animosities that had leeched into the *Wehrmacht* from the Nazis. One study in 1953, for example, asserted that "The Slav psyche—especially where it is under more or less pronounced Asiatic influences—covers a wide range in which fanatic conviction, extreme bravery, and cruelty bordering on bestiality are coupled with childlike kindliness and susceptibility to sudden fear and terror."[5] Today we recognize this as racist nonsense; in 1953, it was packaged as insightful tactical notes.

The man you might call editor-in-chief of all this was not an American official, but a high-ranking former *Wehrmacht* officer named Franz Halder.

General Halder had been brought to the Nuremberg trials for testimony as a former chief of staff of the German Army High Command, and he became embroiled in a subsequent legal proceeding about his role orchestrating Nazi crimes. But before that trial could continue, the Americans, who had already offered him a job in the Historical Division, halted the process by refusing to release him for trial. They deemed him extremely valuable to their work.[6]

Halder vetted the studies that came out of the Historical Division and chose the writers in charge of them, coaching them to hide incriminating information about German war crimes, especially on the Eastern Front (during the war, Halder was one of the leading planners of Operation *Barbarossa* and his office had produced the policies that allowed German soldiers to execute civilians along the way). He created, whether by intent or only effect, the possibility of a kinship between Americans and Germans that was based not just on geopolitics and culture, but a specific conception of shared racial identity.[7]

Halder had, however, also participated in a pre-war plot to overthrow Hitler, which never went anywhere but might have made him a more palatable figure to his American partners. For this and other reasons, Halder was praised from all directions. The Commander in Chief of the U.S. Army in Europe thanked him for providing "valuable material for the organization and training of our military forces to meet the threat of communist aggression ... [his] work has developed another area of alliance between our two great nations for the joint defense of our democratic way of life." In 1961, Halder received the Meritorious Civilian Service Award from an American general in the name of President John F. Kennedy. He is the only German general to be decorated by both Hitler and an American president.[8]

While Halder and others reshaped Western memory from the military outward, popular culture saw a broader and more widespread narrative of German victimization emerge. This was largely driven by Germany's destitution after the war and the subsequent imprisonment of its soldiers. In this version of the story, the Germans—and especially the soldiers—were the unwitting recipients of the war's horrors rather than the perpetrators of them. Hitler's fanaticism and excesses helped postwar observers silo him off as a fringe character, just as it had enabled Franz Halder to separate himself from his more extreme *Führer* even though his war diaries showed his complicity in Hitler's criminal plans.[9] The categories of "the ordinary Germans" and "the Nazis" became more clearly delineated and oppositional, and the Third Reich's racist lunacy was increasingly described as something *imposed* on citizens and soldiers, not something that had been validated and supported by these groups. This was a powerful shift in collective thinking that offered harmonious peace of mind, and it would be decades before historians and the public questioned it methodically.

The victim narrative was propped up in surprising ways. Even the medical diagnosis of dystrophy, often assigned to men like Hartmann who had suffered from various mental and physical ailments as prisoners of war, was part of it. Historian Frank Biess writes:

> By attributing returnees' symptoms solely to the depravations in captivity, the diagnosis precluded, by definition, any extended discussion of the potentially traumatic impact of the military experience itself. Instead dystrophy offered a seemingly objective, scientific justification for ascribing a victim status to returning POWs.[10]

In a cruel twist, there is even evidence that this definition of dystrophy was influenced by Nazi doctors who ran ghastly experiments on prisoners in concentration camps.[11] Today, dystrophy means something altogether different—it describes the degeneration of tissues, as in "muscular dystrophy"—and our understandings of post-traumatic stress are of course much more sophisticated.

## The Radical Sixties

The early insiders who knew Hartmann personally and understood the mileposts of his life had little trouble fitting him into this new German narrative. Shifting views toward the Soviets and the victimization stories gave them the social permission they needed to show their deep fondness for the *Luftwaffe* pilots—especially Hartmann, who had spent an almost unfathomable 10 years as a prisoner of war in Russia. With the most nefarious Nazi actors safely compartmentalized inside Hitler's inner circle, the stage was set for a retelling of the chivalrous air war and the reintroduction of the German knights like Hartmann.

It makes sense that the 1960s was when these *Wehrmacht* narratives were really taking shape and getting published. Early in the decade, a resurgence of war crimes trials taking place in West Germany brought Nazi transgressions and military complicity back into the national conversation, creating an atmosphere of vulnerability for those individual combatants who were still alive and active in the public sphere. The trial and execution of Adolf Eichmann, one of the architects of the Holocaust, in 1961–62, for example, forcefully brought Nazi crimes against humanity into the news and questioned the *Wehrmacht* veterans' reintegration into society, industry, and government. Other prosecutions that came about after the creation of a West German Central Office of the Provincial Justice Administrations did the same.[12] And then 1968 happened.

The cultural upheaval and protests of the time showed that the emerging, younger generation had no time for militarism and harbored precious little veneration of the World War II veterans in question. This undoubtedly gave the *Wehrmacht* commentators their incentive, urgency, and forcefulness.

Today's readers might find the resultant war stories distracting from a writing standpoint. Their tone and language tend to be awkwardly celebratory—the adjectives spill onto the pages and the paragraphs seem written almost breathlessly. Books like *Horrido!* (named after the radio call the *Luftwaffe* pilots used to use to signal that they had made a kill) and *The Blond Knight of Germany* shoehorn glamor and moral clarity into these war narratives, distancing the German heroes from their regime while simultaneously playing up the *Luftwaffe's* historic capabilities and its members' attachment to the institution. The two titles mentioned above are among the most famous and impactful *Luftwaffe* stories, and were both written by Raymond Toliver and Trevor Constable, two of the leading ambassadors from this era. Toliver was an F-100 Super Sabre pilot and a celebrated member of the U.S. Air Force. Constable, among other things, was apparently a dedicated UFO hunter. Together, they adopted a writing approach that was declarative, moralistic, and fiercely protective of their German comrades.

"A fair man and an honest man have nothing to fear from him, for he shakes hands as easily as he locks horns," they write of Hartmann. "His modesty is as much a part of the whole man as his blue eyes and blond hair … He has a will almost fierce in its drive to prevail and conquer. His directness in thought and word are disquieting to the pretender, inspiring to the timid and challenging to the valiant."[13]

The three quotes above came from a span of two pages in the first chapter of *The Blond Knight of Germany*, but a random flip through the remaining text can provide plenty more. The writers use a fantastic array of descriptors and allegories to describe Hartmann and his *Luftwaffe* peers, and they rely on a grab bag of modern heroic traits to endear them to readers: self-reliance, black-and-white morality, disdain for authority, masculinity, and so on. The repetitive celebrations are so shiny they're dull.

Throughout the work, the lush, scenic descriptions and quick pace of the battle stories conceal a severe lack of investigative breadth. There are no citations or source notes in *The Blond Knight of Germany*, *Horrido!* or *Fighter Aces of the Luftwaffe* (which itself isn't so much a new book as it is an expansion of *Horrido!* with copious photos). Of course, in one sense, the research was wonderfully deep—most of the storytelling was paraphrased from what must have been arduous and time-consuming personal interviews with the aces themselves, and nobody else at the time could have inspired the same trust and descriptiveness among this group of soldiers. We really do learn a great deal about tactics, the air battles, and the rigors of the Eastern Front, especially in *Fighter Aces of the Luftwaffe*, which was published in 1996 and offers slightly less gushing versions of these men's stories. (It still leaves no doubt: "In cool blood and calm heart, history should now recognize that the German airman was a brave and fair opponent, whose professionalism is to be admired by all nationalities and generations of fighter pilots.")[14] We also learn a lot about the infatuated scribes who've put together the information. As Christopher Irmscher, a professor of English at Indiana University, once wrote when he reviewed an over-zealous biography of Charles Darwin for the *Wall Street Journal*: "As I was finishing [the author's] book, something rather unexpected had happened to me: I had become more curious about him than about Darwin."[15]

*The Blond Knight of Germany* was translated into German and consumed hungrily by Hartmann's countrymen. Its German title was changed to *Holt Hartmann von Himmel!* which translates roughly to *Bring Down Hartmann from the Sky!* or *Shoot Hartmann Out of the Sky!* The clumsy Aryan connotations in the American title, which apparently didn't satisfy German publishers, might have been a misguided nod to an earlier work on Manfred von Richthofen called *The Red Knight of Germany*. And while the German edition was retitled, the rest of the book is a more-or-less standard translation. Like the original American publication, the book's preface is written by Adolf Galland, who proclaims, still, that this work should be interpreted as something other than a glorification of war.

Toliver and Constable surely aren't alone in their celebrating, nor is their brand of writing confined to World War II pilots. One commentator on the Vietnam air war remembered American ace Robin Olds like this:

> He is being carried jubilantly to the officers' club on the shoulders of the men who have followed him into battle. He is 45 years old and impossibly handsome, with jutting jaw, half smile, handlebar mustache, crow's feet at the eyes and of course a cigarette between his lips. It's 1967, and the man is a fighter pilot.[16]

Scenes and celebrations like these were entirely authentic to the men involved, and there are, as you would hope, plenty of bright moments in these works that showcase human ingenuity, courage, and even bonds between wartime enemies. Hartmann liked to tell the story of learning to warm his engine for start-up in sub-freezing temperatures from a friendly captured Soviet airman—it involved a scary mix of gas and oil—and he always shared his gratitude for having learned the trick. Things like this really did happen in the war, and they really were important to the German combatants.

At times, the insularity of this network of soldiers and their storytellers becomes explicit. From one interview of Hartmann, reportedly his last, comes the following:

> Q: Was this when you first met Dieter Hrabak [your colonel]?
>
> A: Yes, who has been a good friend over the years, as you know. Dieter was the first person to tell me to talk to you [the interviewer], since he and the others trust you. I like you also.[17]

## The Authorities

Today, a 21st-century American aviation fan can put together quite a collection of history books focused on *Luftwaffe* aviators. Many of them are marketed to highlight the mystique of these pilots, and the books are often presented as if they contain some kind of dramatic revelation. Just browse their titles: *The German Aces Speak, The Aces Talk, I Flew for the Führer.* We crack open these book covers with anticipation.

The implications of titles like these probably vary by reader. For some—the biggest fans of these pilots, let's say—*The German Aces Speak* might mean, in effect, *The German Aces [Are Finally Being Allowed to] Speak.* For others less vested in the stories and the *Wehrmacht*, the title implies something even more scintillating: maybe it's *The German Aces Speak [and Divulge Their Dastardly Secrets].* Either way, these books, and the many copycat magazine articles and online missives that have sprung from them, imply investigative tenacity that is missing once you get inside.

Even the marketing and graphic designs build up these expectations. In the case of *The German Aces Speak II*, the volume of the series that includes a long interview with Hartmann, the cover image is of a generic *Luftwaffe* pilot in the cockpit of a Bf 109 fighter, in grainy black-and-white, viewed head-on through the windscreen. Prominent in the photo is what looks like a gunsight pointed directly at the reader—a circle, in the pilot's field of view, that has been photoshopped blood red. It's a striking and purposeful image. Unfortunately, it's also misleading and historically wrong. Not only is the red coloring gratuitous and artificial next to the color treatment of the rest of the photo, but the "gunsight" disc is no such thing. Bf 109 windscreens were designed with small, round cutouts for silica tablets, which absorbed moisture between the clear panes and kept them from fogging during flight. That disc is as innocuous as a seatbelt.

Once you get past the initial posturing of these books (remember that cover designs and even titles can be influenced by a publisher as much as the writer), they usually deliver the tried-and-true anecdotes and revert to the same central messages: that these elite *Luftwaffe* men were misunderstood knights, that we should appreciate their tactical accomplishments independent of ideology, motivation, or impact, and that we shouldn't bother investigating the flyers' National Socialist connections because there usually were none and it didn't matter anyway. Better to assume nobler values, even though many of these values were literally what the Germans were fighting against—recall Hitler and the Third Reich's intolerance of individualism, democracy, and so on, as well as his effectiveness in shaping schools and institutions to abolish these things. This should be profoundly interesting to us, but no; after reading dozens of similar interviews with *Luftwaffe* pilots, you start to crave one that gets anywhere near issues like this.

After a while, the redundancy sets in. One of the forewords to *The German Aces Speak II*, for example—which was published in 2014, 44 years after *The Blond Knight of Germany*—is written by none other than Trevor Constable. Erich Hartmann's chapter in the 2014 book is titled, unsurprisingly enough, "The Blond Knight of Germany." Elsewhere, Heaton and co-author (and wife) Anne-Marie Lewis dedicate the first volume of their German ace interviews, *The German Aces Speak*, to Raymond Toliver. Robin Olds contributes a foreword to that book.[18]

Furthermore, *Horrido!*—for years the go-to resource on the *Luftwaffe* aces—showed up 26 years after its original printing retitled as *Fighter Aces of the Luftwaffe*. The latter book appears to be a new work because of its much larger format and copious wartime photos, but much of the text is lifted from the earlier one. It seems to have been selectively edited the second time around; usually the modifications amount to general wordsmithing, but occasionally there are peculiar additions. One such addition is a comment about the so-called Hamburg Holocaust, which refers to the horrific fire-bombing of the city by American forces in the summer of 1943.[19] The fire-bombing is sometimes invoked by Hitler apologists to morally equalize the warring parties. Its injection into *Fighter Aces of the Luftwaffe* is of unclear purpose or value.

To their credit, Heaton and Lewis included several relevant forewords in their books that offer new insights and some context. One, in *The German Aces Speak II*, is written by Dennis Showalter, a history professor who has taught at Colorado College, the United States Air Force Academy, the U.S. Military Academy, and the Marine Corps University. In it, he gestures toward the harder questions in these aces' lives, rightly discussing how Hitler positioned traditional German cultural norms and values alongside the wretched parts of his ideology, ensuring that the elite fighter pilots could still feel (or at least claim) that they were fighting for something bigger than Nazism. "This may not be a justification. It is an explanation," he writes.[20] So far so good. It's a refreshing way to introduce the rest of the book, even though it feels perfunctory next to the other 270 pages.

Another foreword, in the earlier volume of German ace interviews, is by historian Jon Guttman, who explained his relationship to the authors and Heaton's default attitude toward his interview subjects:

> My job was to edit Colin's manuscripts … In the process, I occasionally had to tone down questions that often reflected the interviewer's awe at being able to converse with "legendary" characters such a as Adolf Galland, Hajo Herrmann, and Erich Hartmann, making them more down to earth.[21]

The inclusion of this (rather frank) commentary is a credit to both Guttman and Heaton.

Truth is, it feels good to normalize the German combatants. People loved *A Higher Call*, a 2012 book about a *Luftwaffe* pilot who escorted a severely damaged American B-17 bomber out of Germany because he saw no good point in killing the crew. The book chronicles a deep and lasting bond between the German flyer and an American bomber crewman (the men reunited decades later as friends), and reviewers described it as "a riveting story of humanity and mercy set against the ghastly backdrop of war."[22] It certainly was all of that, but the German pilot's actions were exceedingly rare and a direct violation of protocol. As a story about the human condition, it's a welcome jolt of inspiration—but this isn't a story about what was normal in World War II.

This is no tiny niche market, either. Chronicles of the *Luftwaffe* pilots have become best-sellers and survived many printings. The most ardently pro-*Wehrmacht* ones often masquerade as deep, penetrating research, typically because they contain lots of granular, technical detail about fighting equipment, tactics, uniforms and camouflage colors, troop movements, and so on. If you want to know what kind of polish a German officer put on his boots, you can find out; but as for how deeply Nazism seeped into the officer corps, that's a much different story.

The most nefarious German combat units are often the most popular, oddly. The *Waffen-SS* is all over bookshelves—because, we're led to believe, of the daring and mystique that defined many of its missions, and the surgical precision of the men who populated its divisions. Its members' extraordinary ruthlessness is often confused for (or manipulatively reframed as) tactical excellence or generic patriotism, and the rhetorical sleight of hand involved in turning such an ethically loaded topic into a neutral discussion of tactics and protocols can be almost invisible.

Here's what American author Mark Yerger had to say:

> My interest in this period is historical ... I have no emotional or social connection to the period. Personally considering politics and politicians of any period [a] non-constructive time expenditure for discussion, I have no interest in either. Politics create the wars that soldiers fight.[23]

Two ideas linger here: One is the implicit definition of politics as "emotional or social"—presumably in contrast to some objective, systematic lining-up of facts that is called history. This returns us to the distinction between preserving history and understanding it; Yerger seems to be arguing that the preservation of artifacts and a chronology is the only necessary—maybe even the only permissible—step when it comes to the World War II German military. The opposite, I would say, is transparently and urgently true: when the artifacts are presented without an awareness of the political and social environments in which they existed, they are emptied of their meaning, relevance, and horror.

The other idea is that soldiers are by definition detached from the political realities that create their missions. It's true that German soldiers inherited a tradition of political non-affiliation (at least in the sense of not joining political parties), and soldiers of many nationalities and periods consider themselves apolitical. But this seems like a limited and uninterested point of view. Especially when the soldiers in question were steeped in the politics from an early age, according to the coordinated efforts of the war-makers, and their reason for fighting was explicitly social/political in nature.

There is also an interesting sleight of hand involved in using the word "politics" to describe things like allegiance to the Nazis, moral complacency, and institutionalized hatred. On the surface, these things are of course political to the extent that they were created and enforced by the German state apparatus. But they're much more than that. They're also broad ideological, social, reactionary, and militarist phenomena that permeated society and the military. This is important because when we label these concerns "politics," we're relegating them to a familiar, undesirable category of discussion—people forgive us for not going there. "We don't need to descend into politics here," commentators might say, and everyone else nods their heads intuitively.

One of Yerger's books includes a foreword written by Otto Baum, a former *SS* commander, who gives us another interesting declaration:

> As little as the German *Wehrmacht* was a criminal organization ... so little also was the *Waffen-SS*. Nothing will change this, neither the foolish and unfair treatment at Nuremberg nor the many false enflamed representations.[24]

No. The *Waffen-SS* was comprised of thousands of men whose soldiering proficiency was matched only by their racist fanaticism, and it was the preferred assignment for the most unashamed and committed Nazi aggressors. Hatred and Hitler's vile political formulations were baked into its very purpose and set-up as an organization—the *Schutzstaffel* as a whole was, as M. Gregory Kendrick puts it, "the *Führer's* executive arm." (Recall that the *SS* was comprised of the *Allgemeine SS*, which was in charge of racial policy and civilian policing at home, and the *Waffen-SS*, which deployed as combat units.) Neitzel and Welzer, with the *Waffen-SS* members' own words in hand, reiterate: "Within the core units of the *Waffen SS*, we find a unique amalgamation of racism, callousness, obedience, willingness for personal sacrifice, and brutality."[25] The *Waffen-SS* was more ideologically homogeneous than the *Wehrmacht*, which was rooted in traditions far predating the arrival of Hitler, and Neitzel and Welzer's empirical assessment here is a concise and useful affirmation of a broadly understood reality.

Put it another way: the *Wehrmacht* had to be infiltrated by the Nazis, but the *Waffen-SS* was birthed by them. This would be beyond dispute in any serious historical meeting of minds. Unfortunately for the apologists and die-hard chroniclers, their militantly non-political approach to their German subjects eventually starts to seem like a political act in itself. When pressed on the issue, they routinely step to the side, as Yerger does, pretending that these issues are tangential topics for someone else to explore. But that's a little like a marine biologist claiming that he doesn't care about fish. Either he's lying, or he's in the wrong field.

Of course, the fact that the soldiers and their chroniclers don't want to talk about these issues doesn't, by itself, mean that anyone was guilty of this-or-that atrocity, or of nefariously sanitizing history. It means that both parties face a particular type of vulnerability related to the Third Reich and their relationship to it. For the soldiers, confronting any of these issues openly means confronting their implication in a horrid war of extermination. And for the writers, exposing the depth of their kinship with Hitler's soldiers, including their own biases and frequently hard-right politics (both of which are easy enough to discern with a Google or YouTube search), might diminish their authority in these conversations and harm their standing in the field of history and elsewhere.

Think of it this way: no opening up of the Nazi politics question is likely to make the *Luftwaffe* aces or their allies feel any safer than they already are. They'll be thrust into a context of complexity and complicity that they haven't had to deal with over the years. Now, it could be that a detailed conversation of these issues would actually clear the air—even exonerate many of the soldiers once and for all. But it rarely, if ever, gets to that. Even though having the conversation doesn't automatically mean they are complicit or guilty, it makes them automatically *vulnerable* to *becoming* guilty. And the established non-political, simple situation is almost always better than that.

Of course, these *Wehrmacht* gurus are positively reasonable alongside other commentators on Germany and the Nazis. The prouder spokespeople of today's far-right are eager to appropriate 20th-century Aryan heroes to prop up their vision of the world, even if there is no reason to think the soldiers would have approved of such a thing.

Not long ago, one such group advertised a magazine with a cover story on Erich Hartmann. I bought it out of research interest but immediately felt slimy about it. The publication itself might as well have been photocopied in a dank basement somewhere—its black-and-white cover and interior pages are printed grainy and off-register, and its binding is obviously hand-done. It smells. The text contains all the celebrations carried over from other works on Hartmann, plus a nice helping of contemporary white nationalism—it's about the strong Aryan man, and so forth. Plus, the magazine arrived in the mail with several enclosures—extra material about various Jewish conspiracies the authors are convinced grip America today. If the authors' motives weren't already obvious, these add-ons remove any doubt. History's refuse has a way of gurgling back up.

## It's a Long Tradition

The contradictions and diversions of these commentators aren't new. They're actually time-tested ways of sidestepping difficult conversations about war, violence, and power. In the aftermath of the American Civil War, for instance, popular reading and reunions of former enemies de-emphasized the political and ideological context (specifically, the institution of slavery) in favor of the strategic and tactical discussions of armaments, missions, and leadership decisions.

In 1913, at a reunion of Northern and Southern veterans held on July 4, Virginia Governor William Hodges Mann prefaced the event like this:

> We are not here to discuss the genesis of the war, but men who have tried to fight each other in the storm of battle are here to discuss this great fight ... we came here, I say, not to discuss what caused the war of 1861–1865, but to talk over the events of the battle here as man to man.[26]

That quote encapsulates it all, really: (1) the "man to man" masculinity that makes these war narratives seem as much like fantasies as histories; (2) the common metaphor of war as a storm—note the rhetorical value in describing war as an external phenomenon imposed on people, not created and perpetuated by them; and (3) the conspicuous, chin-up certainty in the face of decidedly uncertain topics. Here, Mann was engaging in a form of war dramatization echoed by today's Civil War re-enactors who still sprawl prone along hillsides each year with muskets. He's focusing on the bonds among the men and their shared realities as soldiers—true and powerful things—at the expense of the uncomfortable bits.

This kind of remembering is rooted in psychology. Modern-day researchers understand that two of the most consistent parts of being a soldier are (1) the unshakable bond among members of fighting units, and (2) the shared duty to completion of the job, or the work. These two factors, often more than national allegiance or even time and place, determine why soldiers do what they do, and why they often sign up to do it over and over again in the face of mortal horror on the battlefield. The soldiers aren't being belligerent or mindless; they're being human according to the blueprints in our brains.

Historian and journalist Sebastian Junger reports that, during World War II, the U.S. Army Research Branch surveyed scores of soldiers to see what made them so devoted to their job and to one another. "According to their questionnaires," he writes, "the primary motivation in combat (other than 'ending the task'—which meant they could all go home) was 'solidarity with the group'. That far outweighed self-preservation or idealism as a motivator."[27]

Junger continues: "The Army might screw you and your girlfriend might dump you and the enemy might kill you, but the shared commitment to safeguard one another's lives is unnegotiable [*sic*] and only deepens with time."[28]

Here I think of that moment during the war when Hartmann went missing, forced down in a sunflower field only to be taken in by Soviets. His crew chief, Bimmel Mertens, heard of his disappearance, grabbed a gun, and marched right into the woods to find him. No apparent preparation or strategy was involved. This clearly wasn't about protocol or what was safe (it was a reckless and ineffective thing to do), but it *was* about that bond between soldiers. Mertens never got bogged down figuring his odds of finding Hartmann, or the regulations governing his action. The course of action was obvious to him.

These principles show up everywhere in war and in groups of professional combatants. "A study conducted in the mid-1950s," says Junger, "found that jumping out of a plane generated extreme anxiety in *loosely* bonded groups of paratroopers, but tightly bonded men mainly worried about living up to the standards of the group."[29]

Neitzel and Welzer also address this issue, and they perceive it clearly in the captured German soldiers' conversations with one another. "Camaraderie is less about a specific view of the world or ideology than orientation," they write. "Many individuals feel emotionally more at home with their comrades than with family members, who do not share their experiences as soldiers."[30]

This points out a provocative reality about the German World War II combatants. Many of these men—maybe even most of them—weren't a bunch of Nazified snakes out there fighting on behalf of an ideology, even if they had accepted that ideology or its premises enough to fight on its behalf. Hitler bewildered some of them, and to others he was a goon in a mustache. *But that didn't matter to the outcome.* You had honorable men and evil men fighting alongside one another, but the distinction was all but meaningless to their shared contribution to a horrid war and a warped worldview of racism and subjugation. Evil men completed Hitler's missions because they were evil men. Good men completed those same missions because they were soldiers.

So what might be a better way to talk about these soldiers in the future? There are at least two main benefits to probing all the parts of these men's lives—not just the palatable ones, as we've been doing for the last sixty years. First, we get closer to the truth. This is an obvious need. The *Luftwaffe* aces today are basically caricatures of themselves, and that actually keeps them distant from us, serving neither history nor today's interested readers and citizens who hope to use their stories to make better decisions for themselves. Second, we would actually get closer to the aces as men—humanizing them, creating a deeper connection to their time and their trials. Today's readers and commentators are interested in knowing the whole person (consider the rise of the anti-hero—we like fully developed characters, no longer just shiny ones). Ironically, this might allow figures like Erich Hartmann to attain *more* permanence and *more* relevance than they have ever had while shepherded so protectively.

But there is a third, even more pressing, reason to change how we talk about the German soldiers: it is our obligation. As writer Eddie Glaude Jr. puts it: "The language of ideals and perfection obscure what we have done, and continue to do, on the ground."[31] In other words, when we keep talking about a historic topic in terms of noble first principles and moral standards (individualism, honor, chivalry) we often fail to address the practical realities of people's lives (furtherance of oppression, destruction, complexity). Moreover, those who proclaim to adhere to those principles, however earnestly, sometimes have effects in the real world that contradict the principles they claim to own.

In a practical sense, this means that whenever we talk about the German soldiers only in terms of their agreeable principles and beliefs, we ignore how they influenced the world and people around them. Let's assume that Erich Hartmann was always a freedom-loving individualist of the most palatable variety—can we say that his actions really supported that? On the ground (so to speak), he furthered Hitler's war of extermination. He apparently protested little, during or after the war, beyond the scope of his own personal wellbeing; he was unable to publicly show substantive self-reflection or remorse for the millions of Jewish and other lives that his side of the conflict extinguished. Ask the victims of the *Wehrmacht*'s war how consequential the German soldiers' inner principles were to their practical effects in the world.

Another good way to look at this is to acknowledge that it is our practices, not our words, that reflect our real commitments. Although the *Wehrmacht* experts' words do occasionally suggest that they dislike war and that they, echoing their subjects, wish for countries and peoples to get along, their practices have quite a different effect. Taken as a whole, they have tended to obscure history, blanketing a complex and difficult topic with soothing simplicity and urging the rest of us that we needn't go there. These writers' sentimentality and celebration of noble principles has been the easy path—it seems to reflect a desire for a fulfilling resolution, for safety, for clarity.

The resulting historical record is inadequate. Not necessarily because the writers were a bunch of colluding revisionists (there was, as far as we can tell today, no dastardly scheme of historical manipulation), but because the historical record is one-dimensional as a result of their work. They really believed in the honor and high principles of their subjects, and they wished for those principles to inform a durable version of the story to be recognized by the general public. But that was not, ultimately, enough. The insularity and conformity of the commentators points to their central weakness: this slice of history, like Halder's tactical reports, was essentially written by one closely aligned committee.

Importantly, though, the committee wasn't just run by the aces' adoring fans. It was frequently run by the aces themselves.

CHAPTER 14

# In Their Words

My arm and head were bleeding. But I didn't feel any pain. No time for that.[1]

—ADOLPH GALLAND

Even before the war was done, Erich Hartmann's life, and those of all the other German soldiers, had been scrambled. Everything they had been taught to believe impossible had happened; everything they had been taught to believe inevitable had been proven a lie. When the dust settled, they marched ahead into whatever uncertain predicament the future held for them—for Hartmann this meant captivity, but for even the most fortunate of his peers this meant uncertainty in work, family, and everything else.

Although many German soldiers went about their postwar lives silently and as unobtrusively as possible, others chose the opposite approach. Encouraged by the Allied military establishment and their peers, quite a few *Wehrmacht* veterans became chroniclers of their own battles, publishing memoirs and articles that explained their time on the front, what it was like to serve under Hitler and his leadership, and what had, in their view, gone so terribly wrong from a military standpoint. As Halder had done earlier, many also took official roles that made them the war's primary, endorsed storytellers.

These Germans' testimonies meshed with the other laudatory works that were making their way onto bookshelves. There was a certain reciprocity to it all. The friendly chroniclers obtained from the aces the primary research information they needed to write their tales of heroism, while the soldiers received from the friendly chroniclers an established historical framework and the social permission to tell their stories using their own interpretations as the only necessary validating truths.

Many of the resultant memoirs are exaggerated accounts of bravery and chivalry, and they, too, aspire to be politics-free zones. One leading voice from the *Wehrmacht*, *Generalfeldmarschall* Erich von Manstein—considered by many to be the greatest commander in the German Army—published a history that was consumed for decades on both sides of the Atlantic. He was, in fact, a brilliant military mind whose expertise against the Soviets was deep and useful. But he had no time for matters of belief. In his writing, he "reveals early on that he is dealing almost exclusively with military affairs and is going to leave the political arena out," say Smelser and Davies. "This is convenient because it enables him to avoid entirely discussing the war in the East as one of racial enslavement and annihilation, as well as to avoid taking up any relationship he might have had with National Socialism."[2]

Manstein highlights one of the convenient facts about the German soldiers-turned-writers: they were really good at their job, so they had a lot of successes and adventures to talk about without needing to navel-gaze about the issues in the background. Many had led distinguished military campaigns over the course of the war and had ample victories to recall, High Command strategic mistakes to lament, and stories of universalizing human fortitude to share. Hitler's well-publicized late-war blunders were the perfect ways for these writers to superficially critique him while still avoiding much self-inspection in their storytelling.

Manstein, we should note, was eventually brought to trial on charges of war crimes (and convicted on nine counts), but this seems inconsequential to much of his audience. After his trial, his impassioned defense attorney published a book detailing the trial itself and the supposed nobility of his client. That book, not the verdicts, is what many people have remembered over the years.

Elsewhere, Rudel, our *Stuka* pilot and aerial observer, affirms that the air war was the best possible tool for the German curation of history, and that it, too, had its share of hardened converts sprinkled throughout. Rudel was of course a fantastic and amazingly accomplished soldier—as a dive-bomber pilot he destroyed more than 2,000 ground targets, including 519 Soviet tanks, and was the sole recipient of the Knight's Cross of the Iron Cross with Golden Oak Leaves, Swords and Diamonds. His peers said that he was faster than death. But he was also one of the Nazis' most dutiful protectors. After the war, he fled to Argentina, where he made friends with Juan Perón and created an organization called the *Kamaradenwerk* (roughly, "Comrade Operation"), which sheltered Nazis fleeing Germany because of their crimes and affiliations with Hitler. Argentina became a primary hiding spot for old Nazis (and the supposed final destination of Hitler, according to various Hitler-actually-lived conspiracy theorists) in large part because of Rudel's work.

In 1982, Rudel's funeral made the pages of *Der Spiegel* after several attendees were sighted performing Nazi salutes in his honor (an illegal act in Germany). Right after they did so, a pair of *Luftwaffe* F-4 Phantom jets appeared to make a special fly-by over the ceremony, even though such a thing would not have been officially condoned. The funeral site was on a regular flight path, so the jets' arrival could have been incidental—but at least one attendee reported that the Phantoms wagged their wings to those below and then climbed "abruptly upward." The pastor running the ceremony, apparently emotional, had to stop and clear his throat before continuing. A national scandal ensued.[3]

Nazi ties notwithstanding, Rudel's memoir, *Stuka Pilot*, has sold more than a million copies internationally, largely because it is almost 300 pages of breathless, heart-pounding action. It is a tale of gritted-teeth soldiering, and Rudel takes the fighter pilot's swagger to the extreme. "I am not afraid of death," he writes. "I have looked him in the eye for a matter of seconds and have never been the first to lower my gaze."[4] Passages like this might make your heart race or your eyes roll; either way, they sure are entertaining.

One key to Rudel and the other aces' acceptance was that they were legitimized by their former enemies. This often took the form of forewords and introductions that these other pilots wrote for their books. These passages, sometimes short and sometimes rather long, can seem almost conciliatory—*It's ok, reader, this guy isn't so bad.* Douglas Bader, a celebrated British ace who made an appearance in several leading *Luftwaffe* pilots' lives, gingerly endorses Rudel in the foreword to *Stuka Pilot*: "I do not agree with a number of the conclusions he draws or with some of his thoughts ... [but] I am happy to write this short forward to Rudel's book, since although I only met him for a couple of days he is, by any standards, a gallant chap and I wish him luck."[5] These words sound more like Bader dictated them on the way to lunch than as if he sat before a desk and carefully recorded them, but they were all Rudel needed. Even on the cover of the 2016 reprint of *Stuka Pilot*, Bader's name, as the recognizable Allied contributor, is almost as prominent as Rudel's.

Rudel and Manstein show us how permissive readers, military establishments, and aviation fans have been with German soldiers-turned-authors, however obvious their connections to the Third Reich have been. The writers and their fans would have us believe that Nazism was always of minor importance and that the pilots were more or less consistent in their disregard for it. But if you look closer, there is, in fact, a spectrum of belief discernible among the aviators. You can't write a 300-page book and not give away something about your convictions.

At this point, in lieu of trying to be exhaustive in covering these pilots (something that would be impossible in the confines of this book), I'll clarify what that spectrum looked like and where Erich Hartmann might have fitted within it. To do it, I'll go deeper into the writings of three more helpful examples: Adolf Galland, Heinz Knoke, and Elisabeth Hartmann.

## The First

Adolf Galland's status among *Luftwaffe* pilots was cemented when he published *The First and the Last*, one of the most celebrated memoirs to come from a German World War II soldier. Its copyright date of 1954 places it immediately ahead of the reanimated West German Air Force, giving Galland the dual benefits of perspective (a few years of reflection after the war) and authority (no new military narrative to overwrite the one he describes). His writing is spry and detailed; we zoom through the early weeks of the Battle of Britain and follow along as Galland closes in on a troubling realization: that the *Luftwaffe* is filled with spirited combatants but doomed from the start by its leadership.

Galland, almost uniquely, seems to feel a duty to describe the High Command's bullheadedness and Hitler's fatal lack of imagination—something that has endeared him to pilots and historians all over the world. He credits Hitler for a few insights, such as his proper skepticism of the faulty He 177 bomber, but he essentially tells us that if it had ever dawned on Hitler that his *Stukas* would somehow fail to deliver *Blitzkrieg*, Germany might have been able to adapt in time.[6] Throughout the work, Galland markets himself as the realist in a surreal environment. He is very convincing.

The memoir focuses on the Western air war, and it shares some of the limitations in scope that we see in other books on the *Luftwaffe*. Had it been taken out of the first person it could have served as a conventional, linear history of the *Luftwaffe* from about 1935–45—told with detail, masses of tactical notes, and glimpses into the higher leadership. But despite the bookends he imposed on the narrative, Galland's accounts still show his worldview, inner struggles, and personality. He fails, for example, to convincingly repudiate the hateful ideology that propped up his career (Galland appreciated Hitler's fondness for the "Anglo-Saxon race," once lamenting the racial void that would have been left had the Germans ever needed to slaughter the British) even while he provides the best leadership-level critique we have from someone who wore the *Luftwaffe* uniform from before the war to the end.[7]

His writing is fluid and cinematic, echoing the gung-ho action you see in other Germans' accounts. At one point he describes being shot down and nearly killed by a Spitfire, showing us a fascinating running internal narrative:

> Hell broke loose in my crate. Now they've got me! That's what happens when I take my eyes away for a couple of seconds! Something hard hit my head and arm … [t]he wings were ripped by cannon fire. I was sitting half in the open.
> My arm and head were bleeding. But I didn't feel any pain. No time for that.[8]

(Erich Hartmann's biographers say that he would always talk to himself in the heat of battle or in stressful situations, too, and they use that as a similarly effective narrative device.)

In the end, Galland parachuted into a meadow and was rescued by friendly Germans. After a cognac and a cigarette, Galland says, his nerves calmed and a surgeon patched him up at a naval hospital. He made sure to thank the surgeon for letting him smoke on the operating table.[9]

Galland scored most of his 104 kills early in the war on the Western Front, and that total would certainly have been higher had he either flown more missions or moved to the Eastern Front. His kills were interrupted by his promotion to *General der Jagdflieger*—leader of Germany's fighter force—in November 1941, at which time he was prohibited from flying combat missions because his superiors feared he would get shot down over enemy territory or killed. In the role, Galland repeatedly questioned the Nazi higher-ups, but his leadership and experience still earned him trust and deference. One of the more fascinating parts of his career was his simmering feud with Hermann Göring. Galland routinely exposed Göring's shortsightedness and impulsiveness, and was punished for it. "Göring refused to understand that his *Luftwaffe*, this sparkling and so far successful sword, threatened to turn blunt in his hand," Galland wrote.[10] After several years of jabbing Göring and dealing with his bullheadedness (which Galland rightly judged to be costing German lives), Galland was dismissed from his post and, for a time, forced into house arrest. He made it back into action soon enough, though, as the commander of the jet fighter wing that was testing Messerschmitt Me 262s in the last hopeless months of the conflict. This was *JV 44*, the jet unit Hartmann visited but never contributed to. Galland described the Me 262, which whistled through the air with neither the torque nor the deafening rumble of piston engines, as a delightfully different flight experience, and he claimed several kills with it before the war was done.

In some ways, Galland resembled Hartmann. Galland was a decade older and had been flying and fighting as early as the Spanish Civil War, but both were part of the best-trained and best-equipped cohorts that entered the

*Luftwaffe* early and earned it its excellent reputation. Galland helped develop a culture of excellence among the *Luftwaffe's* pilots, whether or not it was sanctioned by his leadership; Hartmann reaped the rewards of that culture and championed it in his own way. Both men could be extremely tactical, focused solely on their objectives and the most efficient ways to achieve them, and they were celebrated by their peers while being begrudgingly admired by some of their enemies.

As a result, Hartmann's biographers describe Galland with a lustfulness they usually reserve for their Blond Knight:

> His heavy black eyebrows, well-trimmed mustache, and strong, square chin form an appropriate setting for his salient physical feature—his eyes. Fiction writers often attribute penetrating eyes to fighter pilots. With Galland, it is no fiction. His eyes have a penetration and sharpness that set him aside from ordinary men.[11]

Even Galland's British obituarists remembered him as an appealing outlier, a figurehead and charming agitator in the *Luftwaffe* hierarchy:

> Adolf Galland was the most famous and dashing of the *Luftwaffe* aces who duelled with Fighter Command ... Galland's career didn't suffer from [his] display of chutzpah, which enhanced an image, carefully fostered in the German press, of a swashbuckling, darkly romantic young flier, chomping on a black cheroot while being prepared by his groundcrew for yet another sortie across the English Channel.[12]

But what of Hitler? Galland described the *Führer* a lot like he described aerial campaigns: factually, almost journalistically. After Galland received his Oak Leaves to the Knight's Cross, he met Hitler privately, and he says he told the *Führer* about the various misrepresentations of the air war circulating in state propaganda and among the *Luftwaffe* leadership. He also told Hitler how much he respected British combatants, fearing, he writes, that the dictator might get irritated at him for complimenting the enemy. But Hitler apparently echoed Galland's admiration for the gentlemen across the Channel. "I must admit that I was highly impressed by the *Führer's* words at the time," Galland recalled.[13]

There are complications in Galland's decades-old disassociation with Hitler and Nazism, however. He, alongside Rudel, spent a lot of time in Argentina after the war, helping the country and its dictator raise an air force. When Adenauer was organizing the *Bundeswehr*, Galland was the most obvious possible choice for leadership—until, apparently, a memo went out from the chief of staff of the U.S. Air Force, General Nathan Twining, warning against bringing in Galland due to his supposed Nazi sympathies. Historian James Corum writes that:

Although a great part of the German effort [during rearmament] seems to have been geared toward reassuring the Western Allies that former Nazis would have no place in the *Bundeswehr*, this was never a major concern among the U.S. or British military staffs. The Americans and British military had been working closely with the Germans for several years at this point, in compiling the historical studies.[14]

Twining also pointed out that "Galland had associated with known Neo-Nazis to include Hans Ulrich Rudel and that Galland had worked in 1948 as an air advisor to the Perón dictatorship."[15] He said that Galland's appointment was "completely their choice" but made it clear that Galland wouldn't have been a favorable option according to American leadership.[16] It's unclear how, or through what paths, the note made its way through the *Bundeswehr* chain of command. Soon after, leaders announced that Josef Kammhuber would lead the new air force. Note that the above doesn't actually say anything about Galland's professed or private convictions—it was probably enough to the American leaders that he had propped up the Argentinian dictator—but you do have to wonder what guided him, and the others, on their forays in South America.

If the pilots' self-proclaimed chivalry and the fact that they spent their days killing each other seem incompatible, Galland's memoir at least helps illustrate how those ideas can coexist among the fighter fraternity. Like Hartmann and many others, Galland liked to tell stories of pilots' generosity toward one another almost as much as he liked to detail how he won dogfights. One such story involves Douglas Bader, who was shot down in 1941 over German-occupied France only to be surprised by the welcome reception he got from the Germans. Bader had become a successful pilot with two artificial legs, after a flying accident when he was young. On top of the misfortune of getting shot down, one of his artificial legs was lost in the wreckage of his Spitfire. Galland immediately ordered the retrieval of Bader's limb from the wreckage and transmitted instructions to the British, over an SOS radio channel, so they could approach with immunity near where Bader was being held and airdrop a spare set of legs that Bader kept tucked away in his bedroom at home.

Unfortunately for the Germans, the British, never ones to waste fuel or a good flying day, delivered the legs but extended their mission to drop some bombs on nearby German targets. "This was not a very friendly reply to our well-meant proposal," Galland said.[17]

After trying to persuade Galland to let him fly a Bf 109 so he could gather intelligence, Bader escaped his imprisonment through a hospital window by climbing down tied-together bed sheets. He later described the events with characteristic frankness: "I am not one of those who regard war as a game of cricket—first to shoot at each other and then to shake hands."[18]

This tension between self-assigned moral values and the practical reality of war was also captured, of all places, on the 1960 reprint of Galland's memoir. On that printing, the publisher decided to use available blank space on the last page to advertise a different book, *The Rise and Fall of Hermann Göring*. The ad copy reads: "As creator of the dreaded Gestapo, Göring was responsible for bloodthirsty party purges, concentration camps and 'extermination' of Jews. Yet his sportsman's code would not permit him to shoot a tame deer."[19] What was undoubtedly a copywriter's attempt at drama provides a good historical lesson. These men—even a snake like Göring—really believed they were conducting themselves according to a set of honorable principles, even (maybe even especially) when their actions and practical effects belied those principles.

## The Last

Heinz Knoke titled his memoir *I Flew for the Führer*, and he meant it. For a member of the *Luftwaffe* writing after the fact he is unusually political and unusually National Socialist. When it came time for him to describe his enthusiasm for the Nazi war, he started as other frank participants have:

> It must be remembered ... that the fundamental principles and ideals [of National Socialism] appealed very strongly to young people. We supported those ideals with unqualified enthusiasm, and we were able to take a real pride in the powerful resurgence of our beloved country during the years when we were young.

Knoke, however, never quite let the enthusiasm go.

He had his first ride in an airplane in 1938, when he was 17, and his first posting orders were to *JG-52*, Hartmann's wing. It's unlikely the two ever flew together, however; Knoke transferred away from the Eastern Front to join *JG-1*, with whom he flew against the United States Army Air Corps and shot down heavy bombers as they came in waves to pummel German factories and other strategic targets.

Unlike Hartmann, Knoke was an explicit supporter of Nazi ideals and wrote his wartime memoir without censoring his lust for the Party. He was a compelling writer, too, which contributed to his book's popularity on both sides of the Atlantic.

In one passage, he describes the death of a Sergeant Schmidt, who was with Knoke as they took their first solos in the Bf 109 before going operational. It's a gruesome reminder of the 109's nasty temperament, as well as the danger of even *training* to be a fighter pilot, much less flying in combat:

> [Schmidt's] aircraft suddenly stalled because of insufficient speed and spun out of control, crashing into the ground and exploding a few hundred feet short of the end of the runway. We all raced like madmen over to the scene of the crash. I was the first to arrive. Schmidt had been thrown clear, and was lying several feet away from the flaming wreckage. He was screaming like an animal, covered in blood. I stooped down over the body of my comrade, and saw that both legs were missing. I held his head. The screams were driving me insane. Blood poured over my hands. I have never felt so helpless in my life. The screaming finally stopped, and became an even more terrible silence. Then Kuhl and the others arrived, but by that time Schmidt was dead.
>
> Major von Kornatzky ordered training to be resumed forthwith, and less than an hour later the next 109 was brought out. This time it was my turn.[20]

Part of what makes Knoke's book so interesting is its diary format. You follow him day by day, through the early times of promise all the way to the final catastrophe. His earlier entries are more wistful about Hitler; later on, his views get a little more complicated and dour. There is a vast middle section of dogfight stories, bonds with comrades, and explanations of the slow crumbling of the *Luftwaffe*.

Then, in a flash at the end, Knoke resumes his political stance. In several fluid steps, he pivots to focus on the new scapegoat—Soviet Russia. It is early 1945 as he writes this, but he is already foreshadowing the rhetorical tactics that others will use:

"It is useless for us to trouble ourselves now over such academic questions as responsibility and war guilt," he writes.[21] "[We] all look forward to the day when the Western Allies will come to realize that it is not Germany which is the real menace to their life and liberty, but Soviet Russia." Here is the most efficient rhetorical distraction you're likely to see from a *Wehrmacht* apologist. First we scoff at questions of responsibility—*How can one really tell who's to blame in war, anyway?* Then comes the quick refocusing on a new enemy. Those blood-coated Soviet spears still point at Germany, Knoke is telling us, and the Soviets will do anything to get their ultimate victory. Without irony, apparently, he writes that "The Russian soldier understands what he is fighting for: Communism has turned every last one of them into a fanatic."[22] This is another pattern that gets more visible with time: the Nazi sympathizer complaining about other people's fanaticism.

Elsewhere, Knoke describes what he calls the "despotism without conscience" of the Nazi leadership, suggesting that he broke with the Party at least on its decisions to embrace "war crimes." He says the Nazis' most evil actions left German combatants feeling "disgusted and indignant."[23] But we also know that this was not a very thorough repudiation of Nazism. After the war, Knoke became a politician and a member of the neo-Nazi Socialist Reich Party. This party was banned in West Germany because it was so explicitly racist and nationalist. Many of its supporters, which included Rudel, saw it as the natural continuation of National Socialism in a new postwar context.

All told, Knoke's outspokenness against the Nazi leadership was episodic and politically expedient. First he was elected as a member of the Socialist Reich Party in 1951, before it was banned. Then he published his memoir in 1952, presumably softening his public image and engendering some level of sympathy for his wartime trials. Then he ran and was elected as a member of the mainstream, right-of-center Free Democratic Party in 1956. Another story reworked; another Nazi ally reintegrated.

## The Family

Galland and Knoke help us understand the spectrum of convictions available to *Luftwaffe* pilots. Galland, essentially a tactician, fashioned himself as a pragmatist with comparatively soft inclinations toward Nazism. Knoke, on the other hand, was an apologist even after the end. Hartmann, as you can tell, was more like Galland by disposition, though he was less of a student of people and leadership. He probably would have championed Galland; it's unclear what he would have had to say about Knoke or Rudel.

If we're really looking to compare the three, the closest thing we have to a memoir from Erich Hartmann is a book by his wife. He apparently helped her put it together over several years during retirement, though his fingerprints on the work are hard to discern (he isn't listed as an author). Around the same time Hartmann sat down with his biographers to interview for *The Blond Knight of Germany*, Ursula must have recognized what a trove of photos and mementos she had to offer, and she published them. The book, *German Fighter Ace Erich Hartmann: The Life Story of the World's Highest Scoring Ace*, is more of a coffee table pictorial than a biography, but because of this, it's a surprisingly comprehensive and refreshing chronicle.

Its introduction is a condensed summary of Hartmann's life, but the vast collection of photos that follow (the book is 296 pages long) show Hartmann in his early years in China, in the Hitler Youth, in flight training, in courtship with Ursula, and of course on the warfront. There are even photos of Hartmann in the Soviet camps—surprising additions—and plenty of shots from his time in the *Bundeswehr*. We learn, interestingly, that while Hartmann was in the *Bundeswehr* he rubbed shoulders with Neil Armstrong and sat in the Gemini space capsule. We learn that his Sabres transitioned from glistening natural metal to muted camouflage under his jurisdiction (but those black tulips stayed). And we learn, amusingly, that while leading *JG-71* he engineered a gizmo affectionately known as the "Bubimat," which attached to the rear end of a Sabre when the tail section was removed and blasted jet exhaust onto the runway to melt ice and snow. (The Sabre's rear fuselage and tail, ingeniously, could be easily detached as a unit and wheeled away on a trolley, fully exposing the jet engine for maintenance and replacement.) Similar to the T-shaped attachment to a household vacuum hose, the Bubimat redirected and spread the jet exhaust over a wide path behind the Sabre as it inched down the runway. Photos of the Bubimat, apparently taken during the first winter at Ahlhorn, show spectacular clouds of steam and dispersed slush created by a few thousand pounds of jet thrust—as well as bare, wet runway where the Sabre had passed by.

The book humanizes Hartmann in a way that his other biographies never did. A photo isn't presumptuous or argumentative; it doesn't exaggerate in the way that an enamored fan might. This photo chronicle, finally, accomplishes for Hartmann what other aces' written memoirs sometimes accomplished for them: it shows him in his element, dealing with diverse challenges and successes, yielding under the strain of such an uncommon military career. You can see the distance in his eyes when, 100 pounds in weight, he returned from captivity to throngs of supporters and townspeople who'd heard of his arrival. If you look hard enough, you can even see a hint of discomfort when he's surrounded by *Bundeswehr* brass at official functions. Elsewhere, you get a clear vision of the closeness between the new *Luftwaffe*'s members and their American counterparts. Hartmann's retraining in the American Southwest wasn't solely (or even primarily) about the planes; it was about aligning the two countries and their Cold War combatants—a crucial task—and the connection and mutual admiration are clear here.

The snapshots from the camps—there are only four of them—all apparently came from Gryazovets. In one, taken in the near-dark, Hartmann looks like an entirely different person. He's worn out, blank, vulnerable. But in the others you can see that there were fleeting times of entertainment on the camp grounds. In one, he's reading one of the few letters from Ursula that made it to him, grinning like he did on the warfront. In another, he sits at what he and his fellow detainees called the *Fliegerecke*—the Pilots' Corner—which appears to be a small table with a checked tablecloth and a photo of someone's wife propped up. The caption says Hartmann would meet there with three other pilots each day, chatting and sitting on a birchwood bench together.

There is also a collection of documents reproduced. Among them are his first telegram to Ursula when he crossed into Germany again, and an excerpt from the speech Hartmann gave to his hometown just after his return. In that speech, he expresses his thanks for such a welcome:

> I can hardly find the words to express the feelings in the heart of an old soldier when, after ten years of slavery, ten years of experiencing cruelty, suppression and no rights, he can suddenly see that he has not lost his human face, but rather that he can once again be a man among men …
>
> It was the sole support from the military members, the town, my schoolmates, which continuously gave me the strength to get through.[24]

After his introduction, he goes into a detailed, almost journalistic, explanation of what happened in Russia—the fake war-crimes trial, the various accusations he faced, his zigzags around the vast country. At one point, he says, he asked a guard if he could at least keep a photo of his wife, since his handlers were confiscating everything else. "It not necessary, she has Americans there, and can keep herself amused," said the guard.[25]

The written and photographic narrative Ursula builds here aligns with the hero-building of the other commentators. "What makes Erich Hartmann stand out from the crowd even by today's standards is that personal integrity and unshakable character which helped him remain true to his convictions while enduring merciless burdens," the inside jacket flap says.[26] But her remarkable images show us Hartmann the person, not just Hartmann the hero, and because of it they bring us closer to him. Thumbing through the photos can bring about all kinds of emotions, partly because they make Hartmann less theoretical—less historical—and more tangible. These emotions might include anger at the sight of the swastika on the young Hartmann's arm (no reference to it in the copy) or sadness at the sight of those photos from Gryazovets. Despite the smile on his face, despite the kitschy Pilots' Corner, it is crushing that any life would be derailed so thoroughly and for so long.

And then there was the telegram Hartmann sent from Herleshausen, reproduced well enough that you can see the teletype, the *Deutsche Bundespost* header, and the penciled notations from those who took and delivered it. That single image says more about the ordeal than anything else in the book. You shudder to put yourself in Hartmann's position: away for 10 years, finally back on your home soil, transmitting a simple, 14-word message to your partner, who you hope is still waiting.

## CHAPTER 15

# The Production of Meaning

Was there ever such a thing as pure memory? I doubt it. Even when we convince ourselves that we're being dispassionate, sticking to the bald facts with no self-serving decorations or omissions, our memory remains as elusive as a bar of wet soap.

—JOHN LE CARRÉ[1]

In 1990, Germans recoiled when a historical exhibit called "War of Extermination: The Crimes of the *Wehrmacht*, 1941–1944" toured the country, tearing off many of the scabs left over from World War II and exposing some of the nastiest actions of Germans on the Eastern Front. At a time that was supposed to be about unification and national healing, the exhibit simultaneously introduced new generations to the moral corruption of the war and reintroduced older generations to topics they thought they'd left behind.

By then, the Berlin Wall had crumbled and Germany was one country again, but for many citizens the integration still felt as if it were only complete politically. The full implications of the end to the postwar partitioning—the "aftermath of the aftermath," someone said—were still developing. People knew that there would be lingering economic and social challenges, and these were easy enough to point to. The GDR (East Germany) and the Federal Republic (West Germany) were vastly different places. Westerners welcomed their embattled neighbors into the last decade of the 20th century from the perspective of the victors of the Cold War, somewhat like the Americans had welcomed so many German émigrés after 1945; those men and women who had stayed in the east, conversely, either willingly or because they couldn't get out, redeveloped the GDR's antiquated and faltering infrastructure with as much tribulation as anyone should have expected. Even the *Luftwaffe* was confused: temporarily, American-made F-4 Phantoms were part of the same air force as Russian-made MiG-29s.

All around, Germans began to reevaluate their place in their own history and their country's place in the world. It was a reasonable time to reopen all kinds of questions about World War II, the conflict that had brought about the split in the first place, and take up related conversations that had gone on in the time since the Cold War began. There was an unavoidable incentive, too, since the elder Germans who could still retrieve first-hand memories were dying.

The exhibit questioned the widespread perception of cleanliness in the German armed forces, mostly in the context of the ground war on the Eastern Front. Interviews with elderly ex-soldiers, as well as thousands of unearthed photographs and written records, promoted fresh assessments of what went on during the war years. Academic historians showed not just that German officers ordered lines of innocent people shot and kicked into mass graves, but also that they could routinely count on the compliance of their subordinates. Infantrymen on the scene posed for the memento as if they were at some famous landmark. These actions, which violated widely and clearly accepted rules of warfare, had always seemed confined to the other side of the Iron Curtain, where the Soviets were the ones who sunk to the lowest levels of conduct.

Moreover, people realized that the atrocities of the Third Reich could never have been carried out by a select group of men. It literally took an army, a navy, and an air force to support the infrastructure of the Holocaust, perpetuate the Nazi program of ideological reform, and strip every city over which the virus of National Socialism had spread of the artwork, traditions, and spirits of discourse that contained its culture.

Several German generations stopped and looked at each other. One was the surviving war generation, dwindling in number; another was the men and women who had been young adults in the hottest days of the Cold War, when a new enemy and a new political discourse had seized their attention. Still another was the late-teens of the 1990s, who were going into national service for a country that had never, in their lifetime, been under fascist control. The elders opened their memories to scrutiny cautiously, not knowing how they would be received. Many in the younger generations weren't really sure how to receive them.

But gradually, conversation brought freer scrutiny. Memories came to the surface, and as they did, complexity, not simple innocence or guilt, became the defining feature of the German war experience. Emerging media, notably the Internet, added depth, new revelations, and many new voices—as well as a good deal of misinterpretation and nonsense. A concurrent revival of third-person historical nonfiction as popular reading introduced us to many previously unknown characters from the Nazi years. Fifty years after the fact, the history of a German century was being recrafted.

There were no pictures of Erich Hartmann among those retrieved by the historians and the old soldiers, and he probably never nailed together a makeshift gallows for partisan dissidents. The fighter pilots followed a much different path than the soldiers fighting it out on the ground—a privileged one, as Hartmann showed us when he ditched his aircraft in 1943 and watched as the *Waffen-SS* unit protecting him mowed down a couple hundred Soviets. But the exhibit is still relevant to him because it clarified just how consistently Hartmann's story has been told using the same cleansing, simplifying habits of mind that have defined our understanding of the Eastern Front more broadly.

"Crimes of the Wehrmacht" exposed much of what we assume about Germany in World War II to be wrong; it also demonstrated, through the reactions of its audiences, that the meaning of the historical record depends not just on the authors of that record, but on the recipients of it. To change the meaning, you need only change one of those variables. Historical content, however accurate or inaccurate, doesn't stick with us because it's composed; it sticks with us because it's consumed.

Historian Seth Cotlar, in a discussion of Thomas Paine and America's early democratic citizens, expresses this idea as the "history of reception." People throughout history show interesting patterns in how they receive and process ideas, and these patterns are based on their time, place, and frames of reference. An American Southerner from 1950 would probably receive any given biography of Abraham Lincoln differently than a New Yorker from 2000, for example.

"When we locate the production of meaning at the point of reception rather than the point of authorship," says Cotlar, meaning becomes about how the work was "reproduced, circulated, received, and contested."[2]

This is a useful insight because it helps us see why the popular version of Hartmann's story has taken hold for 50 years. It was *reproduced* by like-minded advocates who mostly thought the same things about the German aces. It was *circulated* widely because of a hungry market and the prolificness of its authors. It was *received* happily, in part because of the scarcity of competing ideas and because it provided moral clarity just when the West needed it. It was *contested*, as you know by now, fairly little.

## Service Rendered

The Baden Württemberg state library, in Stuttgart, is a heavy gray stone of a building. It's built along a bustling street named after Konrad Adenauer (a heavy gray stone of a man, some might be inclined to say), which in turn is built next to the sprawling and wonderful *Akademiegarten*, a green space fit for all sorts of wanderings. By the time you walk the path to the entrance of the library, the sounds and distractions of the city have mostly faded off, soaked up or concealed by long-established tree canopies.

When I visited, a couple of days after I had visited Weil im Schönbuch, I was struck by the airy architecture, abundant light, and extensive use of glass. This library is a degree grander than most U.S. libraries and archives, and the mood that day was calm and businesslike. Analysis happens there, you can't help but think. A few employees metered out important documents and resources to users searching for all sorts of answers.

One of those employees, a smiling woman whose name I never wrote down, took an interest in my project and promptly provided a list of resources that any German resident or researcher might encounter on Erich Hartmann. We assessed those available works and picked out the ones that promised the most depth. Most of these still contained brief, perfunctory encyclopedia-type blurbs—you can find profiles of all the great aces, each with the obligatory wartime mug shot and a couple of dry paragraphs—and anything deeper was harder to come by. Among the lengthier, more detailed works, a pattern stood out: they're translated from American English and written by the same people.

The main source for Germans, just like Americans, is still the Toliver/Constable biography. We found an old, creased copy of *Holt Hartmann von Himmel!* easily enough, and holding the book highlighted the fact that what Germans read about Erich Hartmann is essentially what Americans read about him. This is not to say that their reception of him is the same—German education, for example, provides context, detail, and nuance about the war that are unavailable to even the most interested young American students—but the same central messages persist. This says something about how integrated the West German and American ways of thinking became, and how little these carefully curated and translated conversations have been supplanted over time.

People are starting to notice the obsolescence of these works, both within and outside Germany. A 2016 workshop organized by the *Arbeitskreis Militärgeschichte* ("Working Group [for] Military History") in Munich singled out Toliver and Constable's book for lacking critical reflection, relying on old stereotypes of Russians and Germans, and altogether excluding "the political and social consequences of the Second World War."[3] Smelser and Davies offer a corroborating view: "The Cold War made possible the success of the German accounts of the war. By the 1990s, as the Cold War was coming to an end, the narrative produced by these works had long since achieved canonical status and nourished the spate of books published."[4]

Smelser and Davies' book, *The Myth of the Eastern Front*, is cited increasingly often in the context of the German war effort and provides what appears to be the most direct critique of the biography in circulation, save for some eye-rolling book reviews out there that muse about Toliver and Constable's lust for their protagonist. It suggests a bit of a pendulum swing away from the earlier works, particularly within academia.

These authors see Hartmann's biography as a quintessential piece of Cold War historicization, and they seize on its vulnerabilities as a historical document:

> Hartmann's story, the writers assure the reader somewhat gratuitously, should be seen "as an indictment of war," which it certainly is not …
>
> Sketching Hartmann's character as it was revealed in Russian captivity, the authors describe characteristics that the Nazis themselves always admired in leadership …
>
> There is also a strain of the Nazi antipathy to modernity as expressed by the authors in characterizing Hartmann. His values are traditional, not modern …
>
> Nor is there missing an ingredient of the nonspecific religiosity favored by the Nazis.[5]

Hartmann's fans will recoil at the brashness, and you can imagine them deploying that ultimate curse word in history—*revisionism!*—to discredit these arguments before they're taken in. They will continue to lean into the positive and the inspirational, and with some good reason. They will point out that Hartmann furthered a system of fighting that sought to locate inspiring moral codes in war (oxymoronic to some, sensible and necessary to others); that he clung to the Geneva Conventions in captivity, arguing forcefully for their uniform and even expanded application to soldiers of any nation, in any war; that he resisted oppressive Communism and at least gestured toward disavowing his *Führer*; that he was a faithful companion to Ursula under unimaginable conditions; and that he said some of the right things, after the fact, about hatred and prejudice and resisting judgment of entire groups of people.

But change is setting in. As Smelser and Davies conclude:

> One wants to take nothing away from Hartmann in terms of his skill and daring as a fighter pilot. However, to divorce his exploits from the regime, which he loyally served and from

whose leader he accepted its second highest decoration, renders no service. Nor does placing him not in the historical context of a war of racial conquest and annihilation, but rather in a romanticized feudal joust between knights.

I'll go a step further than "renders no service." It's not just that the many earlier stories haven't done us any good: as a historical inheritance from which we're supposed to put together our view of the world, they have set us back. They are damaging to the truth, damaging to our assessment of Hartmann, Germany, the war, and all kinds of related issues, and—most importantly—damaging to its readers' understanding of history itself as something complex, ambiguous, and fluid. These writers submitted their work to the historical record with the intent that it be taken seriously as fact and used to guide our understandings of the war. They made specific truth claims about the soldiers, the war, and history—claims that they support using little more than anecdotal testimonies from the German aces themselves. The inadequacy of this approach has become clearer over time.

The French writer Laurent Binet, in his account of Reinhard Heydrich's assassination, wrote: "I just hope that, however bright and blinding the veneer of fiction that covers this fabulous story, you will still be able to see through it to the historical reality that lies behind."[6] Binet's key insight was that the veneer is there no matter what, and any work of history tells you about the author just as it tells you about the subject.

I think now of Eric Vuillard, another French writer, who described the fateful meeting in 1933 of the German and Austrian captains of industry who helped Hitler consolidate his support and quickly destroy Austria's self-determination. "I don't know who was first in line," Vuillard tells us, recounting the walk those important men made up gilded stairways to seal their country's dark fate, "and ultimately it doesn't matter: all twenty-four had to do exactly the same thing, follow the same path."[7] Vuillard was telling us about two things at once: the fascinating setting through which these men passed on their way to the meeting with Hitler, and the moral impotence with which they made the walk.

We can end where we started, in a sense, which is with Manfred von Richthofen. William E. Burrows, in his biography of the World War I ace, concludes:

> Heroes—war heroes—may be invented by government and the press, but they are "built" by the ordinary men who live vicariously through them ... But the cost of war heroes is very high.[8]

Burrows might have meant to say that hero-building is costly because it is complacent. It tugs us toward the sensational, the warped, the uncritical. The utility in our hero stories, if you think about it, is also their weakness: they're simple, easily remembered, decadently assuring. They can inspire us to act in remarkable and transformative ways, but because they so frequently prefer simplicity to rigor, conviction to doubt, they don't always prepare us for a complex world.

They condition us, instead, to recoil at difference. To comfort ourselves with talk of universality, moral simplicity, and resolution when, in fact, the tools we need to develop most today have more to do with adaptability, tolerance, and complexity. This could be one reason why the anti-hero has emerged alongside the superhero. We want to see layers, conflict, even failure in our main characters. We want to see them doing the difficult moral work. We want to see a little more of ourselves in them.

There's a practical element to all of this. The more we treat our historical characters as if their lives were black and white, the more we expect our own lives to be black and white. This harms us. It harms us as citizens, as leaders, as professionals, and as commentators. It provides little value for navigating an increasingly complex world. But when, on the other hand, we treat our historical characters as if they were complicated, worthy of care, and occasionally messy, we can see our own lives in the same way.

This does more than get us closer to the truth in history. It helps us know ourselves and our neighbors, and helps us create a future that is intelligently informed by the past and those all-too-frequent, all-too-horrid mistakes we've made—so that we might see the next one coming.

# Conclusion

I always try to keep faith in my doubts, Sister Berthe.

—Mother Abbess, *the sound of music*[1]

I visited Hartmann's gravesite one morning between squalls, when the cemetery grass was wet and dark. The sky was the same. I seemed to be the only one around, presumably because the other visitors could choose whether or not to brave the weather; I had a schedule to keep before flying home.

I found Hartmann's grave easily enough because I recognized the large, whitish boulder that served as his headstone. I'd seen photos of it online, usually taken by other visitors who posted captions to the shots with messages of admiration or gratitude. My reaction to seeing Hartmann's place of rest was more conflicted, though. I was excited, for sure, but also tentative. I noted how the rain changed his site, giving it an energy. Water sprinted down the vertical crevasses in the boulder as if drawn to the earth by some additional accelerating force.

I saw then that there were two women tending someone else's grave nearby, and they glanced over to me as I approached. They had a small wheeled cart for trucking in a few new flowers, and on impulse I diverted toward them.

In the moment or two it took to reach them, I did a mental review of the several ways to express "I'm a writer" in German. I felt vaguely uncomfortable interrogating them in a cemetery (*Is this insensitive? What are the customs in these situations?*) but by this point I was invested. The women were a generation apart, one middle-aged and one probably in her seventies, so this seemed like a good chance to gauge generational understandings. Maybe they'd be experts, or maybe they wouldn't even know who Hartmann was.

They didn't speak much English, but they gave me the space to form my German sentences and stumble around for expressions. We shared some of those tension-relieving chuckles that come when communication is hard, and they gave me patience and smiles. I had the immediate impression that maybe these ladies were, or had been, teachers.

The older woman remembered when Hartmann was a townsman following his time in the *Bundeswehr*. He was a quiet, but constant, presence in town and was undetachable from his wife, she said. She recalled Hartmann foggily but with interest, a little like how someone might think back to who the old police chief or local preacher had been.

The younger woman—the daughter, I learned—knew less about him personally but more about his gravesite. His was one of the more elaborate ones. She was the one doing the planting, and she pointed me toward his site and encouraged me to take my time there. When I told her I was from the U.S., she asked what I did for a living (magazine editor), how long I'd been interested in Hartmann (two years), and why I persisted with the project (it's difficult).

It's an interesting thing to stand before someone's grave when you never knew them. I have to admit it felt a little presumptuous at the time, almost self-serving. What did I really have to say in this moment? What offering of respect or acknowledgment, past some superficial admiration for someone else's hero, could I contribute? I never really answered those questions for myself. I decided to observe the site as a journalist might, be as mindful of the experience as I could, and figure out the meaning later.

I returned to the women, told them that this had been a valuable experience, and wished them well. I didn't get any revelations from them because, to be honest, I left far too many questions unasked. But they learned quite a bit about me, and in an interesting way this actually helped me clarify my approach. I became more aware of my own distance from Hartmann, and I understood my preconceptions about him better. I became aware of my own love for stories, and the unknown, and being a small part of history's search crew.

I left with a clear lesson, and it informed every month and year that remained in this project: history is about listening, and it matters what kind of listener you are. It's about standing and observing in the rain when you're not yet really sure what you're doing. It's about asking questions so that you might get answers, not affirmations. It's about proceeding even if you're nervous and you can't fully form your sentences. It's about resisting some grand assessment until you've done the work.

# What We Can Say

Today I'm no more settled in my beliefs about "Erich-Hartmann-the-Man" than I was when this project started. If anything, I'm even less inclined to categorize him, to define him for people, or to submit a black-and-white judgment. I'm tired of those.

What I do understand, far better than when I started, is the nature of Erich Hartmann's story and his legend. And that, after all, was my real mission. "Hartmann-the-Man" will keep eluding us, slipping out of our sights, as it were, just when we think we've got him; but "Hartmann-the-Legend" will remain alive, discoverable, traceable, observable, documentable. I hope that I have contributed in some way to broadening its appeal and reach, and to enabling today's readers to inspect it and get some lessons from it.

One such lesson, which I've taken to heart and will be trying to apply to my own life, is that the complacency I discussed earlier isn't exactly the absence of interest or investment. Complacency is in fact a decision—an unearned indulgence, as the German writer Michael Sontheimer might say.[2] When the Waffen-SS chronicler shrugs his shoulders at the mention of German politics, he is committing a political act. When the politician claims "Not my thing" as hate groups appropriate his words and platforms in search of legitimacy, he is committing a legitimizing act. When I, the self-proclaimed researcher, turn away from a legitimate objection to my work because it feels threatening, I haven't earned the job title.

Let me try, at least, to shrug off some of the ambiguity that has flowed through this book so far. Empirically, the only way to really decide "what kind of person" Erich Hartmann was at his core, if our context is a system of acidic beliefs that killed millions and reshaped the 20th century, is to say something meaningful about how his beliefs corresponded to, were driven by, and supported that system. We can certainly say something about how his actions supported it (highly effectively), but as we know by now, participation is a faulty way to judge belief.

What can we really say, then?

We can say that Erich Hartmann unambiguously aided Hitler's quest of racial annihilation.

We can say that this was largely because the military system he was embedded in ensured it.

We can say that whether or not a German soldier *believed* in his appointed mission had, at best, a secondary influence on whether he *completed* it.

We can say that this reality extends to all kinds of militaries in all kinds of wars.

We can say that Hitler desired for every man like Hartmann to believe in the Nazi cause fanatically, because Hitler was a fanatic.

We can say that Hitler never actually needed to succeed at this in order to decimate a continent and tear up several generations of families and communities all over the globe.

We can say that, whatever uniforms he wore, there are parts of Erich Hartmann that we might relate to, find fascinating, or admire.

We can say that there are many of us who, insulated by our privileged racial and religious identities, might have chosen the same path he did had we been born into the same time, place, and influences.

We can say that Hartmann's life, like most people's, is a reminder that neatness is something we impose on history, not something that's particularly natural in it.

When I was leaving the cemetery, soon to return to the Stuttgart airport, I headed downhill and glanced up at the cloud cover. It was going to be a rough flying day. There was a stack of storm clouds, angry-looking things the color of camouflage, headed toward town. And I had that same thought again: that I could almost see Erich Hartmann up there, twisting, turning, evading.

Almost.

# Bibliography

"'A Beautiful Death'—For the Fatherland?" ("'*Ein Schöner Tod*'—*Fürs Vaterland?*") in *Der Spiegel* (30 August 1982), http://www.spiegel.de/spiegel/print/d-14349673.html. Retrieved August 21, 2017.

"A Higher Call: An Incredible True Story of Combat and Chivalry in the War-Torn Skies of World War II" in *Publishers Weekly* book review, https://www.publishersweekly.com/978-0-425-25286-4. Accessed January 2, 2018.

Applebaum, Anne. *Gulag* (New York: Doubleday, 2003).

Basu, Sammy. Personal interview (July 2010).

Bark, Dennis and Gress, David. *A History of West Germany. Volume 1: From Shadow to Substance: 1945–1963* (Cambridge: Blackwell, 1989).

Bergman, Jay. "Valerii Chkalov: Soviet Pilot as New Soviet Man" In *Journal of Contemporary History*, Vol. 33, No. 1 (January 1998).

Binet, Laurent (trans. Sam Taylor). *HHhH* (New York: Farrar Straus and Giroux, 2012).

Blackburn, Gilmer W. "The Portrayal of Christianity in the History Textbooks of Nazi Germany" in *Church History*, *49* (Cambridge: Cambridge University Press, 1980), pp. 433–45.

Boym, Svetlana. *The Future of Nostalgia* (New York: Basic Books, 2001).

"Brigadier General Robin Olds (2)—Fly/In Cruise/In" video interview, https://www.youtube.com/watch?v=qPCFeVpVXew. Accessed May 26, 2019.

Burrows, William E. *Richthofen: A True History of the Red Baron* (New York: Harcourt, Brace & World, 1969).

Cadbury, Deborah. *Space Race* (New York: Harper Perennial, 2005).

Campbell, Joseph. *The Hero With a Thousand Faces* (Princeton, New Jersey: Princeton University Press, 1949).

Caygill, Peter. *Jet Jockeys* (Shrewsbury, England: Airlife, 2002).

Corum, Robert (Ed.). *Rearming Germany* (Leiden, The Netherlands: Koninklijke Brill NV, 2011).

Cotlar, Seth. "Tom Paine's Readers and the Making of Democratic Citizens in the Age of Revolutions" in *Thomas Paine: Common Sense for the Modern Era* by King, Ronald F. and Begler, Elsie (eds) (San Diego, California: San Diego State University Press, 2007), pp. 121–37.

Crossland, John. "Obituary: General Adolf Galland" in *The Independent* (February 14, 1996), http://www.independent.co.uk/news/people/obituary-general-adolf-galland-1318925.html. Accessed January 9, 2018.

Daso, Dik A. "The Red Baron" in *Air Force Magazine* (March 2012).

"Erich Hartmann, German Ace of World War II, 71," *The New York Times* obituary (October 23, 1993), https://www.nytimes.com/1993/10/23/obituaries/erich-hartmann-german-ace-of-world-war-ii-71.html. Accessed April 10, 2018.

Evans, Richard J. *The Coming of the Third Reich* (New York: Penguin Books, 2003).

Evans, Richard J. *The Third Reich at War* (New York: Penguin Books, 2008).

Evans, Richard J. *The Third Reich in Power* (New York: Penguin Books, 2005).

Feldmann, Hartut. *Jagdgeschwader 71 "Richthofen"* (Erlangen, Germany: AirDOC, 2013).

Ford, Daniel. "A Man On a Mission," *Wall Street Journal* book review of *Fighter Pilot* by Christina Olds and Ed Rasimus (April 12, 2010), https://www.wsj.com/articles/SB1000142405270230 33825045751648417404144472. Accessed July 12, 2019.

*Foundations of Air Power: ROTC Handbook* (Washington: U.S. Government Printing Office, 1958).

Galland, Adolf. *The First and the Last* (New York: Ballantine Books, 1954).

"Günther Scheel," *The Luftwaffe 39–45*, http://www.luftwaffe39-45.historia.nom.br/ases/scheel.htm. Accessed July 22, 2018.

Fengler, Kurt. Personal interview (March 2010).

Haffner, Sebastian. *Defying Hitler* (New York: Picador, 2000).

Haffner, Sebastian. *The Meaning of Hitler* (Boston: Harvard University Press, 1979).

Hampton, Dan. *Lords of the Sky: Fighter Pilots and Air Combat, From the Red Baron to the F-16* (New York: William Morrow, 2014).

Hardesty, Von and Grinberg, Ilya. *Red Phoenix Rising: The Soviet Air Force in World War II* (Lawrence, Kansas: University Press of Kansas, 2012).

Hartmann, Ursula (trans. James Cable). *German Fighter Ace Erich Hartmann: The Life Story of the World's Highest Scoring Ace* (Atglen, Penn.: Schiffer, 1992).

Head, R. G. Lecture to Wings Over the Rockies Air and Space Museum (March 10, 2018).

Heaton, Colin D. and Lewis, Anne-Marie. *The German Aces Speak: World War II Through the Eyes of Four of the Luftwaffe's Most Important Commanders* (Minneapolis, Minnesota: Zenith Press, 2011).

Heaton, Colin D. and Lewis, Anne-Marie. *The German Aces Speak II: World War II Through the Eyes of Four More of the Luftwaffe's Most Important Commanders* (Minneapolis, Minnesota: Zenith Press, 2014).

Heck, Alfons. *A Child of Hitler: Germany in the Days When God Wore a Swastika* (Phoenix: Renaissance House, 1985).

Housden, Martyn. *Resistance and Conformity in the Third Reich* (London: Routledge, 1997).

"How Whiteness Distorts Our Democracy, With Eddie Glaude Jr.," *The Ezra Klein Show* podcast. Accessed June 17, 2019.

Irmscher, Christopher. "Origin of the Specious?," *Wall Street Journal* book review of *Charles Darwin: Victorian Mythmaker* by A. N. Wilson (Saturday/Sunday, December 9–10, 2017).

"Irving v Penguin Books Limited," http://www.bailii.org/ew/cases/EWHC/QB/2000/115.html. Accessed 10 September 2018).

"Interview with Erich Hartman, WWII's Greatest Ace" in *Wings* magazine (October 5, 1975).

Johnson, Eric and Reuband, Karl-Heinz. *What We Knew* (Cambridge, Mass.: Basic Books, 2005).

Junger, Sebastian. *War* (New York: Twelve, 2010).

Kammen, Michael. *Mystic Chords of Memory: The Transformation of Tradition in American Culture* (New York: Knopf, 1991).

Kater, Michael. *Hitler Youth* (Cambridge, Mass.: Harvard University Press, 2004).

Kattago, Siobhan. *Ambiguous Memory* (Westport, Connecticut: Praeger, 2001).

Khazanov, Dimitri. "Erich Hartmann, un total contesté: 352 victoires ou 80?" in *Le Fana de l'Aviation #423* (February 2005).

Klemperer, Victor. *The Language of the Third Reich* (New York: Bloomsbury Academic, 2013).

Knoke, Heinz. *I Flew for the Führer* (London: Greenhill Books, 1997).

Knopp, Guido. *Hitler's Children* (Gloucestershire, England: Sutton Publishing Limited, 2002).

Koch, H.W. *The Hitler Youth: Origins and Development 1922–1945* (New York: Cooper Square Press, 2000).

Leckie, Robert. *Helmet for My Pillow* (New York: Bantam Books, 1957).

Le Carré, John. "John le Carré: 'I was a secret even to myself'" in *The Guardian* (April 12, 2013), http://www.guardian.co.uk/books/2013/apr/12/john-le-Carré-spy-anniversary. Accessed February 5, 2017.

Le Carré, John. *The Pigeon Tunnel: Stories from My Life* (London: Penguin Books, 2017).

Lewis, William F. "Telling America's Story: Narrative Form and the Reagan Presidency" in *Quarterly Journal of Speech #73* (August 1987), pp. 280–302.

"Little War on the Prairie (Seeing White, Part Five)," *Scene On Radio* podcast. Accessed April 12, 2017.

"Lockheed's Defiance: A Right to Bribe?" in *Time* magazine (August 18, 1975).

Macdonald, Alastair. "Vatican Plays Down Pope's Hitler Youth Past" in *Reuters* (May 10, 2009). Accessed June 18, 2019. http://in.reuters.com/article/2009/05/12/us-pope-mideast-hitleryouth-sb-idINTRE54B3B020090512.

Mahoney, Barbara S. *Dispatches and Dictators: Ralph Barnes for the Herald Tribune* (Corvallis, Oregon: Oregon State University Press, 2002).

Matthews, Johannes and Foreman, John. *Luftwaffe Aces: Biographies and Victory Claims, Vol. 2 G–L.* (Walton on Thames, U.K.: Red Kite, 2015), p. 485.

Mayer, S. L. and Tokoi, Masami (ed.). *Der Adler: The Official Nazi Luftwaffe Magazine* (New York: Thomas Y. Crowell, 1977).

Meinecke, Friedrich (trans. Sidney Fay). *The German Catastrophe* (Boston: Harvard University Press, 1950).

"Michelle Bachmann's Baseless Attack on Huma Abedin" in *The Washington Post* (July 19, 2012), https://www.washingtonpost.com/opinions/michele-bachmanns-baseless-attack-on-huma-abedin/2012/07/19/gJQAFhkiwW_story.html?utm_term=.855dee3879ed. Accessed June 5, 2019.

Mosier, John. *Cross of Iron: The Rise and Fall of the German War Machine, 1918–1945* (New York: Henry Holt and Company, 2006).

Nees, Greg. *Germany: Unraveling an Enigma* (Boston: Intercultural Press, 2000).

Neitzel, Sönke and Welzer, Harald (trans. Jefferson Chase). *Soldiers: German POWs on Fighting, Killing, and Dying* (New York: Vintage Books, 2012).

"No Shooting Please, We're German" in *The Economist* (October 13, 2012), http://www.economist.com/node/21564617. Accessed February 5, 2017.

Notheisen, Laura. "*So war der deutsche Landser. Die populäre und populärwissenschaftliche Darstellung der Wehrmacht,*" conference report for the *Arbeitskreis Militärgeschichte e.V.*, https://www.hsozkult.de/conferencereport/id/tagungsberichte-6959. Accessed May 14, 2019.

"Otto Wels: 'You cannot take our honour', speech against Hitler's Enabling Act—1933" in Speakola, https://speakola.com/political/otto-wels-cannot-take-our-honour-1933. Accessed July 16, 2019.

Pine, Lisa. *Hitler's "National Community"* (London: Hodder Arnold, 2007).

Reese, Willy Peter. *A Stranger to Myself* (New York: Farrar, Straus and Giroux, 2003).

"Reunion WWII Pilots in Dayton and Interview with Colonel Erich Hartmann," https://www.youtube.com/watch?v=6WExpN8nW7c. Accessed May 9, 2019.

Richthofen, Manfred Freiherr von. *The Red Battle Flyer* (Johannesburg, South Africa: CruGuru, 2011).

Sampson, Anthony. "Lockheed's Foreign Policy: Who in the End, Corrupted Whom?" in *New York Magazine* (March 15, 1976).

Saueier, Hans. "The Generals of Yesterday" ("*Die Generäle von Gestern*") in *Die Zeit* (November 5, 1976), https://www.zeit.de/1976/46/die-generaele-von-gestern. Accessed May 23, 2018.

"Scandals: The Lockheed Mystery (Contd.)" in *Time* magazine (September 13, 1976).

Sims, Edward. *The Aces Talk* (New York: Ballantine Books, 1980).

Sontheimer, Michael. "Why Germans Can Never Escape Hitler's Shadow" in *Der Spiegel* (March 10, 2005), http://www.spiegel.de/international/germany-s-nazi-past-why-germans-can-never-escape-hitler-s-shadow-a-345720.html. Accessed June 5, 2019.

Smelser, Ronald and Davies II, Edward J.. *The Myth of the Eastern Front* (New York: Cambridge University Press, 2008).

Stephenson, Scott. "The Myth of the Great War: A New Military History of World War I," book review from *Military Review*, https://www.questia.com/read/1P3-323516871/the-myth-of-the-great-war-a-new-military-history. Accessed July 16, 2019.

Teschke, John P. *Hitler's Legacy* (New York: Peter Lang Publishing, 1999).

"The Geneva Conventions: To Whom Do the Conventions Apply?," pbs.org, https://www.pbs.org/wnet/wideangle/uncategorized/the-geneva-conventions-to-whom-do-the-conventions-apply/615/. Retrieved July 20, 2018.

"The Last English Language Interview With Eric [*sic*] Hartmann," https://youtu.be/oPsYKOahKMU. Accessed May 14, 2019.

"The Last Interview With Erich Hartmann," Migflug, https://migflug.com/jetflights/final-interview-with-erich-hartmann/. Accessed July 12, 2019.

"The Myth of the Great War: A New Military History of World War I," book review from *Publishers Weekly* (April 16, 2001), https://www.publishersweekly.com. Accessed July 16, 2019.

Tillman, Barrett. "Shot down or out of gas?" in *Flight Journal* (August 2006).

Toliver, Raymond F. and Constable, Trevor J. *The Blond Knight of Germany* (Pennsylvania: TAB AERO Books, 1970).

"Training the Luftwaffe" in *Flight International* (December 10, 1942).

Vuillard, Éric (trans. Mark Polizzotti). *The Order of the Day* (New York: Other Press, 2017).

"West Germany: Watchman on the Rhine" in *Time* magazine (December 19, 1960).

Wette, Wolfram (trans. Deborah Schneider). *The Wehrmacht: Myth and Realities* (Boston, Mass.: Harvard University Press, 2006).

Winkler, Heinrich. *The Long Road West, Vol. 2* (New York: Oxford University Press, 2000).

Wolfe, Tom. *The Right Stuff* (New York: Picador, 1979).

# Endnotes

## Introduction

1. "Little War on the Prairie (Seeing White, Part Five)," *Scene On Radio* podcast, accessed 12 April 2017.

## Chapter 1

1. William E. Burrows, *Richthofen: A True History of the Red Baron* (New York: Harcourt, Brace & World, Inc., 1969), p. 199.
2. Ibid, p. 201.
3. Ibid, p. 203.
4. Ibid, p. 205.
5. Ibid, p. 204.
6. Ibid, p. 205
7. Mark Wilkins, "The Dark Side of Glory," in *Air & Space* magazine, February/March 2018, pp. 54–59.
8. Dan Hampton, *Lords of the Sky: Fighter Pilots and Air Combat, From the Red Baron to the F-16* (New York: William Morrow, 2014), p. 124.
9. Richard Griffiths, "Fellow Travelers of the Right: British Enthusiasts for Nazi Germany 1933–1939," accessed April 30, 2019, https://tinyurl.com/y4yxh2n2.
10. Mike Spick, *Aces of the Reich* (London: Greenhill Books, 2006), p. 18.
11. John Keegan, *The First World War* (New York: Knopf, 1999), p. 4.
12. Michael R. Marrus, "Final Solutions," review of *Mirrors of Destruction*, by Omer Bartov, *New York Times*, September 10, 2000, https://archive.nytimes.com/www.nytimes.com/books/00/09/10/reviews/000910.10marr.html.

## Chapter 2

1. M. Gregory Kendrick, *The Heroic Ideal: Western Archetypes from the Greeks to the Present* (Jefferson, North Carolina: McFarland & Company, 2010), p. 2.
2. Ursula Hartmann, *German Fighter Ace Erich Hartmann: The Life Story of the World's Highest Scoring Ace* (Pennsylvania: Schiffer Publishing, 1992), p. 7.
3. Raymond F. Toliver and Trevor J. Constable, *The Blond Knight of Germany* (Pennsylvania: TAB AERO Books, 1970), pp. 15–16.
4. Ursula Hartmann, *German Fighter Ace Erich Hartmann*, p. 43.

5. Colin Heaton and Anne-Marie Lewis, *The German Aces Speak II: World War II Through the Eyes of Four More of the Luftwaffe's Most Important Commanders* (Minneapolis: Zenith Press, 2014), p. 8.
6. Toliver and Constable, *Blond Knight of Germany*, p. 16.
7. Ursula Hartmann, *German Fighter Ace Erich Hartmann*, p. 8.
8. Toliver and Constable, *Blond Knight of Germany*, p. 18
9. Brian Murdoch, *The Germanic Hero: Politics and Pragmatism in Early Medieval Poetry* (London: The Hambledon Press, 1996), p. 37.
10. Ibid, p. 43.
11. Ibid, p. 5.
12. Ibid, p. 72.
13. Ibid, p. 4.
14. Kendrick, *The Heroic Ideal*, p. 105.
15. Ibid, p. 203.
16. Richard J. Evans, *The Third Reich in Power* (New York: The Penguin Press, 2005), p. 4.
17. "Realpolitik," *Encyclopedia Britannica*, accessed April 30, 2019, https://www.britannica.com/topic/realpolitik.
18. Kendrick, *The Heroic Ideal*, p. 147.
19. Ibid, p. 148.
20. Sammy Basu, personal interview, July 2010.
21. Éric Vuillard (trans. Mark Polizzotti), *The Order of the Day* (New York: Other Press, 2017), p. 24.
22. Evans, *The Coming of the Third Reich*, p. 34.

# Chapter 3

1. Walter Capps, ed. *The Vietnam Reader* (New York: Routledge, 1990), p. 70.
2. Anthony Lane, "Loyalty Oaths," *The New Yorker*, January 15, 2012.
3. Toliver and Constable, *Blond Knight of Germany*, p. 20.
4. Ibid, p. 23.
5. Evans, *The Coming of the Third Reich*, p. 340.
6. "Otto Wels: 'You cannot take our honour', speech against Hitler's Enabling Act— 1933," Speakola, accessed July 16, 2019, https://speakola.com/political/otto-wels-cannot-take-our-honour-1933.
7. Hartmann, *German Fighter Ace Erich Hartmann*, p. 55.
8. Lisa Pine, *Hitler's "National Community": Society and Culture in Nazi Germany* (London: Bloomsbury Academic, 2007), p. 44.
9. Victor Klemperer, *The Language of the Third Reich* (New York: Bloomsbury Academic, 2013), p. 3.
10. Gilmer W. Blackburn, "The Portrayal of Christianity in the History Textbooks of Nazi Germany," in *Church History, 49* (Cambridge: Cambridge University Press, 1980), pp. 433–45.
11. Pine, p. 47
12. Laurent Binet (trans. Sam Taylor), *HHhH* (New York: Farrar Straus and Giroux, 2012), pp. 202–203.
13. Sönke Neitzel and Harald Welzer, *Soldiers* (New York: Vintage Books, 2012), pp. 27, 29–30.
14. Rudi Florian, "My Story," unpublished essay.
15. Ibid.
16. Toliver and Constable, *The Blond Knight of Germany*, p. 23.

17. School website, accessed prior to March 2018. Due to a website refresh, previous content is unavailable for direct linking, despite the author's efforts to retrieve it.
18. Heaton and Lewis, *The German Aces Speak II*, p. 11.

## Chapter 4

1. Michael Kater, *Hitler Youth* (Cambridge: Harvard University Press, 2004), p. 6.
2. Toliver and Constable, *Blond Knight of Germany*, p. 206.
3. Knopp, *Hitler's Children*, p. 1.
4. Kater, *Hitler Youth*, p. 23.
5. Toliver and Constable, *Blond Knight of Germany*, p. 21.
6. H. W. Koch, *The Hitler Youth: Origins and Development 1922–1945* (New York: Cooper Square Press, 2000), p. 86.
7. Kater, *Hitler Youth,* p. 1.
8. Ibid.
9. Pine, pp. 62–63.
10. Evans, *The Third Reich in Power*, p. 322.
11. Knopp, *Hitler's Children*, x (Introduction).
12. Alastair Macdonald, "Vatican Plays Down Pope's Hitler Youth Past," in *Reuters*, 10 May 2009, accessed June 18, 2019, http://in.reuters.com/article/2009/05/12/us-pope-mideast-hitleryouth-sb-idINTRE54B3B020090512. Retrieved January 7, 2012.
13. Alfons Heck, *A Child of Hitler: Germany in the Days When God Wore a Swastika* (Phoenix: Renaissance House, 1985), p. 17.
14. Ibid, p. 16.
15. Ibid, p. 19.
16. Ibid, p. 13.
17. Barbara S. Mahoney, *Dispatches and Dictators: Ralph Barnes for the Herald Tribune* (Corvallis, Oregon: Oregon State University Press, 2002), p. 136.
18. Ibid, p. 127.
19. See http://e-militaria.com/catalog/germany_third_reich/NSFK_DLV/index.htm; https://www.jewishvirtuallibrary.org/military-organization-of-the-third-reich. Accessed June 18, 2019.
20. "Training the Luftwaffe," in *Flight International*, December 10, 1942, p. 639.
21. "Behind the Lines: Luftwaffe Aces," in *Flight International*, September 7, 1944, p. 265.
22. Kater, *Hitler Youth*, pp. 4–5.
23. Ursula Hartmann, *German Fighter Ace Erich Hartmann*, p. 9.
24. Ibid.
25. Toliver and Constable, *Blond Knight of Germany*, p. 19.
26. Ibid, p. 332.

## Chapter 5

1. Keegan, *The First World War*, p. 73.
2. Ibid, p. 22.
3. Burrows, *Richthofen*, p. 50.
4. Hampton, *Lords of the Sky*, p. 36.
5. R. G. Head, lecture to Wings Over the Rockies Air and Space Museum, March 10, 2018.

6. Ibid.
7. Toliver and Constable, *Blond Knight of Germany*, p. 28.
8. Ibid, pp. 30–31.
9. "Flieger und Soldaten," in *Der Adler: The Official Nazi Luftwaffe Magazine* (New York: Thomas Y. Crowell, 1977), Mayer, S.L. and Tokoi, Masami (ed.), unnumbered page.
10. John Mosier, *Cross of Iron: The Rise and Fall of the German War Machine 1918–1945* (New York: Henry Holt and Company, 2006), pp. 17–18.
11. "The Myth of the Great War: A New Military History of World War I," book review from *Publishers Weekly*, accessed July 16, 2019, https://www.publishersweekly.com/; Scott Stephenson, "The Myth of the Great War: A New Military History of World War I," book review from *Military Review*, accessed July 16, 2019, https://www.questia.com/read/1P3-323516871/the-myth-of-the-great-war-a-new-military-history.
12. Mosier, *Cross of Iron*, p. 26.
13. Keegan, *The First World War*, p. 424.
14. Mosier, *Cross of Iron*, p. 59.
15. Neitzel and Welzer, *Soldiers*, p. 237.
16. Friedrich Meinecke, *The German Catastrophe* (Boston: Harvard University Press, 1950), p. 51.
17. Neitzel and Weltzer, *Soldiers*, p. 7.
18. Ibid, p. 6.
19. Heaton and Lewis, *The German Aces Speak II*, p. 60.

# Chapter 6

1. John Weal, *Jagdgeschwader 52: The Experten* (Oxford: Osprey Publishing Limited, 2004), p. 57.
2. Weal, *Jagdgeschwader 52*, p. 70.
3. Toliver and Constable, *Blond Knight of Germany*, p. 33.
4. Weal, *Jagdgeschwader 52*, p. 7.
5. Heaton and Lewis, *The German Aces Speak II*, p. 44.
6. Ibid, p. 16.
7. Christer Bergström, *Graf & Grislawski: A Pair of Aces* (Hamilton, MT: Eagle Editions, 2003), p. 141.
8. Bergström, *Graf & Grislawski*, p. 161.
9. Toliver and Constable, *Blond Knight of Germany*, p. 290.
10. Heaton and Lewis, *German Aces Speak II*, pp. 22–23.
11. Ibid, p. 23.
12. Dimitri Khazanov, "Erich Hartmann, un total contesté: 352 victoires ou 80?," in *Le Fana de l'Aviation #423*, February 2005.
13. Toliver and Constable, *Blond Knight of Germany*, p. 293.
14. Johannes Matthews and John Foreman, *Luftwaffe Aces: Biographies and Victory Claims, Vol. 2 G–L* (Walton on Thames, U.K.: Red Kite, 2015), p. 485.
15. Barrett Tillman, "Shot down or out of gas?," in *Flight Journal*, August 2006, pp. 48–56.
16. Dik A. Daso, "The Red Baron," in *Air Force Magazine*, March 2012.
17. "Brigadier General Robin Olds (2)—Fly/In Cruise/In," video interview, accessed May 26, 2019, https://www.youtube.com/watch?v=qPCFeVpVXew.
18. Toliver and Constable, *Blond Knight of Germany*, pp. 64–68.

19. Ibid, p. 70.
20. Heaton and Lewis, *The German Aces Speak*, p. 34.
21. Ibid, p. 35.
22. Ibid, p. 36.

## Chapter 7

1. Von Hardesty and Ilya Grinberg, *Red Phoenix Rising: The Soviet Air Force in World War II* (Lawrence, Kansas: University Press of Kansas, 2014), p. 5.
2. Adolf Galland, *The First and the Last* (New York: Ballantine Books, 1954), p. 54.
3. Hardesty and Grinberg, *Red Phoenix Rising*, p. 8.
4. Ibid, p. 111.
5. Ibid, p. 20.
6. Ibid, p. 53.
7. Hampton, *Lords of the Sky*, p. 293.
8. Ibid, p. 288.
9. "Aviation History: Interview with World War II Soviet Ace Ivan Kozhedub," HistoryNet, accessed January 3, 2017, http://www.historynet.com/aviation-history-interview-with-world-war-ii-soviet-ace-ivan-kozhedub.htm.
10. Ibid.
11. Ibid.
12. Jay Bergman, "Valerii Chkalov: Soviet Pilot as New Soviet Man," in *Journal of Contemporary History* Vol. 33, No. 1 (January 1998), p. 139.
13. Hardesty and Grinberg, *Red Phoenix Rising*, p. 253.
14. Ibid, p. 253.
15. HistoryNet interview.

## Chapter 8

1. Heaton and Lewis, *German Aces Speak II*, p. 49.
2. Toliver and Constable, *Blond Knight of Germany*, p. 10.
3. Ibid.
4. Heaton and Lewis, *German Aces Speak II*, p. 40.
5. Ibid, p. 42
6. Ibid, p. 44
7. Ibid, p. 49.
8. Mosier, *Cross of Iron*, p. 58.
9. Ibid.
10. Toliver and Constable, *Blond Knight of Germany*, pp. 149–152.
11. Ibid, p. 155.
12. Mike Spick, *Aces of the Reich*, p. 195.
13. Toliver and Constable, *Blond Knight of Germany*, p. 296.
14. John Weal, *Bf 109 Aces of the Russian Front*, pp. 80–81.
15. Mathews and Foreman, *Luftwaffe Aces*, p. 485.
16. Ibid, p. 156.

17. Ibid.
18. Ibid, p. 159.
19. Ibid, p. 155.
20. Kurt Fengler, personal interview.
21. Toliver and Constable, *Blond Knight of Germany*, p. 176.
22. Heaton and Lewis, *The German Aces Speak II*, p. 120.
23. Toliver and Constable, *Blond Knight of Germany*, p. 57.
24. "Interview with Erich Hartman, WWII's Greatest Ace," in *Wings* magazine, October 5, 1975, p. 38.
25. Edward Sims, *The Aces Talk* (New York: Ballantine Books, 1980), pp. 233–34.

## Chapter 9

1. Willy Peter Reese (trans Michael Hofmann), *A Stranger to Myself: The Inhumanity of War: Russia, 1941–1944* (New York: Farrar, Straus and Giroux, 2005), p. 49.
2. Christer Bergström, *Graf and Grislawski*, p. 256.
3. Ibid.
4. Toliver and Constable, *Blond Knight of Germany*, p. 186.
5. Heaton and Lewis, *German Aces Speak II*, p. 78.
6. Ronald Smelser and Edward J. Davies II, *The Myth of the Eastern Front* (New York: Cambridge University Press, 2008), p. 41.
7. Toliver and Constable, *Blond Knight of Germany*, p. 188.
8. Ibid, p. 192.
9. Ibid, p. 194.
10. Ibid, p. 195.
11. Heaton and Lewis, *German Aces Speak II*, p. 82.
12. Toliver and Constable, *Blond Knight of Germany*, pp. 270, 297.
13. Ibid, p. 197.
14. Ibid, p. 196.
15. Bergström, *Graf & Grislawski*, pp. 265–66; Toliver and Constable, *Blond Knight of Germany*, p. 207.
16. Ibid, p. 198.
17. Toliver and Constable, *Blond Knight of Germany*, p. 206.
18. David Hosford, Pamela Kachurin and Thomas Lamont, "Gulag: Soviet Prison Camps and Their Legacy," curriculum prepared by the National Park Service and the National Resource Center for Russian, East European and Central Asian Studies, Harvard University, accessed February 3, 2018, http://gulaghistory.org/nps/downloads/gulag-curriculum.pdf.
19. Indirect citation of Erich Maschke, *Zur Geschichte der Deutschen Kriegsgefangenen des Zweiten Weltkrieges Bielefeld, E. und W. Gieseking, 1962–1974, Vol. 15*, p. 207.
20. G. F. Krivosheev, "Russia and the USSR in the Wars of the 20th Century: Loss of the Armed Forces" ("*Россия и СССР в войнах XX века: Потери вооруженных сил*"), Table 198, accessed May 8, 2019, http://lib.ru/MEMUARY/1939-1945/KRIWOSHEEW/poteri.txt#w02.htm-186.
21. Frank Biess, *Homecomings: Returning POWs and the Legacies of Defeat in Postwar Germany* (New Jersey: Princeton University Press, 2006), p. 3.
22. Bergström, *Graf & Grislawski*, p. 266.

23. Toliver and Constable, *Blond Knight of Germany*, p. 215.
24. Ibid, p. 217.
25. Heaton and Lewis, *German Aces Speak II*, pp. 81–82.
26. Ibid, p. 83.
27. Ibid, p. 88.
28. Ibid, p. 85.
29. Toliver and Constable, *Blond Knight of Germany*, p. 246.
30. Ibid, p. 247.
31. Ibid, p. 249.
32. Ibid.

## Chapter 10

1. Ursula Hartmann, *German Fighter Ace Erich Hartmann*, p. 178.
2. Heaton and Lewis, *The German Aces Speak II*, p. 108.
3. Ibid, pp. 108–109.
4. Ibid, p. 109.
5. Toliver and Constable, *Blond Knight of Germany*, p. 264.
6. Ibid, p. 263.
7. Frank Biess, *Homecomings*, p. 73.
8. Ibid.
9. Frank Biess, *Homecomings*, p. 8.
10. Heaton and Lewis, *The German Aces Speak II*, p. 110.
11. Richard J. Evans, *The Third Reich at War*, p. 749.
12. Ibid, p. 748.
13. Heinrich Winkler, *The Long Road West, Vol. 2* (New York: Oxford University Press, 2000), p. 156.
14. Alexandra Möckel, "Auschwitz – The Betrayal of Humanity (2)" (*Auschwitz – der Verrat an der Menschlichkeit (2)*), bundeswehr.de, accessed May 8, 2019, https://www.bundeswehr. de/portal/a/bwde/start/aktuelles/weitere_themen/!ut/p/z1/hY_RC4IwEMb_ I29OzfmoSSCISWblXmK4YYZtMpb00B_fRuBbdA8f3Pfd_4DChegki3jw- MyoJJts39HNNSPlscQJxmVLECrKiuwjjHwUhnCC878RamP0o1IEDRfQWUb- 8mxFAAxQoF16vpDBOjZBmtDpoZpT2ZqXN5JKn1jbxRg4d8vPMj9dT_jtt6xx- vkyDMi-zggHe2sNe6y3r3NHQ3Jvkkat WnX2N-7EhVRcMHFDMi0g!!/dz/d5/ L2dBISEvZ0FBIS9nQSEh/#Z7_B8LTL2922LU800ILN8O5201043.
15. John le Carré, *The Pigeon Tunnel* (New York: Penguin Books, 2016), p. 26.
16. Ibid.
17. John le Carré, "John le Carré: 'I was a secret even to myself'," in *The Guardian*, accessed February 5, 2017, http://www.guardian.co.uk/books/2013/apr/12/john-le-Carré-spy-anniversary.
18. Biess, *Homecomings*, p. 1.
19. Ibid, p. 6.
20. Ibid, p. 7.
21. Ibid, p. 56.
22. Ibid, p. 57.
23. Ibid, p. 67.

## Chapter 11

1. "West Germany: Watchman on the Rhine," *Time* magazine, December 19, 1960.
2. Dennis Bark and David Gress, *A History of West Germany. Volume 1: From Shadow to Substance: 1945–1963* (Cambridge: Blackwell, 1989), p. 370.
3. Toliver and Constable, *Blond Knight of Germany*, p. 266.
4. Indirect citation of Peter Stockert, *Die Eichenlaubträger 1939–1945 Band 5 (The Oak Leaves Bearers 1939–1945 Volume 5)* (Bad Friedrichshall, Germany: Friedrichshaller Rundblick), accessed via Wikipedia, May 19, 2019, https://en.wikipedia.org/wiki/Erich_Hartmann#CITEREFStockert2007.
5. Toliver and Constable, *Blond Knight of Germany*, p. 208; Ibid, p. 206.
6. Ibid, p. 271.
7. Robert Coram, *Boyd: The Fighter Pilot Who Changed the Art of War* (Boston: Little, Brown and Company, 2002), chapter two (eBook).
8. Toliver and Constable, *Blond Knight of Germany*, p. 274.
9. Ibid, p. 275.
10. Hartut Feldmann, *Jagdgeschwader 71 "Richthofen"* (Erlangen, Germany: AirDOC, 2013), p. 17.
11. Ibid.
12. Ibid, p. 36.
13. Toliver and Constable, *Blond Knight of Germany*, p. 278.
14. Heaton and Lewis, *The German Aces Speak II*, p. 117.
15. Hans Saueier, "The Generals of Yesterday" ("*Die Generäle von Gestern*"), in *Die Zeit*, November 5, 1976, accessed May 23, 2018, https://www.zeit.de/1976/46/die-generaele-von-gestern.
16. "No Shooting Please, We're German," in *The Economist*, October 13, 2012, accessed February 5, 2017, http://www.economist.com/node/21564617.
17. Ibid.
18. Toliver and Constable, *Blond Knight of Germany*, p. 286.
19. Ibid, p. 56.
20. Ibid, . 283.
21. "'A Beautiful Death'—For the Fatherland?" ("'*Ein Schöner Tod*'— *Fürs Vaterland?*"), in *Der Spiegel*, August 30, 1982, retrieved 21 August 2017, http://www.spiegel.de/spiegel/print/d-14349673.html.
22. Toliver and Constable, *Blond Knight of Germany*, pp. 283–84.
23. Ibid, p. 285.
24. "Lockheed's Defiance: A Right to Bribe?" in *Time* magazine, 18 August 1975.
25. Anthony Sampson, "Lockheed's Foreign Policy: Who in the End, Corrupted Whom?," in *New York Magazine*, March 15, 1976.
26. "Scandals: The Lockheed Mystery (Contd.)" in *Time* magazine, September 13, 1976, pp. 32–33.
27. Toliver and Constable, *Blond Knight of Germany*, p. 285.
28. Ibid, p. 278.
29. Heaton and Lewis, *The German Aces Speak II*, pp. 117–18.
30. Toliver and Constable, *Blond Knight of Germany*, p. 287.

# Chapter 12

1. Joseph Campbell, *The Hero With a Thousand Faces* (Princeton, New Jersey: Princeton University Press, 1949), p. 382.
2. "Reunion WWII Pilots in Dayton and Interview with Colonel Erich Hartmann," accessed May 29, 2019, https://www.youtube.com/watch?v=6WExpN8nW7c.
3. "The last English language interview with Eric [*sic*] Hartmann," accessed May 14, 2019, https://youtube/oPsYKOahKMU.
4. Heaton and Lewis, *German Aces Speak II*, p. 78.
5. "Irving v Penguin Books Limited," accessed September 10, 2018, http://www.bailii.org/ew/cases/EWHC/QB/2000/115.html.
6. Matthews and Foreman, *Luftwaffe Aces*, p. 485.
7. "Erich Hartmann, German Ace of World War II, 71," in *The New York Times* obituary, 23 October 1993, accessed April 10, 2018, https://www.nytimes.com/1993/10/23/obituaries/erich-hartmann-german-ace-of-world-war-ii-71.html.

# Chapter 13

1. Smelser and Davies, *Myth of the Eastern Front*, p. 2.
2. Ibid, p. 47.
3. Ibid, p. 49.
4. Ibid, p. 48.
5. Ibid, p. 69.
6. Ibid, p. 65.
7. Ibid, p. 70.
8. Ibid, p. 73.
9. Ibid, p. 65.
10. Frank Biess, *Homecomings*, p. 74.
11. Ibid.
12. Richard J. Evans, *The Third Reich at War*, p. 748.
13. Toliver and Constable, *Blond Knight of Germany*, pp. 5, 7.
14. Raymond Toliver and Trevor Constable, *Fighter Aces of the Luftwaffe* (Atglen, Pennsylvania: Schiffer Publishing, 1996), p. 9.
15. Christopher Irmscher, "Origin of the Specious?," in *Wall Street Journal* book review of "Charles Darwin: Victorian Mythmaker," by A. N. Wilson, Saturday/Sunday, December 9–10, 2017.
16. Daniel Ford, "A Man On a Mission," in *Wall Street Journal* book review of "Fighter Pilot," by Christina Olds and Ed Rasimus, accessed July 12, 2019, https://www.wsj.com/articles/SB10001424052702303382504575164841740414472.
17. "The Last Interview With Erich Hartmann," Migflug, accessed July 12, 2019, https://migflug.com/jetflights/final-interview-with-erich-hartmann/.
18. Colin Heaton and Anne-Marie Lewis, *The German Aces Speak: World War II Through the Eyes of Four of the Luftwaffe's Most Important Commanders* (Minneapolis, Minnesota: Zenith Press, 2011), pp. x–xi.
19. Toliver and Constable, *Fighter Aces of the Luftwaffe*, p. 26.
20. Heaton and Lewis, *The German Aces Speak II*, p. 4.
21. Heaton and Lewis, *The German Aces Speak*, p. ix.

22. "A Higher Call: An Incredible True Story of Combat and Chivalry in the War-Torn Skies of World War II," in *Publishers Weekly* book review, retrieved January 2, 2018, https://www.publishersweekly.com/978-0-425-25286-4.

23. Smelser and Davies, *Myth of the Eastern Front*, p. 161.

24. Ibid, p. 159.

25. Neitzel and Welzer, *Soldiers*, p. 315.

26. Smelser and Davies, *Myth of the Eastern Front*, p. 83.

27. Sebastian Junger, *War* (New York: Twelve, 2010), pp. 239–40.

28. Ibid, p. 239.

29. Ibid, p. 240.

30. Neitzel and Welzer, *Soldiers*, p. 22.

31. "How Whiteness Distorts Our Democracy, With Eddie Glaude Jr.," *The Ezra Klein Show* podcast, accessed June 17, 2019.

# Chapter 14

1. Adolf Galland, *The First and the Last* (New York: Henry Holt and Company, 1954), pp. 58–60.

2. Smelser and Davies, *Myth of the Eastern Front*, pp. 94–95.

3. "Letzter Flug," in *Der Spiegel*, January 3, 1983.

4. Hans Ulrich Rudel, *Stuka Pilot* (London: Black House Publishing, 2016), p. 56.

5. Ibid, p. I.

6. Galland, *The First and the Last*, p. 31.

7. Ibid, p. 35.

8. Ibid, pp. 58–59.

9. Ibid, pp. 58–60.

10. Ibid, p. 28.

11. Toliver and Constable, *Horrido!*, p. 25.

12. John Crossland, "Obituary: General Adolf Galland," in The *Independent*, February 14, 1996, accessed January 9, 2018, http://www.independent.co.uk/news/people/obituary-general-adolf-galland-1318925.html.

13. Galland, *The First and the Last*, p. 36.

14. James S. Corum, "Adenauer, Amt Blank, and the Founding of the Bundeswehr 1950–1956," in *Rearming Germany*, James S. Corum (ed.) (Leiden, The Netherlands: Koninklijke Brill NV, 2011), p. 45.

15. Ibid.

16. Ibid.

17. Ibid, p. 71.

18. Ibid.

19. Ibid, p. 280.

20. Heinz Knoke, *I Flew for the Führer* (London: Greenhill Books, 1997), pp. 28–29.

21. Ibid, pp. 185–87.

22. Ibid, p. 49.

23. Ibid, p. 187.

24. Ursula Hartmann, *German Fighter Ace Erich Hartmann*, p. 186.

25. Ibid, p. 178.

26. Ibid, inside jacket flap.

# Chapter 15

1.  John le Carré, *The Pigeon Tunnel*, introduction, unnumbered page in ebook edition.
2.  Seth Cotlar, "Tom Paine's Readers and the Making of Democratic Citizens in the Age of Revolutions," in *Thomas Paine: Common Sense for the Modern Era*, Ronald F. King and Elsie Begler (eds) (San Diego, California: San Diego State University Press, 2007), pp. 121–37.
3.  Laura Notheisen, "*So war der deutsche Landser. Die populäre und populärwissenschaftliche Darstellung der Wehrmacht*," in conference report for the Arbeitskreis Militärgeschichte e.V., accessed May 14, 2019, https://www.hsozkult.de/conferencereport/id/tagungsberichte-6959.
4.  Smelser and Davies, *Myth of the Eastern Front*, p. 131.
5.  Ibid, p. 173.
6.  Binet, *HHhH*, p. 4.
7.  Vuillard, *The Order of the Day*, p. 3.
8.  Burrows, *Richthofen*, p. 244.

# Conclusion

1.  Robert Wise, director, *The Sound of Music* (Beverly Hills: Twentieth Century Fox, 1965).
2.  Michael Sontheimer, "Why Germans Can Never Escape Hitler's Shadow," in *Der Spiegel*, March 10, 2005, accessed June 5, 2019, http://www.spiegel.de/international/germany-s-nazi-past-why-germans-can-never-escape-hitler-s-shadow-a-345720.html.

# Index

References to images are in *italics*.

*Adler, Der* (magazine) 48–9
*Aeroplane, The* (magazine) 4, 5
aircraft
    DeHavilland Mosquito 80
    Eurofighter Typhoon 82
    F-4 Phantom 69, 171, 182
    F-11 Tiger 134
    F-86 (and Canadair) Sabre 128, 130–134
    F-100 Super Sabre 134, 157
    F-102 Delta Dagger 134
    F-104 Starfighter 133, 134–6
    Fw 190 43, 78, 80, 141
    He 177 76, 172
    I-16 75
    Il-2 *Sturmovik* 57, 62, *67*
    Ju 87 *Stuka* 60
    La-7 78, 80
    La-9 78
    Lagg-3 63
    Me 163 *Komet* 87–8, 89
    Me 262 86, 87, 89, 103, 127, 129, 135, 173
    MiG-29 182
    P-38 Lightning 69
    P-39 Airacobra 76
    P-47 Thunderbolt 45, 46, 141
    P-51 Mustang xv, 45, 46, 66, 69, 90, 127
    Spitfire 44, 45, 141, 173, 175
    Yak-3 78
    Yak-7 xv, 90
    *see also* Bf 109; Lockheed scandal
American Civil War 164–5
anti-Semitism 15, 16, 30, 53
*Arbeitskreis Militärgeschichte* ("Working Group [for] Military History") 184–5
Argentina 170, 174

Austria 14, 97, 186
*Autobahn* 27–8

Barkhorn, Gerhard 83
Bartov, Omer 6
Baum, Otto 162–3
Benedict XVI, Pope 28
Bf 109 xv, 43, *47*, 57–8, 75, 78, 91
    and design 40, 44, 45, 128, 159
    and *JG-52* 59–60
    and Knoke 176–7
    and Kozhedub 79–80
    and last Hartmann mission 93–4
    and performance 64, 69
Bismarck, Otto von 10, 14–15, 16, 50, 114
black tulip paint scheme xv–xvi, 130–1
*Blitzkrieg* 73, 172
*Blond Knight of Germany, The* (Toliver & Constable) 22, 70, 86, 99, 101, 160
    and *Bundeswehr* 138
    and Goebel 66
    and interviews 178
    and research 157–8
    and Soviet Union 97, 126
Böblingen (Germany) 88
Bölcke, Oswald 6, 40–1, 68
Bong, Dick xiii
Brown, Roy 5
"Bubimat" device 179
*Bund Deutscher Mädel* (League of German Girls) 27
*Bundeswehr* ("civil defense") xvii, xviii, 123–6, 131–3, 136, 138–9, 179
    and Galland 174–5

capitalism 78, 115
Capito, Günther 90–1, 133
China 8–9, 10–11, 127, 178

Chkalov, Valery 79, 80
Cold War xix, 80, 102, 103, 151–3, 181–2
  and aircraft 76, 134
  and Germany 185
  and U.S.A. 126, 127, 179
Communism 78, 80, 107, 152, 177, 185
Concordia 7
Constable, Trevor 97, 101, 157, 158, 160,
  184–5
"Crimes of the Wehrmacht, The" (exhibition)
  181, 183

Darwin, Charles 16, 158
Deutsche Bundespost 180
dystrophy 115, 156

Eichmann, Adolf 156
Erhard, Ludwig 115–16
Experten xiii, xix, 5

Fengler, Kurt 87, 88, 89
Flieger-Hitlerjugend 31–2, 33
Flight Journal (magazine) 66
Florian, Rudi 22, 146
Fokker, Anthony 39–40
Foreman, John 66, 86
Free Democratic Party 178

Galland, Adolf 75, 87, 158, 161, 172–6, 178
Geneva Conventions 71, 104, 106, 185
German Army see Wehrmacht
German Flying Corps 3; see also Luftwaffe
Gestapo 176
Gleichschaltung (coordination of the citizenry)
  17
gliding programs 31–2
Göbbels, Joseph 19, 53, 85
Goebel, Robert 66
Goldwater, Barry 151
Göring, Hermann 32, 37, 48, 53, 85, 173,
  176
Graf, Hermann 87, 94–5, 97–8, 99, 100, 102
Grey, C. G. 5
Grislawski, Alfred 62, 63
Gryazovets (Russia) 99–101, 102, 105, 112,
  179, 180
Günsche, Otto 107

Hadubrand 11
Hahn, Assi 99–100, 112
Halder, Franz 154–5, 167, 169
Hartmann, Dr. Alfred 8–10, 112
Hartmann, Alfred, Jr 17–18
Hartmann, Elisabeth 8–10, 31, 107, 111–12
Hartmann, Erich xiii–xiii, xxv–xxvi, 13, 14,
  36, 167, 189–92
  and Barbarossa 74, 76, 77–9, 82–3
  and books 157, 158–9, 164, 178–80,
    184–6
  and Bundeswehr ("civil defense") 124–6,
    132–3, 136–9
  and China 7, 10–11
  and Cold War 152
  and death 146–7
  and F-104 Starfighter 134–5
  and frame of reference 52–4
  and Galland 172–5, 178
  and Hitler 83–5
  and Hitler Youth 25–7, 28–9, 30, 32–5
  and Holocaust 142–6
  and JG-52 59–63, 69–72
  and JG-71 130–2
  and kills 63–9
  and Knoke 176
  and Luftwaffe 42–4, 48
  and marriage 85–6
  and Me 262 87–8
  and missions 57–9, 89–92, 93–5
  and Porsche 116–17
  and prisoner of war 95–109, 114–15, 120,
    156, 165–6, 169
  and release 111–14
  and Richthofen 5
  and school 16, 17–20, 21, 22–4
  and U.S.A. 126–30
  and West Germany 121
Heaton, Anne-Marie 160
Heaton, Colin 90, 160–1
Heck, Alfons 29, 30
heroic vitalism 14–15
heroism 12–13, 30, 152, 169
Heydrich, Reinhard 21, 186
Higher Call, A (book) 161
Hildebrand 11–12
Hitler, Adolf xv, xviii, xx, xxiv–xxv, 28

and aircraft 76, 87, 89
and Chancellorship 18
and combatants 163–4, 166
and death 107, 115
and education 19, 20, 24
and Germany 11, 12, 13, 15, 21–2, 25,
  116, 117
and Halder 155
and Hartmann 82–5, 191–2
and Holocaust 144
and *Luftwaffe* 37, 41–2, 49, 160–1
and *Mein Kampf* 17
and paternalism 78
and postwar 119–20, 133
and Soviet Union 73, 77
and testimonies 169, 170, 172, 174, 177,
  186
and *Wehrmacht* 51, 53
*see also* Hitler Youth
Hitler Youth *(Hitlerjugend)* xix, 19, 22, 25–7,
  28–9, 30–5, 53
and Hartmann 85, 101, 144
Holocaust 6, 22, 28–9, 144–6, 156, 182
Hrabak, Dieter 53, 125, 159

Irving, David 145

Jews 33, 50, 96, 176
  and Hartmann 143–4, 146, 164, 167
  and Nazism 19, 20, 21, 118, 119
  *see also* anti-Semitism; Holocaust
Junger, Carl 64
Junger, Sebastian 165–6

*Kamaradenwerk* (Comrade Operation) 170
Kammhuber, Josef 131, 134–5, 138, 175
Karaya One (call sign) 93, 95
Kennedy, John F. 151, 155
Khazanov, Dmitri 65–6
Klemperer, Victor 19
Knight's Cross of the Iron Cross 82–3, 130,
  170, 174
Knoke, Heinz 172, 176–8
Kozhedub, Ivan 78–80
Krupinski, Walter 83, 87, 125, 132–3

Le Carré, John 118
League of German Girls (*Bund Deutscher
  Mädel*) 27
Lockheed scandal 134, 135–6
Loveland (U.S.A.) xxiii, xxv
Luftwaffe 37, 88–9, 156, 166
  and aircraft 48, 134–5
  and books 157–8, 159–61, 171, 172–8
  and Hartmann xiii–xiv, xv–xvi, xviii, 42–3,
    53
  and *Jagdfliegerheim* (Fighter Pilot's Home)
    85–6, 125
  and *JG-52* 59–61, 64, 65, 66, 86, 87, 176
  and *JV-44* 86, 87, 92
  and kills 65–6
  and Nazism 32, 49
  and organization 59–60
  and Soviet Union 73–8, 79–80, 82
  and Spanish Civil War 41, 64
  and U.S.A. 126, 130, 181–2
  *see also Experten*

Maginnis, John 153
Mann, William Hodges 164–5
Manstein, Erich von 170, 171
masculinity 157, 165
Matthews, Johannes 86
Mertens, Bimmel 72, 94, 165
Messerschmitt, Willy 44
Mölders, Werner 42

National Socialism *see* Nazism
Nazism xxiv–xxv, 12, 19–24, 27, 154–7,
  182–3
  and anti-Semitism 16
  and apologists 145–6
  and Galland 173, 174–5
  and Hartmann xviii, xix, 11, 53, 185
  and Knoke 176, 177–8
  and Rudel 132–3, 170–1
  and Soviet Union 100
  and *Wehrmacht* 48–9, 51–2, 161, 162–4
  and West Germany 117–18, 119–20,
    123–4
  *see also* Hitler, Adolf

NKVD (People's Commissariat for Internal Affairs) 100–1, 102, 103, 132

Obleser, Friedrich 64
Olds, Robin 69, 158, 160
Operation *Barbarossa* 60, 74, 76, 77, 155

Paine, Thomas 183
Pätsch, Ursula 23
Porsche, Ferry 117
post-traumatic stress 115, 156

Ratzinger, Joseph *see* Benedict XVI, Pope
Reagan, Ronald 151–2
Red Baron *see* Richthofen, Manfred von
Richthofen, Manfred von xvi, xvii, 3–6, 13, 67, 130, 186
    and books 158
    and death 79
    and Fokker 40, 41, 44, 82
    and missions 37–8
Rossmann, Edmund "Paule" 58, 62
Rottweil (National Political Reformatory) 18–19, 22, 33, 42
Rudel, Hans-Ulrich 82, 84, 143, 178
    and Nazism 132–3, 145–6, 170–1, 174, 175

Schirach, Baldur von 26
Schumacher, Kurt 118, 120
Shakespeare, William 17, 23
Shakhty labor camp 105–6
Social Democratic Party 118
Socialist Reich Party 178
Spanish Civil War 41, 64, 173
*Spiegel, Der* (newspaper) 171
Stalin, Joseph xvi, 77, 80, 106, 107
    and air force 76, 78, 79
Steinhof, Johannes "Macky" 87, 135

Third Reich xix, 21, 138, 160, 163, 171; *see also* Nazism
Toliver, Raymond 97, 101, 157, 158, 160, 184–5
Twining, Nathan 174–5

U.S. Army
    82nd Airborne Dvn 89
    90th Infantry Dvn xvi
    Operational History 154

Vatican, the 28

*Waffen-SS* xxiv, xxv, 71, 161, 163, 191
    and Hartmann 96, 183
war fondness 28–9
*Wehrmacht* xxiii, 12, 41, 49–52, 53, 77
    and Holocaust 144
    and Soviet Union 100, 101–2
    and veterans 123–4, 132, 154–5, 156–7
    see also *Luftwaffe*; *Waffen-SS*
Weil im Schönbuch (Germany) xx, 10, 147, 184
Wiese, Johannes 83
World War I xiv, xxv, 3, 6, 15, 49–51, 108
    and Germany 116, 119
    and Hartmann 7–8
    and Hitler 13
    and Hitler Youth 25
    and *Luftwaffe* 37, 41
    and machine guns 39, 46

Xiang River (China) 8

Yerger, Mark 162–3